Japan Among the Powers

Japan Among the Powers
1890–1990

Sydney Giffard

Yale University Press
New Haven & London   1994

For Kazuyoshi, forty years on.

Set in Sabon by Best-set Typesetter Ltd., Hong Kong
Printed and bound in Great Britain by Biddles Ltd., Guildford and Kings Lynn

Library of Congress Cataloging-in-Publication Data

Giffard, Sidney.
 Japan among the powers 1890–1990 / Sidney Giffard.
  p. cm.
 Includes bibliographical references and index.
 ISBN 0–300–05847–0
 1. Japan—History—1868– 2. Japan—Relations—Foreign countries.
 I. Title.
 DS881.9.G54 1994
 952—dc20   93–36806
                                                                       CIP

A catalogue record for this book is available from the British Library.

Contents

List of Abbreviations

APEC	Asian-Pacific Economic Co-operation
ASEAN	Association of South-East Asian Nations
CCP	Chinese Communist Party
DSP	Democratic Socialist Party
ECAFE	Economic Commission for Asia and the Far East
EPA	Economic Planning Agency
GATT	General Agreement on Tariffs and Trade
IMF	International Monetary Fund
IRAA	Imperial Rule Assistance Association
JCP	Japan Communist Party
JSP	Japan Socialist Party
JTU	Japan Teachers' Union
LDP	Liberal Democratic Party
LTTA	Long Term Trade Agreement
MITI	Ministry of International Trade and Industry
MOF	Ministry of Finance
MSA	Mutual Security Assistance
NYK	Nippon Yusen Kaisha, a leading shipping line
OECD	Organization for Economic Cooperation and Development
PECC	Pacific Economic Cooperation Conference
PRC	People's Republic of China
SCAP	Supreme Commander for the Allied Powers
SEATO	South-East Asia Treaty Organization
SMR	South Manchurian Railway

Far off like floating seeds the ships
Diverge on urgent voluntary errands;
And the full view
Indeed may enter
And move in memory as now these clouds do,
That pass the harbour mirror
And all the summer through the water saunter.

From 'Look, Stranger!'
by W.H. Auden

Introduction

Nowadays, an outline of the background to the history of modern Japan is well known; in particular, how the policy of seclusion and exclusion established for over two centuries under the Tokugawa Shogunate was abandoned in the mid-nineteenth century, and how, following the Meiji Restoration of 1868, Japan was made fit for survival. A popular slogan calling for a rich country and a strong army (*fukoku kyohei*) accurately encapsulated the aims of the statesmen who served the Emperor Meiji. When the Empire had been lost, the new inspiration, of equal popularity, was the idea of overtaking the industrial countries of the West, the United States above all.

These were the dominant ideas determining Japan's economic development, and overshadowing all other considerations in the conduct of foreign relations. Many other themes of the greatest social and constitutional importance were also competing for attention. The whole period since 1868 could, for example, be seen as a struggle for supremacy between those who championed the authority of the state (*kokken*) and those who believed in the primacy of the people's rights (*minken*). There were continuing and changing tensions, contests and alliances between and within a variety of classes, factions, policies and interests. There was persistent uncertainty about the relationship between the country's place in Asia and its place in the larger world; with the West, or against it.

There were those, too, who consistently accorded priority to economic, financial and commercial considerations. In recent decades, especially, it has sometimes seemed necessary only to analyse the output of the industrial sector, and to study the roles of the banks and finance houses, in order to understand where Japan is going. In truth, we should not be surprised to find that the outlook from Japan offers both wider and narrower perspectives.

Introduction

It is in the world's market-places that we meet Japan. At the same time, we are aware of the continued existence of a separate market within Japan, for traditional products belonging to a particular, indigenous way of life, which may itself seem vulnerable, but with which most of the people of Japan still feel at home, in the sense in which many individuals feel at home in the places where they grew up, or spent their childhood. These traditional products, still in common daily use, such as umbrellas of oiled paper, or crested ceramic roof-tiles, straw matting (*tatami*) or wooden clogs (*geta*) may now serve an additional function in the setting of the modern world, as reminders of much that is left unspoken, in the background, in our worka-day, international exchanges.

Such an impact has been made abroad by Japanese industrialists, designers and artists that some acquaintance even with this inner aspect of Japan has now entered the core curriculum in the experience of Europeans, although in this they have lagged some way behind North Americans, and behind some of Japan's Asian partners. The full integration of Japan as part of the great, expanding community of those engaged in international commerce and finance has been widely taken for granted, and has also been carefully studied; but there is much disagreement about its implications, both for Japan and for Japan's partners in the world's business. There is still greater uncertainty in areas of international activity in which the influence of post-war Japan has been manifested less vividly.

The groups of remarkable men who between them determined the aims as well as the structure of Meiji Japan thought of their country as a state, which they would make into a Power; and for which they aspired, in due course, to the status of a Great Power. This determination and these aspirations seem perfectly natural in the context of the nineteenth century. We may therefore proceed, at one level of enquiry, to consider how they got on: we do not need to keep on asking why they were trying to achieve objectives which were common to their peers and contemporaries in other states, at least to those comparable with them in ambition and ability.

Variants of the question how was it done? nevertheless linger: there has been much stimulating examination of the background to the emergence of modern Japan, and of the process of emergence itself. The terms of art used to describe this process, modernization and Westernization, are themselves controversial, and can be misleading, but they have long been in common use in Japan and among scholars everywhere. It may now seem to be an old-fashioned view that the personalities of the leaders of Meiji Japan were themselves crucial determinants of the course taken by their country. It is, however, an assumption of the present account that these men were actors in their own right, not puppets manipulated by impersonal forces.

It is also assumed here that Japanese history is not peculiarly recondite. What is hidden is no more deeply hidden than missing clues might be in another country, continent, or culture. To say this is not to disparage investigation into the unique character of the Japanese people (the pursuit which has come to be known as *nihonjinron*); but only to equate it with research into the characteristics of other peoples or countries.

National character is a dangerous subject, on which worthwhile pronouncements are rare. The influence of their historical experience on the Japanese people is, by contrast, a rewarding subject for study. As with any other people, past experience is reflected in present conduct. Partly because there was such an unusually drastic change in Japan's circumstances from the end of the Tokugawa period, it is necessary to stress the relevance of the earlier history to any understanding of subsequent events, if only by way of an introductory note. Equally, there is the background of centuries of Confucian morality, and Buddhist teaching, the former with its profoundly conservative message for the social and political order of society, uniquely influential among secular philosophies; and there are the distant antecedents of State Shinto, itself seemingly susceptible throughout most of the first half of the twentieth century to political and sectional manipulation. In addition to these conditioning elements, those of family, class and clan may be assumed to have had some influence on individuals active in our period, and those of the institutions, services and corporations to which they belonged and with which they came into contact. The most superficial acquaintance with individual careers reveals a great richness and variety of character, contrasting and coexisting with an unmistakable, but never unquestioned, social conformity.

Like the personalities, the documents sometimes exhibit a certain ambivalence, and may sometimes be suspected of concealing as much as they reveal. This, again, is not a national peculiarity. The purport of Mr Yoshida's famous letter to Mr John Foster Dulles about one rather than two Chinas, for example, was transparent; the circumstances in which it came to be written were pretty clear; but even the principals' own later reports of the transaction whose conclusion was signified by the letter may seem to have left plenty of room for speculation about deeper motives and intentions, on either side.

A similar case, of thirty years earlier, would be the voluminous papers concerning the then British government's decision to let the Anglo-Japanese Treaty die, so that a new international order might be brought into the world. The considerations governing this decision, and the British approach to the Washington Treaties, were of the greatest complexity, and global in their ramifications. They were argued comprehensively and perceptively, with scrupulous reasoning; and also with some passion. Grave concepts like honour and loyalty were weighed in the balance against the tonnage of warships; and were rightly found to be incomparable, but not necessarily invincible. For Japan, the issues were perhaps more nearly clear-cut;

certainly, they were more nearly vital, to use the word which is most often overworked in discussions of national interests. In neither London nor Tokyo, nor in Washington (though more nearly there) were the doubts which had been expressed in the long course of the prior, private consultations extinguished by their formal and public outcome.

In this book the idea is to try to look at such events, and at a substantial period of Japan's modern history, not from a Japanese point of view – to attempt that would be neither practicable nor consistent with the ideal of objectivity – but in a geo-political and strategic context which has Japan at its centre. In imagination, a position is taken on a platform suspended high above the Japanese Islands, from which it is possible to look out *à tous azimuths*, as the years since 1890 go by. The aim is to avoid looking at Japan primarily from the standpoint of other Powers. A question would be, for example, not what Japan's attendance at the Paris Peace Conference signified for the other delegations, though that would be relevant and important, but what attendance meant for the development of Japan's foreign policies, for Japan's influence or standing, and for the subsequent balance between forces contending for dominance in Tokyo.

The choice of standpoint has many consequences, not least for vocabulary. There may be no way of avoiding constant references to the left and the right in Japanese politics, or to conservatives and socialists. These are alien terms (except to the potentially misleading but reassuringly distant extent that a court noble of the Heian period or a grandee under the Shogunate might have aspired to become Minister of the Right), but they have long been in use in Japan, and are part of a universal political vocabulary. Where Japanese labels seem to have distinctive connotations, it may be preferable not to translate them. The greatest danger lies in the use of expressions which may suggest spurious analogies. For example, the transformation effected in Japan in a few years, leading up to the Meiji Restoration of 1868, could be said to have been the rough equivalent of a telescoping of the experience of the British people over three and a half centuries, say, between the Battle of Bosworth Field in 1485 and the passage of the Reform Act of 1832. Yet the word feudal as a basic description of Japanese society under the Tokugawa seems to us today much more liable to mislead than we considered its use for this purpose forty years ago. This is partly because the Japanese economy in the latter part of the Tokugawa period is now shown to have been more highly sophisticated than we had supposed.

All the same, it is essential to retain a keen sense of the sheer speed at which society has evolved in Japan throughout the century since the Meiji Constitution came into force. Personal experience may assist the imagination here, even vicarious experience. It is not unusual to come across people whose well-remembered grandparents could themselves recall the earliest years of Meiji. The recollections of the older generation in Japan, at least until only yesterday, frequently included some fading memory of the Russo-Japanese War, most often of public dissatisfaction with the terms of the Treaty of Portsmouth of 1905. In order to develop a perspective, it may be helpful to bear in mind that we were further in 1990 from the end of the Second World War than we were in 1945 from the Treaty of Portsmouth and the end of the Russo-Japanese War, or than they were then, in 1905, from the end of the Tokugawa period.

It would no doubt go without saying that the balance and emphasis of the account given in the following chapters are wholly dependent upon subjective judgement as to the relative significance of particular features and developments for an understanding of the course of events as a whole, in an essentially political context. It is the same with assessments of evidence relating to particular personalities, motives, decisions and actions. It will be equally apparent that there are whole areas of Japanese life, notably the arts and literature as well as religious and intellectual developments in modern Japan, which it has not been found possible to accommodate worthily in the available space; and other areas of both social and economic activity of which the coverage must seem extremely perfunctory to those who know them at all well. The balance will be redressed easily by any readers who care to extend their acquaintance with the excellent material now abundantly available in English, on every aspect of modern and contemporary Japanese life.

This material is no longer limited to the work of foreign students of Japan. Talented and accurate translations of Japanese academic studies, as well as much original work in English by Japanese experts, are to be found in every library and bookshop. Moreover, the great Japanese novelists of this century have been deservedly fortunate in their interpreters. Their work affords the best possible introduction to the texture and flavour of Japanese life, especially to the styles of life which are just beginning to look old-fashioned, but which predominated in the society in which the leaders of contemporary Japan passed their formative years, and in the earlier society of which their parents spoke to them, as parents do, with such compellingly vivid descriptions that it came to seem their own. Oral tradition is one of our few defences against the potentially stunning effect of a continuously brisk pace of change.

It must be said that the Japanese people are good at not being stunned by the mere rapidity of change. This is one of the few generalizations which it is permissible to make about them, generalizations about any people being otherwise even more odious than comparisons between peoples. The reason for the privileged status of this generalization is that the Japanese Islands are prone to earthquake, typhoon and flood, and their buildings have been liable to catch fire, to such a degree that it cannot have failed to endow their inhabitants with a certain natural resilience and adaptability. It is necessary only to read Tanizaki's novel *The Makioka Sisters* (*Sasameyuki*) to understand something of this quality.

That brilliant novel, apart from the incidental account of reactions to a great natural disaster in the Kansai, deals with moderately well-to-do family life in the period shortly preceding the Second World War, a period which it may be particularly difficult for those familiar only with post-war Japan to picture at all clearly in the mind's eye. Given that the serial publication of this novel was discontinued by order of the authorities, during the war, presumably on account of some deficiency of patriotic spirit, it may also convey, indirectly, some feeling for the atmosphere in Japan in those days of wartime, almost equally difficult to understand for those who did not experience them.

The events of that time were so traumatic that it has seemed to many that there must have been some kind of break, which was presumably concealed somewhere in the story; or that a complete reel must be missing , as it were, in the received documentary film about the evolution of modern Japan. We run it through again, in the belief that, on re-examination, the succession of events may be seen to provide its own explanation. However, these passing events also have to be seen in relation to processes detectable and definable only in a longer and slower timescale.

The choice of 1890 as the year from which to begin the account in this book was governed by the consideration that the opening of the Imperial Diet in Tokyo and the coming into force of the Meiji Constitution jointly marked, in practical administration, the momentous decision by Japan's leaders that the future social and political development of the country should be along lines parallel with those being followed in dominant Western countries. In detail, their programme was eclectic, but its general orientation was unequivocal. It was justified in terms of power: it was to provide security then, and empire thereafter.

At the time, among the Powers, there was a common outlook amounting to an imperial culture (imperialist, if use of that term is now separable from commitment to Marxist doctrine). Within the conventions of that culture, there was a close understanding, in the language of power, between the leaders of Meiji Japan and those of Western countries, even during the years of recrimination and confrontation over Japan's demand for revision of the unequal treaties. By the time of the conclusion of the Anglo-Japanese Treaty of 1902, mutual understanding, not only between Baron Hayashi and Lord Lansdowne, but also between the two governments, in Tokyo and London, could certainly have been described as close, extending as it did to their understanding of nuances of deliberate ambiguity. This close mutual understanding applied, however, only to a strictly defined area of intense mutual interest. Outside that area, and beyond the purview of the treaty, there was undeniably a certain mutual ignorance and incomprehension, giving large scope for misunderstanding. And even where the best understandings were achieved between governments, in those not so far off days, they were the property of a few individuals or small groups in each state. Governmental authorities might or might not command respect: they seldom saw any necessity to expose to the public the full rationale of their policies.

Nevertheless, it is certainly arguable that those few statesmen who between them controlled the development of relations between the Powers knew each other's minds better during the two or three decades immediately prior to the outbreak of the First World War than their successors were to do until many years after the conclusion of the Second World War. In science and in the arts, it might be quite different. Improved communications meant vastly and continuously improved facilities for cultural exchanges. They also, however, enabled rigidly authoritarian and ideologically fanatical regimes to exercise an unprecedented degree of control over the lives of individual citizens.

It is a conventional view that the importance attached, in European and North American societies, to the individual's need for fulfilment in life has its closest parallel, in Japanese society, in the priority given to the need for harmony within the group. This view identifies, if in oversimplified form, a contrast which is generally agreed to be significant for the broader analysis of social and cultural differences. The emphasis laid upon the group, as opposed to the individual, has been an enduring feature of the Japanese tradition, owing especially to its foundation in Confucian ethics, if also to more mundane factors, such as the density of the population in the towns and cities. It has been a major contributory factor in Japan's industrial and economic success, especially in facilitating teamwork and communication, and has also affected the nature of political organization, though in the latter's evolution the tradition of personal loyalty to the group's leader has perhaps been equally significant, not least because of its share of responsibility for the persistence of factionalism. The homogeneity of Japanese society has served to sustain tradition; but to be homogeneous is certainly not, in this case, to be monolithic.

Indeed, the heroic dissident, of whom the nineteenth-century scholar-samurai Yoshida Shoin, of Hagi in the Choshu fief, may be regarded as a most notable exemplar, also has an honoured place in the Japanese tradition. Moreover, many of the most widely respected religious teachers and artists, in every period of the country's history, have been distinguished for the originality of their individual achievements and of their personalities and characters, not as the embodiments of ideal stereotypes. The homogeneity of the society as a whole, and the central importance of group activity are of considerable value as general ideas in the background to the study of every aspect of Japanese history; but other characteristics of this background, which must also be borne in mind, are its depth, complexity and variety.

Introduction

It is not only the background features which are liable to be distorted by oversimplification: the main narrative itself is at risk from all the pitfalls lying in wait for summarizers. In its broadest outline, from the point of view adopted here, this main narrative is an account of Japan's drive for the status and security of a Great Power; and of how an alternative route was found, after the failure of the imperialist approach. Much was learned in the course of the first expedition which was to prove invaluable on the second; just as much of the original equipment proved adaptable to the later purposes.

Thus, it is not sufficient, for an understanding of this story, to see the years 1931–1945, from the beginning of the Manchurian Incident to the end of the Second World War, as a break in continuity, or a diversion. Much ground was covered in those years, especially in the development of technology and of production engineering, and in the management of large enterprises, which was necessary for the subsequent, post-war economic and industrial advances. The deviation of the political system was not merely the sudden product of the great depression: there were contributory causes far back in history. The dislocation of the all-important conventions of constitutional monarchy, to the functioning of which the Emperor Showa was manifestly attached, was the result of a deviant pseudo-loyalty prevalent among certain of his subjects, which was redolent of much earlier periods of Japanese history. The fabric of conventions surrounding the British constitutional monarchy might be regarded as a model (and may at times have been so regarded in court circles in Japan) but it would be easy to forget how painfully it was constructed. Nor did the deviation by which the Emperor Showa's reign was afflicted take a coherent course.

The direction of policy was inconsistent, and the militarists themselves were divided. Tojo's career did not remotely resemble those of Hitler or Mussolini, nor was he ever in a position to exert dictatorial power. The failure of Prince Konoye and his associates, and of other opponents of the dominant military cliques, has all the pathos of dramatic tragedy: the conclusion seems inescapable that disaster could and should have been averted. It is particularly striking, with the advantage of hindsight, that the economic growth achieved by Japan from the beginning of the century right up to the outbreak of war with China, despite the effects of the great depression, was not given greater weight in considering future policy.

By comparison, the uncertain development of the parliamentary system is more easily predictable, given the doubts so clearly entertained by the leaders of Meiji Japan as to its capacity to provide the strong government which they rightly judged to be a prerequisite for the national advance, and probably for continued independence, even perhaps for national survival. That parliamentarians as robustly independent as, for example, Ozaki

Yukio were nevertheless forthcoming was in keeping with a certain tradition; at the same time, in the longer perspective, it is hardly surprising to discover that the Diet as a whole should have been unable to assert the commanding role which the Meiji Constitution had so carefully avoided giving it.

Most observers would agree that the temper of the people of Japan became progressively more favourable towards democracy, and that this reflected a maturity of political experience, not merely a reaction to defeat in war. A recognition was common, for example, that the treatment of Professor Minobe in the 1930s, just because his theory of the Constitution did not suit the dominant military factions, had been wholly unjust. The popular favour accorded to his son, Minobe Ryokichi, as the avowedly socialist Governor of Tokyo for many of the post-war years of steadily increasing prosperity under conservative administrations, appeared to be a kind of tacit acknowledgement of this. The policy of the Occupation must also certainly receive much credit for the renewal of the strength of the democratic spirit in Japan. It is something of an irony that the consciousness of foreign influence over the structure of the political system adopted after the Second World War, and of the Constitution itself, should have made it easier for criticism of the system to develop, and to be expressed. When the economic recovery reached a plateau of achievement, the demand for political reform, and specifically for a way to be found of escaping from the toils of 'money politics' became more insistent.

The common desire in Japan for an equitable and 'clean' system of parliamentary democracy is coupled with a strong tradition of nationalism. These two components are also prominent in the make-up of other societies; their combination is by no means peculiar to Japan. The strength of nationalist sentiment in Japan is a feature of the historical narrative from the beginning of modern times. The circumstances of Japan's emergence made this inevitable. The temper of the people was roused by the challenge from the West, and found repeated cause for expression, just as in Europe national tempers might respond to a Fashoda Incident or an Agadir crisis, to the Boer War or to the Boxer Rising.

The struggle for treaty revision served to unify Japanese opinion, after painful internal divisions. Moreover, this struggle with the Powers was to culminate in their acceptance of Japan as a Power, if without any formal recognition of equality. The Triple Intervention, however, was a plain humiliation, the memory of which could not be wholly effaced. The Boxer rising brought a renewed sense of prestige; and the conclusion of the Anglo-Japanese Treaty amounted to certification of Great Power status, confirmed by victory in the field, and triumph at sea, in the Russo-Japanese War, but in public esteem less than convincingly endorsed by the terms of the Treaty of Portsmouth. The beginnings of racial friction over immigration to the

United States in the first decade of the twentieth century, though seriously disturbing to the Japanese public, were as nothing compared with the shock of the Exclusion Act of 1924. This shock was in no way diminished by reflections upon the shortcomings of Japan's treatment of people of other Asian races. What was intolerable, after Japan's clear recognition as a Power, was for Japanese nationals not to be treated accordingly by the other Powers. By the international standards of the time, such thinking was unexceptionable.

Japan's determination to rank as a Great Power was allowed to conflict with the idea of representing the Asian peoples in world politics, and becoming above all the champion of their interests. The episode of the Twenty-One Demands presented to China by Okuma's government in 1915, though not out of line with the earlier attitudes of Okuma himself towards China, was as damaging psychologically as it was politically. In other respects Japan's experience of participation in the First World War, and at the Peace Conference in Paris, was equivocal; and therefore was not wholly reassuring to public opinion, which was subsequently affronted and cast down by the termination of the Anglo-Japanese Treaty, and was suspicious of the Washington Treaty system from its inception, and of the whole motivation in the West for the limitation of naval armaments. These broad public reactions, here crudely summarized, were to influence the later course of events. The deterioration of Japan's relations with Britain and the United States which followed the economic slump and the Manchurian adventure was not unheralded. The Japanese people were not mentally unprepared for it.

To anyone looking back on those days, and especially on the late 1920s and early 1930s, and comparing what then passed for close consultation with the unending flow of information and advice available to statesmen two generations later, the scope for misunderstanding, even between governments disposed in favour of mutual co-operation, is plain. It was enlarged by disagreement about the role of the League of Nations. Japanese statesmen found it hard to assess the impact of the ideas put forward by President Woodrow Wilson. Some of these proposals would be repudiated in Washington by Congress, but retained a certain validity in the wider international community. The world had changed as a result of the First World War, in ways which it was not easy to perceive, for a country like Japan, a participant in the hostilities on the side of the victorious Allies, yet a participant whose population had been only partially committed, whose armed forces, even, had not been deeply engaged.

Nor was it easy, from the other side of the world, to appreciate the scale of the fighting on the main battlefronts of the First World War, or of the losses suffered by the principal combatants. The appalling figures – for example that the British alone lost, in the four months of the Somme battle in 1916, 400,000 men, very substantially more than the total strength of the combined Japanese armies brought together before Mukden under General Oyama in the last campaign of the Russo-Japanese War; and that both the French and the Germans suffered casualties on the same scale over a similar period of time at Verdun alone, in the same year – would have been hard, even impossible, fully to comprehend.

It was therefore not only the new idealism of President Wilson that the Japanese delegation in Paris, and Japanese policy thereafter, had to take into account. It was also the unacknowledged or inadequately defined revisions, which were coming to be adopted in the West, of previously accepted ideas about the conduct of the Powers, and of their imperial interests. In the West, also, statesmen were greatly preoccupied with the consequences in Europe of what had been done at Versailles; and these preoccupations were easily made to look like an opportunity by those in Japan who favoured a policy of expansion on the Asian continent. This in turn, combined with a willingness to use the methods of terrorism, facilitated the gradual encroachment by groups of ambitious army officers on the prerogatives of central government. Blame for the failure of collective security lies primarily elsewhere. In Japan, disaster was the result of a failure of the machinery of government, that is to say of those to whom it had been intended by the authors of the Meiji Constitution to entrust its operation.

What happened in the Asian and Pacific theatres during the Second World War needs no introduction, since we are still reminded of it in general terms every day in the cinema and on television screens. It left deep scars, both moral and material, and severely weakened Japan's international credit. It was a common view in Japan that the country's defeat must be ascribed above all to the superior technology and logistical organization of its enemies, as manifested, to take possibly the most decisive example, in the ability of the United States Navy to maintain its carriers for unprecedentedly long periods at sea. The importance subsequently attached in Japan to technological innovation gave a great stimulus to economic recovery.

Economic factors had contributed powerfully to the breakdown of the Washington system, but they were never so compelling in the Pacific or in East Asia as in Europe. In particular, the pressure of population on resources, even when full allowance is made for the paucity of cultivable land in the Japanese Islands, was not sufficient to have caused the pursuit of expansion by Japan in the manner or on the scale chosen by its military advocates and protagonists. In the early post-war period, Japan's rising birth rate was believed once again to be likely to pose a threat to stability in the country and the region. As soon as Japanese standards of living began to rise, these apprehensions melted away.

The fear of revolution in Japan, entertained by Prince Konoye and his circle before the end of the war, and by Allied governments in its aftermath, faded similarly. The poverty in cities which would have been overcrowded even if they had not also been utterly devastated seemed to provide the classic setting for an uprising by the proletariat, as foreseen in Marxist textbooks. Great demonstrations took place. Hard work was soon found to be more rewarding; but both politicians and industrialists concluded that the sovereignty of the people, now enshrined in the Constitution, was not to be flouted.

Consultation with the workforce became one of the distinguishing characteristics of Japanese industrial success, with benefits to productivity as well as to relations between workers and managers. In politics, the precept was much easier to master than the practice. The continuing popular demand for political reform, which meant release from 'money politics', proved genuinely difficult to satisfy. Japanese Diet members were no less solicitous of their constituents' best interests than other parliamentarians were in other democratic countries. But there was a sense in Japan that politicians and public alike were trapped within a system they disliked: they could not yet find the right way in which to change it.

The priority given to this problem of political reform is easily rationalized. Continued industrial and technological advance can be achieved only on the basis of social harmony. The Constitution provides satisfactory machinery: a way must be found to operate it in the common interest, not in the interest of the richest faction. The bureaucrats and the judiciary are sound. The influence of industry is in favour of reform. It might be a mistake to expect the adjustment eventually adopted to owe its character to some model already working in another country. Japanese democracy has its own ethos; it may devise its own formal structure, on original lines. (Given the capability of Japanese information technology, it would not be surprising to see the adoption of methods of consulting public opinion which drew on this: instantaneous referenda, for example, might have a place in a new system.) The attachment of the sovereign people to the principles of democratic government seems assured.

The success of Japan's post-war economic policy and of the leading industries is well known indeed and has been intensively studied. Even if it were to turn out that the peak of Japan's economic achievement had been passed, as some observers were predicting in the early 1990s, the retention of a place of leadership in economic performance seemed assured. In the talk of internationalization there was growing recognition that success at one level might conflict with harmony at another: the need to provide for coexistence (*kyosei*), not only with potential enemies but also with friends, was a new theme. In particular, although the incentive which superpower rivalry had provided for sustaining a co-operative relationship with the United States no longer applied, it was perceived in Tokyo that economic considerations argued powerfully to the same effect.

The strains that had been imposed on this crucial relationship were not immediately relieved by the weakening of Soviet power, nor by its subsequent dispersal. The dangers of nuclear proliferation were apparent, not least in North Korea. It was still argued in Washington, as it had been argued for so many years, that Japan should make a greater direct contribution to the maintenance of international peace and security. The example of Japan's massive financial support for the operations undertaken under United Nations auspices in the Gulf War was evidently not regarded there as an adequate earnest of Japan's will to uphold the authority of the United Nations in the new international order. In Tokyo, the strength of the sovereign people's attachment to Article 9 of the Constitution, renouncing the use of force in international affairs, necessarily remained the prime consideration.

The Japanese people were mindful of the international responsibilities which went with their economic strength. They strongly approved the emphasis put by successive Japanese governments on participation in the work of the United Nations and its agencies. They wished to make their contribution to the new international order in the ways of peace. They approved the development aid programme, which had become the largest in the world. They also naturally longed for better amenities for their children, and believed that technological advance could bring advantages for their own way of life, with new and exciting developments (those many-storeyed artificial islands projected to be built in Tokyo Bay, when the economy picked up again, as it surely would). They had learned that optimism could bring its own fulfilment.

They were also conscious of problems, including that posed by the 'greying' of the population, though they thought they had got the better of industrial pollution in their own islands, after a stiff fight. They found it hard to believe in the possibility of serious deterioration in relations with the United States, assuming that the series of annual compromises over trade and finance would surely be resumed. Meanwhile, they noted with some regret that Peking had come to seem more distant than Paris; and reflected upon their shared obligations in respect of so much unfinished business in East Asia.

These circumstances combined, in the early 1990s, to suggest that there were bound to be substantial changes in the new Heisei era. Even as we look forward to these changes, it may be helpful to look back also, over a hundred years of modern Japan.

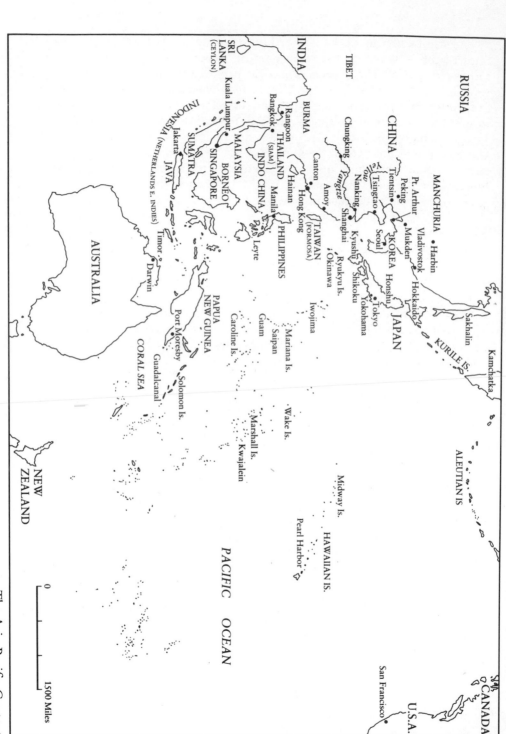

The Asia-Pacific Context

1

A Place Among the Powers, 1890–1900

This was the age of the Powers, the civilized world and the march of progress. Japan assumed a place as a Power among the Powers during the 1890s. To the Japanese leaders, seeking both to justify and to control radical change in their own society, this seemed a necessary stage in a natural process of growth. Japan's new status was rapidly coming to be accepted in similar terms by contemporary opinion at large. The impact of Japanese art and design was already reverberating throughout the salons and galleries of the civilized world.

In Japan, the 1880s closed with the promulgation of the Imperial Constitution in 1889 and its coming into operation in November 1890; with the first convening of the Imperial Diet, also in November 1890, following elections for the House of Representatives, in July; and with the Imperial Rescript on Education.

In the elections for the lower House, little more than one per cent of the adult male population qualified for the vote. An electorate of half a million men in Japan in 1890, out of a total population of about 40 million, compares with an electorate of some 5 million men in Britain at that time, with its smaller total population of about 30 million. The size of the British electorate in the late 1880s, however, had more than doubled since before the Second Reform Act of 1868, that is to say, since the Meiji Restoration of that same year. Despite their long parliamentary tradition, British governments had been cautious about extending the franchise. Those who had struggled to learn how to govern Japan since the Meiji Restoration had good cause to be doubly cautious; but they had themselves designed the Meiji Constitution. It sanctified the position of the Emperor himself, and thus conferred legitimacy upon the actions they had taken, and would take, in his name. It should enable them to ensure that there was a sufficient, continuing degree of domestic stability, and in so doing to achieve one of their two primary objectives.

Their second preoccupation was to secure the independence of the state from foreign interference or domination, and to achieve that recognition of equal status with the Powers which this entailed. Longer-term objectives, such as the greater prosperity of the people, must be subordinate to these aims.

It is true that there had been an early appreciation in Japan, at the practical and instinctive levels of daily transaction, that industrial and economic development would offer the prospect of growing general prosperity. The idea that strength would depend on economic as much as on defensive capability was not new.

Indeed, pressure for economic advance had contributed at least as much as any threat from outside the country to the weakening of the rigidities of *bakufu* government and of confidence in the competence of Tokugawa officials to sustain the social and administrative systems which they had created. Nevertheless, it was foreign pressure which had been most keenly felt and most widely discussed. For nearly a generation before the Meiji Restoration there had been growing disquiet over reports of foreign, and especially of British, action in China, and its consequences. It was the United States which had forced concession on the Shogunate. But the perception of a generalized threat from foreign Powers had been, and remained, widespread and intense. It was magnified and distorted by a deep consciousness of putative disadvantage. In this atmosphere, an equally sharp awareness of certain national priorities had developed, and had been encouraged to develop by a leadership anxious to disown an inconvenient inheritance of factional division.

It was generally accepted, then, that the country needed to be strong, in order to survive and ultimately to compete with the established Powers; and that strength should be founded, ideally, on unity. In their simplest expression, these were the ideas which dominated political life in Meiji Japan, both foreshadowing and reflecting the primary objectives of policy as conceived by the leadership. The complexity of the Japanese language made, paradoxically, for simplification in the presentation and communication of basic ideas. The spirit of a long campaign could be encapsulated in a few Chinese characters, to be memorized and disseminated in three or four syllables, or displayed in confident and economical brushstrokes. For a time, the cry had been 'Revere the Emperor and Expel the Barbarian' (*Sonno joi*). Then, with the overthrow of the Tokugawa accomplished, the evident need for imported ideas and techniques found expression in the call for 'Civilization and Enlightenment' (*Bummei kaika*). The subsequent craze for almost everything foreign, which had reached a peak in the mid-1880s, was soon felt to court dangers of decadence and subversion. It was not as though the Powers themselves were ready to concede equality. The surest hope lay in 'A Strong Army and A Rich Country' (*Fukoku kyohei*). Progress would be achieved by applying the 'Japanese Spirit to Western Knowledge' (*Wakon yosai*).

Broad agreement about national priorities had not served to eliminate protest or even revolt by the oppressed and disadvantaged, nor to prevent the outbreak of bitter disputes among the leaders themselves. Living conditions remained extremely harsh for the poor, while the man of spirit was still faithful to his own convictions rather than to majority opinion. Numerous uprisings of desperate peasants, often promoted and led by disillusioned samurai, were easily quelled by the agents of those who had entrenched their positions in the central government. The Saga Rebellion of 1874 was an expression of various lines of political opposition, both reactionary and progressive in character, but it was a small outbreak, extinguished before it could spread. The expedition to Formosa, mounted in the same year, had also served, in addition to its punitive purpose, to give temporary employment to otherwise dangerously idle samurai. Kido, almost isolated among the leaders in his opposition to this expedition, had taken the view that what was not worth attempting in Korea was certainly not to be indulged in elsewhere.

It was frustration over the aborting of the earlier plan to invade Korea which largely fuelled the Satsuma Rebellion of 1877. This had been inspired and directed by Saigo Takamori, the most charismatic of all the original leaders of the Meiji Restoration. It took six months to suppress, giving his former colleagues in the central government the need to demonstrate, with great reluctance, that the new conscript army was sufficiently well armed, trained and led to overcome fanatical disaffection, even at the centre of Satsuma power, in Kagoshima. All the same, Saigo Takamori was to remain a popular hero, and his statue in Ueno, close to where he had received the surrender of Edo Castle by its *bakufu* garrison, was to approach the status of a national shrine. His was a character at once rock-like and impulsive, an individual paradox, whose physical animation was such as to suggest a spiritual force, a character perhaps best compared with that of Benkei as portrayed in Kanjincho, in the Kabuki theatre. That his quarrel with others in the central leadership had stemmed from an insistent sense of national purpose, expansionist and ambitious, was neither criticized nor held against his memory in the inner circles of Meiji society, nor in public esteem. His brother, Tsugumichi, who had conceived it his duty to take command of the Imperial Guard against Takamori's forces, was also to enjoy continued respect, if never the same *réclame*.

The history of this period is in large part the history of gifted and determined individuals. Another outstanding leader from Satsuma, Okubo Toshimichi, assassinated after a brilliant career, by a discontented samurai in 1878, may perhaps be regarded as the most distinguished, if an indirect, victim of his fellow-clansman's stubborn and headstrong apostasy. The toll

3

exacted from the leadership in the early years of Meiji by samurai resentful of their loss of status and unable to adapt to rapid and radical social change, was heavy indeed. The first public advocate of a conscript army and of the abolition of samurai privileges, Omura Masujiro, himself a lower samurai from Choshu, had been one of the earliest targets of this resentment, in 1869.

Twenty years later, the most scholarly and intellectual of the Satsuma reformers, a seminal influence in the development of education, who had also been Minister at the legation in London from 1879 to 1884, Mori Arinori, was murdered as he left his house in Tokyo to attend the ceremony of the promulgation of the Constitution. Mori had overseen the introduction of a sound, basic school system, later to be expanded on unchanged lines. In his own views, he had moved, not unlike the influential scholar and publicist Fukuzawa Yukichi, towards a position on the conservative wing of radical thinking. This did not protect him.

In the same year of 1889, Okuma Shigenobu, founder of one of the earliest significant political parties, the Kaishinto, and opponent of the monopolizing of power by representatives of the dominant fiefs of Satsuma and Choshu, was also attacked by a bomb-thrower, and wounded so seriously that he lost a leg. As Foreign Minister, he was judged to have shown weakness in pursuit of revision of the unequal treaties. The other principal early critic of Satcho domination, Itagaki Taisuke, founder of the rival opposition party, the Jiyuto, had survived a murderous attack in 1882, as, in 1884, had Iwakura himself, probably the most highly regarded single figure of the early Meiji period, the arbiter of convention for a constitutional monarchy in Japan, and of the new orthodoxy.

Such episodes illustrated the turbulence and harshness of the first two decades after the Restoration. It was perhaps only the perception of a deadly threat from the hostile foreigner which could have reduced dissension to a level permitting central government to function at all. That the centre not only functioned but succeeded in introducing administrative, social and financial reforms of a fundamental character is in itself proof of the quite extraordinary energy, resourcefulness and panache of those in charge; and of the power of the Emperor's name, on which their authority depended. The prestige and wisdom of Iwakura Tomomi and the imaginative depth of Kido Koin were lost to the country before the consolidation of the reforms which they had done so much to initiate and nurture; and the stabilizing dignity of Prince Sanjo Sanetomi, first Lord Privy Seal and temporary Prime Minister, was extinguished within a year of the coming into force of the Constitution. These were men who established, by their own examples, a new pattern of service.

Iwakura inspired and promoted the preparation of the Meiji Constitution. He had also taken a keen interest in the development of Japan's industrial capabilities. Through Iwasaki Yataro of Tosa, government agents under Iwakura's guidance had, in effect, brought both Mitsubishi and NYK into being. It was a generous policy towards the entrepreneur and manager, open to challenge; but it was not seriously disputed, on account of its novelty and because it undermined the foreigners' near-monopoly of the import and export trades. Before his death in 1885, Iwasaki had expanded his original shipping interests to take in shipbuilding, insurance and mining as well. Meanwhile, the expansion of the Mitsui interest in finance, which had antedated the Meiji Restoration, and in commerce, had greatly benefited from connection with Inoue Kaoru, one of the most versatile and subtle of the leaders from Choshu.

In the development of banking, manufacturing industry, mining, commerce and transport, giant strides had been made in these early years of the Meiji period. So much so, that many of the 4,000 or so specialists brought in from Europe and the United States to instruct and advise had already been found redundant by the late 1880s. The opening of the trunk railway line along the Tokaido, the historic route between Tokyo and the cities of the Kansai, in 1889, symbolized, as it were, Japan's graduation in the study of imported technologies, and in their application. At the same time, the direct participation of government agencies in commercial and industrial enterprises was being withdrawn, deliberately and gradually.

A key to the success of Japan's industrial policies was the zest of the public for progress in this field. Few of the deep reservations held about foreign influence in social and political affairs were allowed to detract from the popular enthusiasm for new technology. Enterprising and adaptable samurai saw in these developments their opportunity to preserve a leading place in society, and to assert their presumed superiority in careers which would have been unthinkable even to the immediately preceding generations of their class. Some reconciled themselves, in their need for mere subsistence, to humbler jobs in industry and commerce. There was to be in principle no inferiority in social status for the industrialist, nor for the engineer, nor for the scientist. Everyone knew (as all know still) who was of noble descent, even among the workforce at large, but the respect due to your own learning and to your own achievements did not depend primarily upon connections, family background or material inheritance.

For the peasant, labourer, craftsman or artisan unable to find a livelihood in agriculture, traditional manufacture or construction, there were openings in the new factories. Factory conditions were to become barely tolerable for some workers, but for the landless peasant, as for the penniless gentleman, the mills and foundries represented at first a welcome source of assured or supplemented subsistence. For a time, peasant families were even able to take advantage of gaps in the system, contriving, for example, to promise their daughters to two or three textile mills concurrently, and to pocket a contract fee from each, but life was soon to become as hard for the factory hand as it had always been for the peasant. Supervision was oppressive; leisure and amenities, if available at all, were basic; employers often took advantage of the weak; minimal regulation offered hardly any protection from exploitation. The concerted work-stoppage (*domei hiko*) was not yet a manifestation of power, only of resentment.

The conditions endured by the poor, both in agriculture and in industry, make the achievements of the early years of the Meiji period the more remarkable, and give the popular enthusiasm for novelty and technical change an ironic tinge. Iwakura had said that, in trying to create employment for the samurai, first importance must be given to the development of industry. The observation has implications for an understanding of the priorities and values of his time. Though the structure of society was changing in every other aspect, a profound sense of hierarchy was to persist. Modern Japan was, and remains, as deeply rooted in the country's history as any society in the world; more than most, given the combination of geographical isolation with centuries of varying degrees of deliberate seclusion.

By trial and error, the Meiji leaders had found that the stimulation of industrial development by government subsidy and patronage, gradually reduced and withdrawn as private managerial competence and financial capacity grew, was a sound route to the progressive achievement of economic goals. Denied tariff autonomy, they concentrated on import substitution wherever natural and human resources made this possible, as in the production of textiles. Exports were facilitated and stimulated by the standardization of quality in the manufacture of goods with promising overseas markets. By the early 1890s silk accounted for over 30 per cent of Japan's total exports by value, and this was preponderantly raw silk. The weaving and dyeing of silk piece-goods remained in the hands of craftsmen. The production of raw silk, though still based substantially on village labour, in small units, was on a massive scale overall. For forty more years it was to remain an essential element in the livelihood of whole regions. In the 1890s large filatures also came into production. The central authorities, who had earlier encouraged the establishment of reeling plants, could now leave the further development of this staple export industry in private hands. The major Tomioka silk mill, first set up by government investment, was sold to Mitsui interests in 1893. The authorities kept a stricter control over the continuing performance of military and strategic industries, but even here they were content to see shipbuilding, as well as merchant shipping, pass into competent private ownership.

The link between industrial and financial policy was understood at first in Meiji Japan partly by reference to what had happened in other parts of Asia, where the collapse of traditional, handicraft industries had led, by way of financial instability, to foreign domination. Matsukata Masayoshi of Satsuma was most prominent among the Meiji leadership in economic affairs. He had gained undisputed authority in this sector through his management of the commutation of samurai stipends; his reform of the land tax, on which government revenue largely depended; and of the deflationary policy of retrenchment (named after him) to regain control of price levels in the early 1880s; together with his supervision of the establishment of the Bank of Japan in 1882 and of the centralization of the issuing of notes. He was insistent that the growth of industrial production would be the key to financial stability, thus demonstrating a maturity of judgement which would have done credit to contemporary economic management in any of the most advanced countries of his time, and setting an enduring template for the design and operation of the national economy.

Matsukata's skill enabled the leadership to increase defence expenditure steeply in the 1880s, improving armaments, equipment, training and conditions of service substantially, in both the army and the navy. The dominant personality in the formulation of defence policy, both in its strategic and in its administrative aspects, was Yamagata Aritomo. Coming from a lower samurai family in Choshu, Yamagata had learned in the kiheitai militia, before the Restoration itself and the Boshin War which accompanied it, that discipline and organization were even more important than birth, in the ordering of military affairs. He had been largely responsible for the introduction of conscription, and his administrative flair had also been brought to bear effectively on the problems of local government in the reorganized clan territories. Yamagata was a builder; steady, thorough, accurate, determined. What he constructed, in government administration generally, and in defence policy and practice, was not to be disturbed lightly. The political constituency which he also aimed to build was to be considered no more than his due. He personified the concept of patriotic duty under the Emperor's authority. Liberty was for him the occasional indulgence of legitimate pleasures in moments of relaxation from dedicated and disinterested service. His political influence was to last, with some decline from the time of the First World War, until his death in 1922. (Matsukata outlasted him physically, but not in his impact on public affairs.) There may have been bolder commanders, perhaps with greater breadth and flexibility of mind; but there was none to whom the armed services of Japan owed a more comprehensive debt. He combined great qualities of leadership, as these were assessed in his own time, with a capacity for the measured appraisal of strategic and political issues. His concepts of 'the cordon of sovereignty' and 'the cordon of advantage' were basic to strategic thinking in Japan for two generations.

Ito Hirobumi, however, whose background was similar to that of Yamagata but whose experience in government was even wider, and the cast of whose mind was subtler, must be regarded as the member of the leadership who came to bear the greatest single share of responsibility for the consolidation of the Meiji Restoration. As the principal architect of the new cabinet system of government, which he was the first to lead, in 1881, and of the peerage, he was entrusted, under Iwakura's guidance, with preparatory work on the Meiji Constitution itself, of which he came to be regarded as the author.

Having outmanoeuvred Okuma, his chief rival for pre-eminence in politics, in the controversy about the Hokkaido colonization assets at the beginning of the decade, Ito also knew better than any of his active contemporaries in the late 1880s how to turn developments to his advantage. His first Foreign Minister, Inoue Kaoru, having run into the expected difficulties in negotiations for treaty revision, thus exciting popular unrest, Ito's cabinet introduced Peace Regulations which greatly handicapped their political opponents.

Political divisions were complex. A most significant difference lay between those who wished to see effective power transferred to political parties, and those who were determined that it should be retained in the hands of transcendental or non-party governments. The former emphasized the need to define and entrench popular rights (*minken*), while the latter were intent upon consolidating the authority of the state (*kokken*). To a large extent, these divisions coincided with those between the opponents of continuing Satcho dominance, and the leadership themselves from Satsuma and Choshu, who felt that they had earned the right, as they alone were qualified, to carry on the government in the Emperor's name. It was they who were already devising indispensable constitutional processes, designed to command the necessary degree of consent in the country, when the time came to introduce them. They had already undertaken to reconcile conflicts of interest, and to revive a proper sense of national cohesion. It was they who were providing for the practical expression of this sentiment of unity in military strength, underpinned by industrial expansion, in order to secure the country's independence against the undiminished threat of foreign encroachment. They were building and buttressing for Japan an appropriately prominent place in Asian affairs, from which the country could exert a worthy influence throughout the civilized world. Collectively, they presented the patronizing face of benevolent tyranny.

Their claims put the political parties in the position of seeming to oppose virtue. The whole vocabulary of party politics on a national scale was unfamiliar, the basic concepts strange, liable to be misunderstood, easily misrepresented. The strongest surviving advocates, from among the original Meiji leadership, of the early establishment of representative institutions had been Itagaki Taisuke and Okuma Shigenobu. Itagaki had broken with his colleagues over the same issue as that which had led Saigo Takamori towards the Satsuma Rebellion, namely the need for an assertion of Japanese authority in Korea. Itagaki had expressed his dissent in political activity, dissociating himself from any plans for armed uprising. Nevertheless, the circumstances of his disaffection were used to discredit his proposals. He had put forward a powerful memorial calling for the setting up of an elective assembly. It was widely debated in the press, this debate itself being a significant novelty, and was refuted by government spokesmen, who characterized it, on the whole, as premature rather than fundamentally mistaken. It became clear that Itagaki himself would have favoured giving the franchise initially only to samurai and to the richer farmers and merchants. Such formulae, however sensible at a time when democracy itself was still a dirty word in much of Europe, to say nothing of other parts of Asia, were scarcely calculated to arouse enthusiastic support among the bulk of the people.

The movement for popular rights had nevertheless become sufficiently strong to evoke, in 1881, the promise of a constitution and a parliament. Ito recognized from the outset that his preparatory work must lead to the adoption of a system which would be consistent both with Japan's historical experience and with the new social order which he and his colleagues had already inaugurated. From either viewpoint, the position of the Emperor would be the key to success.

Ito did not, therefore, think in terms of the introduction ready-made of a constitutional model already in operation elsewhere. He was, however, particularly attentive to developments in Prussia from an early stage in the period of Bismarck's ascendancy. He had been impressed favourably there from the time of his tour of Europe with the Iwakura mission in 1871–73. He was not sympathetic with the view of Okuma, Itagaki and others that the British style of parliamentary government might be adopted, or even adapted, for use in Japan. He bore in mind that a number of other highly influential Meiji leaders, in earlier consultations with men of learning and with representatives of regional opinion in Japan, had concluded that the British system was too heavily dependent on unique historical experience, and on conventions evolved over centuries in circumstances wholly unparalleled by those of contemporary Japan, to provide much guidance of direct, practical value, let alone to constitute a model. The conduct of the monarchy as such was a different matter, in which there should be a close study of British custom. Presidential systems were less likely to repay detailed investigation. At the same time, the trend of political evolution in the United States of America, evidently accelerated by the outcome of the Civil War, was towards what seemed an extreme of democratic theory, and its pace might be dangerously fast. It was to be watched rather than imitated.

During his constitutional study visit to Europe in 1882–83, Ito had been receptive to the views of von Gneist and von Stein, and after his return to Tokyo he had preferred the advice of Roesler to that of Boissonade. He had met, and greatly admired, Bismarck. (So far as we know, there had been no opportunity to meet Gladstone during Ito's stay in London.) Not all his German-speaking advisers were wholly favourable to the influence of Prussia in the German Empire. Although Ito spoke of using a German model, the drafts produced under his supervision, within his department while he was Minister of the Imperial Household and in subsequent consultations with the Privy Council, were designed to reflect and so far as possible to embody Japan's historical inheritance. His assistants in the work on the Constitution, including Ito Miyoji, Inoue Kowashi and Saionji Kinmochi, and his private secretary, Kaneko Kentaro, were all to remain among his closest political associates. The vision of Japan's development which they shared was that of a constitutional monarchy, but one in which the Constitution was the gift of the monarch to his people; a constitutional monarchy, to put it paradoxically, in which the divine right of the monarch was unimpaired.

The Emperor himself presented the Constitution to Count Kuroda Kiyotaka, from Satsuma, the Prime Minister, on 11 February 1889, together with laws and ordinances governing the procedure of the two Houses of the Diet, of elections for members of the lower House, the House of Representatives, and of the administration of public finance. The Constitution, which was to come into force in November of the following year, characterized the Emperor, in the eternal succession of his line, as 'sacred and inviolable'. A strong emphasis on his powers was its most prominent feature. Those of the Diet were circumscribed. The Cabinet was independent of the Diet. Ministers were appointed by the Emperor, and were responsible to him, both individually and collectively. His legislative powers were superior to theirs. The Emperor was also Commander-in-Chief of the armed forces, the army and navy being directly responsible to him, through their professional chiefs, who enjoyed the privilege of immediate access to the presence.

The promulgation of the Constitution was accompanied by ample formal and official explanation of the importance of sustaining transcendental government and thus averting any risk of the domination of policy by party or partisan interest. Powers given to the House of Peers and, especially, to the Privy Council were designed to ensure that these exhortations were not merely rhetorical, and that there was an apparatus of institutional control interposed between the House of Representatives and the Emperor, an area in which his most experienced and most loyal servants could see to it that his will and his interests were paramount. It was in this area that various informal arrangements of constitutional significance were to be made subsequently, seemingly *ad hoc*, and it was in this area that ambiguities and distortions were to appear. At various times, there would be good or bad reasons why attempts should be made to conceal exactly by whom the Emperor's will and interests were being interpreted or implemented.

The Meiji leadership saw themselves as custodians of the Emperor's supreme prerogatives. So, from the mid-1890s, did the group of elder statesmen known as the Genro, a group endowed with immense prestige but entirely lacking in constitutional endorsement. Co-opting their own membership, the Genro provide an informal definition of the leadership. Regarded as an institution, the Genro have tended to transcend definition, as the powers which they arrogated to themselves transcended not only those of the Diet and of the parties but even those of the Cabinet. Later it was to be so with the Privy Council, at times, either as a whole or acting in committee, as for example in the Gaiko Chosakai; later still, with the Jushin. Similar claims were to be made later also by the Supreme Command, by the army and navy separately, by individual commanders, ultimately even by groups of comparatively junior officers. It was to be the same outside the structure of government, on the fringes of political life, with various influential groups and secret societies. For their part, the bureaucrats soon felt themselves to be closer to the guardians of central authority than members of the House of Representatives could hope to come simply by virtue of popular election. Officially, indeed, senior civil servants enjoyed precedence before members of the lower House.

The rights and duties of the people were covered briefly in the Constitution. Their duties were also expressed with great clarity in the Imperial Rescript on Education, itself ranking with the Constitution in popular esteem, with its presumption of selfless patriotism as the basic motivating force in both individual and social conduct. It was left by implication to the political parties to secure any necessary further definition of the rights of the people, but without interfering with the transcendental administration of public affairs. It became the practice to refer to the national polity (*kokutai*) as if it were a transcendental entity; and for many of those who invoked it to do so on the basis that the interpretation of its requirements was self-evidently safe in their understanding, and its mysteries in their keeping. Such attitudes were not wholly out of line with metaphysical doctrines fashionable, though not without detractors, elsewhere in the civilized world.

However, although the entry into force of the Meiji Constitution legitimized the position of the leaders, it succeeded only very imperfectly in stabilizing domestic politics. The political parties, reconstructed for the purpose, naturally set out to test the limits of their constitutional licence against the unconcealed reluctance of the national leadership to share with them the management of government and public business or the direction of policy. As party chiefs, Itagaki and Okuma were forced into rivalry in pursuit of acceptance as partners in government by the Satcho establishment; but they were later to combine uneasily in the first, brief, so-called party government, in 1898. Meanwhile, Ito himself gradually came to acknowledge that the parties' demand that they should at least participate

11

in government must eventually be conceded. Yamagata held out for the principle of transcendental government, but he was a shrewd master of the tactical compromise in politics and had enlisted Goto Shojiro, of Tosa, one of the most prominent party men, as Minister for Communications in the cabinet which he formed in December 1889, to see in the new Constitution.

Yamagata also never lost sight of the mutually supportive relationship between efforts to attain Japan's external objectives and the fostering of a sense of domestic unity. This relationship, which had been critical in the debate known as the *seikanron*, when the leadership had been confronted with Saigo's drive for intervention in Korea twenty years earlier, reasserted itself soon after the Constitution came into effect, though in an altogether changed social context. For Saigo, the maintenance of the traditions and privileges of the warrior class had been uppermost among considerations motivating his demand for a forward policy; but he had told Itagaki at the time that his plan would benefit the country by diverting those who still wished to fight for revival of the cause and system of the *bakufu*. It would, in other words, keep things quiet at home.

Foreign adventure was not yet back on the agenda, as the first general elections for the House of Representatives passed off in reasonably good order, in November 1890. Itagaki's Jiyuto and Okuma's Kaishinto, together with Goto's party, won 160 of the 300 seats. Most of the 140 independents were as keen as the parties to oppose the government, however, so that friction was unavoidable. Goto's followers were not deterred from confrontation by his having joined the Cabinet. Despite its many inbuilt safeguards, it became clear that the Constitution would permit the lower House largely to frustrate the government's budget proposals. Some heavy-handed transactions by Yamagata contrived a compromise by which Diet business was enabled to continue, but did not produce a solution satisfactory to the government. He handed over the premiership to Matsukata who, however, for all his reputation in financial affairs, was equally unable to obtain approval for the budget, and was obliged to dissolve the lower House in December 1891.

The elections held in February 1892 were disfigured by violence and corruption. In the country, divisions between and within the opposition parties exacerbated a tense atmosphere. Adherents of the Jiyuto, for example, in addition to their animus against both the central authorities and the Kaishinto, suffered from a long-standing rift within their own organization, in which landlords and industrialists were fighting to protect their interests against peasant farmers. Moreover, the apparent success of the Meiji leaders in having set up elective assemblies in the prefectures years in advance of the inauguration of the Imperial Diet at the centre, had had the effect of leading local officials and the police under their control to share the government's hostility to the political parties. The Home Minister, Shinagawa Yajiro,

resigned after the elections in acknowledgement of government responsibility for the casualties suffered in the campaign, which had left 25
people dead and 400 wounded. During the elections, Okuma had accused
Inoue Kaoru publicly of venality in his dealings with Mitsui, disregarding
his own well-known family ties with Iwasaki, and so with Mitsubishi. One
positive effect of these proceedings was to influence Ito in the direction of
power-sharing with the parties, even of abandoning the principle of transcendental government, if perhaps by slow degrees. As Yamagata would
evidently not do this, the parties sensed that the cohesion of the leadership
was weakening. Ito took over from Matsukata as Prime Minister in August
1892, but despite his having invoked the authority of the Emperor in the
Cabinet's defence, following a lower House motion for their impeachment
in February 1893, a further dissolution proved unavoidable in December,
and yet another in June 1894, after elections in March. Ito remained Prime
Minister.

These years of unanticipated domestic political complication were not
years in which the leaders could afford to neglect Japan's international
position, and treaty revision remained a major preoccupation, somewhat
lightened from 1893, when a hopeful new round of negotiation was
launched by Count Mutsu Munemitsu, as Foreign Minister. New pressures,
however, had been felt from 1891, as the result of the inauguration of
Russia's great programme for the Trans-Siberian Railway. In the same year,
the Tsarevich, invited to pay an official visit to Japan in the hope on his
hosts' part that this would promote an easier relationship, was attacked and
wounded in the head by a mad policeman, at Otsu, near Kyoto. As he made
a good recovery, the incident itself was not so disastrous as at first seemed
likely, though damaging to national pride and prestige. The Japanese government was able subsequently to gain some credit for refusing to press the
judiciary to sentence the assailant to be hanged. The death penalty was not
imposed by the courts, despite some clamour from abroad, and some
attempted prompting from outside government circles at home. In the
substance of their relations with Russia, the Japanese leaders had already
improved their position, in 1875, by agreeing to renounce their claim to
Sakhalin in return for Russian acceptance of Japan's title to the northern
Kuriles. They were nevertheless increasingly concerned about the ultimate
intentions of the Russians in the Far East. They saw the railway plans as
a direct threat to their interests, and conclusion of the Franco-Russian
Alliance, also in 1891, compounded their suspicions. Furthermore, both
British and French activities in China had been regarded consistently as
prejudicial to Japan's interests and freedom of action, if for the most part
indirectly. By comparison with these activities, neither Chinese recognition, from the 1870s, of Japan's sovereignty over the Ryukyus, nor the
uneasy stalemate in Korea following the agreement reached by Ito with

Li Hung-chang (Hongzhang) in 1885, gave a balancing satisfaction to the Japanese leadership.

It was a situation in which apprehensions and ambitions were mutually supportive. Both focused most sharply on the Korean peninsula, and on the strategic approaches to it both from China and from Russia, by way of Manchuria. The military strength which it had been possible to build up in Japan under the financial and budgetary management of Matsukata now made it possible to contemplate the sort of action from which the majority of the leadership had drawn back twenty years before, at such heavy cost to the consolidation of national unity.

The Japanese leaders had long seen what was then called the backwardness of Korea as a kind of provocation to themselves, because it constituted an invitation to China, and to any of the Powers, to establish positions of influence which might come to threaten their own security or independence. Since the unsatisfactory agreement of 1885, the Chinese had not only stepped up their own activity, especially in trade, but had also encouraged European Powers to establish relations with and interests in Korea. The energy and skill of China's representative in Seoul, Yuan Shih-k'ai, had put the Japanese at something of a disadvantage there. When the traditionalist revolt of the Tonghaks broke out in Korea in June 1894, the Chinese responded promptly to the Korean king's appeal for help. The Japanese countered this response by reinforcing their own troops in Korea and demanding that the Korean government undertake major reforms favourable to Japanese influence. By warning China to refrain from further troop movements on her part, and by taking over the palace in Seoul, the Japanese government left the Chinese with the alternatives of resisting these aggressive moves as best they could, or effectively abandoning their claim to exercise suzerainty over Korea. The internal situation in China was such as to preclude major concessions, which would have had disastrous domestic consequences. War began in August. The circumstances in which hostilities broke out and the course which they took left no doubt as to the readiness of the Japanese leaders for a showdown in Korea and with China.

Embarking on this course involved a series of policy decisions in which Ito and Yamagata were in broad agreement, perhaps for the last time on matters of such range and consequence. The implications of these decisions were far-reaching and long-lasting, and were recognized as such. The leaders were committing themselves, above all, to a view of the regime in China. They had become resigned to the decay of the Empire. They were accepting that, rather than help the existing authorities in Peking to resist the depredations of the Powers, they would seek to secure a position for Japan on the mainland of continental Asia which would enable them to compete with, and if necessary contest encroachments on their own interests by, the other Powers. Yamagata's preliminary formulation in 1890 of the concepts of a

14

cordon of sovereignty and a cordon of advantage had presupposed the extension of Japanese influence at least, if not also of Japanese authority, in North-East Asia. The rejection of Saigo's forward policy in the early 1870s by his colleagues in the leadership had been on the grounds that it was premature and risky; not that its aims were undesirable. At the same time, there was some belief that Japan would be acting in the interests of the peoples of Asia generally if she set an example of assertiveness in the face of European and American imperial pretensions. For Yamagata himself, it was also a basic premise of policy that 'Asia exists as Asia of the Asians'. There was an underlying contradiction here, which was to persist. Yet this was the age of teachers and pupils, of lessons to be taught and learned. The Japanese leaders were following in what European and American leaders had demonstrated to be the way of the Powers. They may have noted a word of caution from London, but they also noted that it was not pressed.

For Ito, there were additional considerations. He had been responsible personally for the deficient agreement of 1885 with China over Korea, and it was desirable to have that episode overlaid and superseded. He was facing an unexpected degree of difficulty with the Diet. Although the expense of repeated election campaigns was beginning to deter the political parties from pressing the role of opposition at every opportunity, and although Ito himself was increasingly inclined towards some form of accommodation with the parties, it would be useful to have a success close at hand to distract attention from domestic wrangles. He could press home the great advantage at last obtained by Mutsu's achievement of treaty revision in his negotiations in London. Mutsu's success would mean the end of extraterritoriality, with the coming into force of Japan's new Civil Code, in 1899; and would lead eventually to tariff autonomy. These long-sought benefits would come not only with Britain, but inevitably and consequentially in relations with all the other Powers, even if not immediately. The revised Treaty of Commerce and Navigation with Great Britain was signed in July 1894, on the eve of the outbreak of hostilities with China. There was a sense of advance in the country's interests, which Ito was naturally keen to enhance. Bismarck and Yoshida Shoin would surely both have applauded.

The prosecution of the military campaign itself showed how thoroughly the Japanese planners had prepared for it; and how well they had learned from other empire-builders that comparatively modest, well-equipped forces of disciplined men may exert an unfailing superiority over a less well organized, less well led and less determined opposition, almost regardless of the total resources available to either side. The Chinese Navy, whose guns were reportedly supplied with only one round of ammunition each, was rapidly disabled. The whole of Korea was brought under Japanese military control without serious difficulty. In October, Yamagata himself led two divisions into south Manchuria. Oyama, in command of three divisions,

15

invaded the Liaotung peninsula, capturing Port Arthur in November. A force was then detached for operations in the Shantung peninsula, and Weihaiwei was taken in February 1895. This latter move followed the recommendations of Marshal Yamagata, who himself, however, had been recalled by Ito, in order to restrain his ambitions in Manchuria. The principal objectives of the entire campaign were attained, almost with ease. The conduct of the Japanese troops was evidently exemplary. There was no opening for foreign critics to argue that standards had been observed to fall below those acceptable in the civilized world. Readers in Britain, for example, were assured by the *Times* correspondent that, despite barbarous provocation on the past of their enemies, the treatment of prisoners of war by the Japanese military forces was a model of correctness.

The Chinese having acknowledged defeat, Li Hongzhang went to Japan to sign the Treaty of Shimonoseki with Ito, in April 1895. For Ito, this more than compensated for the shortcomings of their agreement of ten years before. It consisted of a series of painful concessions by China in terms of territory, as well as in the surrender of the claim that Korea lay within China's sphere of influence; in the grant of access to Chinese ports hitherto closed to foreign commerce; and of a substantial indemnity. But the scale of the territorial concessions – besides Formosa, they included the whole of the Liaotung peninsula, with Port Arthur – was such as to alarm the Russians and their French allies, and to excite the envious disapproval of Germany. No sooner had popular rejoicing in Japan over the prizes won in the war reached a climax, than news broke of the Triple Intervention. The Japanese government felt compelled to accede to professedly friendly but unmistakably threatening advice that they retrocede the Liaotung peninsula to China. Complete humiliation was averted by the negotiation of a compensating increase in the war indemnity to be paid by China, but an unforgettable slight had been inflicted on the national pride of Meiji Japan. The significance of the Triple Intervention was underlined in the spring of 1898, when the European Powers exacted concessions for themselves from China, the Russians actually securing the lease of Port Arthur, together with China's recognition of their special position in Manchuria. The exactions of the Powers in that year, precipitated by German demands following the murder of two Roman Catholic priests in China, were a prelude and an incitement to the Boxer Rising, which in turn offered Japan the opportunity to reassert her claim to a leading place among the Powers, in East Asia, and especially *vis-à-vis* China, and to do so in circumstances which brought her considerable international credit and *réclame*.

In 1895, however, when obliged to back down in the face of threats of active intervention by both the Russians and the French, if not also the Germans, the Japanese government reacted by initiating a new programme of further greatly increased defence expenditure. The regular army's strength was doubled, the fleet substantially enlarged, with a building programme extending well into the next century, and the manufacture and provision of armaments and equipment improved and expanded proportionately. The government itself saw to the setting up of an iron and steel industry which would be capable of production on a scale appropriate to a first-class Power. All this reflected the temper of the country.

Sir Ernest Satow, who believed that it was primarily concern about the Trans-Siberian Railway, and resolve to prevent Russia from gaining free access to the Pacific, which had motivated Japan's approach to the war with China, noted subsequently that Japan was 'arming with greater rapidity and secrecy' than she had prior to that war. One of his Japanese informants, well placed to know, told Satow in the spring of 1896 that 'Japan does not want to move again for another eight or nine years, till she is ready'.

It was Japan's actions which had now exposed the full reality of China's weakness, and at the very period of the most intense worldwide competition between the established Powers. Despite heavy preoccupations in other regions, none felt able to ignore developments in East Asia. The prospects here were of what came to be known as the slicing of the Chinese melon; of adjusting to, or opposing, the eastward expansion of Russian influence and authority; of accommodating reasonable aspirations on the part of Japan, as a newcomer among the Powers; of securing loans and, increasingly, of protecting investments; of building railways and spheres of influence; of developing trade; and of calculating advantage in commercial arrangements, and in political combinations and alliances. These prospects were to absorb energies and resources on a scale which may seem, in retrospect, disproportionate to the prizes available, either immediately or after long years of persistent if in most cases intermittent endeavour. In this competition, Japan's geographical advantage was underestimated, because her standing among the Powers was so recently recognized and its implications were so imperfectly assimilated.

Furthermore, the Japanese leaders controlled their resentment of the Triple Intervention, and soon learned to practise the low posture and the cautious, gradual advance. At first, however, seeking to consolidate the gains still remaining to them from the war with China, they pressed too hard the advantage won in Korea. The implication of their agents in the murder of Queen Min, presumably with authority from Tokyo, amounted to a serious setback. It led to the assumption by the Russians of a dominant position in Seoul, building on their response to the appeal of the Korean king. Competition with China for influence in Korea was thus exchanged for renewed competition with Russia, which grew spasmodically keener.

Efforts for the mutual recognition of equal rights in Korea were expressed in agreements negotiated between Komura and Weber, and again between Yamagata and Lobanov, in 1896, but concurrence was of the letter rather

17

than the spirit. Yamagata's formal visit to Russia for the coronation of Tsar Nicholas II, on a journey which also included calls in Washington and in European capitals, was the occasion for his negotiation. Yamagata coincided in Russia with Li Hongzhang, who concluded a secret agreement with Lobanov designed essentially to inhibit Japanese expansion, in part by facilitating Witte's strategy of advancing personal and national interests together, in the construction of railways. Japan achieved some further improvement of her position in Korea, and renewed Russian confirmation of Korea's technical independence, through the Nishi-Rosen agreement of 1898, but this scarcely began to make up for the Russian lease of Port Arthur and its environs. Friction with Russia in Korea persisted, reaching the level of a war scare after an incident at Masampo in 1900. This was followed in turn by a secret agreement over the island of Koje. But mutual suspicion was growing. Ito was converted to the idea of exchanging recognition of Russia's position in Manchuria for an unequivocal acknowledgement by the Russians of Japan's superior position in Korea, the concept known as *ManKan kokan*; but the Russians tended to pocket the recognition without giving the reciprocal acknowledgement.

While the Russians secured Port Arthur in 1898, and the Germans Kiaochow, the British succeeded the Japanese in temporary occupation of Weihaiwei. This was not at the expense of Japanese interests, since Japan's withdrawal was made by agreement, on completion of payment of the war indemnity by China, and this payment had been dependent upon a loan to China in which British banks took the lead. Before he left office in 1898, Ito sought to promote Japanese interests in China by the negotiation of a non-alienation agreement for the province of Fukien, opposite the Japanese colony of Taiwan, and thus to gain a new sphere of influence. Shortly afterwards, during Okuma's first, brief premiership, when he was also Foreign Minister, rights were obtained for Japan in the foreign settlements at a number of additional ports on the China coast.

It had been noted with interest and satisfaction in Tokyo that Britain's approach to trade with and foreign rights in China had led her to withhold support from the Triple Intervention. The commercial provisions of the Treaty of Shimonoseki were acceptable in London, even welcome, and the likely consequences of the treaty as a whole were not found objectionable there. In Japan, Britain's recent willingness to proceed with treaty revision, seen as a decisive if belated move in Japan's favour, together with the success of certain personal and institutional links, for example in finance and naval training, had prepared the way for speculation about a possible alliance of convenience. The containment of Russian expansion remained Japan's principal common interest with Great Britain. The temporary establishment of facilities for the Royal Navy at Port Hamilton was evidence of recognition of the strategic importance of the Korean peninsula. In 1899 the

British government reached agreement with the Russians whereby the latter would abstain from seeking railway concessions in the Yangtse basin, and from obstructing British activity there, in exchange for British acceptance of limits on their own support of railways and associated projects north of the Great Wall. However, by the time the Boxer Rising reached serious proportions, in mid-1900, the British were heavily preoccupied in South Africa. This led them to come out strongly in favour of maximum Japanese participation in operations for the relief of the legations in Peking (Beijing). Yamagata had insisted at first on a cautious policy, but he was ready for Japan to respond energetically, once it was clear that this was what a number of sufficiently influential Powers favoured.

Before this necessity arose, however, Secretary of State Hay had launched the United States' Open Door proposals, in an attempt to regulate competition between the Powers in China, to preserve the integrity of the Chinese Empire, and to indicate indirectly that there was likely to be some co-ordinated resistance to any further Russian pressure upon Peking. The Japanese leaders were not among those consulted in the preparation of these proposals. Nevertheless, Yamagata was able to welcome them. The idea that a combination of the United States, Great Britain and Japan was beginning to challenge Russian ambitions in the Far East, and above all in Manchuria, suggested that Japan might indeed find, in developing positive relations with other Powers, help in containing the single threat to which her interests were most vulnerable.

This was not a view which prevailed throughout the leadership. There were those who would have preferred to develop a partnership with China than with any of the Powers. There were those who would have persevered in the search for a *modus vivendi* with Russia, among whom Ito was certainly to be numbered at a later stage. A unified view on foreign policy did not long survive the war of 1894–95 with China.

Nor was the welcome given to the United States' Open Door proposals unqualified. Yamagata's Foreign Minister, Aoki Shuzo, was to draw attention to certain unsatisfactory features of the responses of the Powers. The intentions of the United States were not themselves unambiguously favourable to Japanese interests. Indeed, a tentative American bid for a preferential position in Fukien had to be warded off. Earlier designs on Formosa, promoted notably by Commodore Perry, were not forgotten in Tokyo. More recently, the annexation of Hawaii, when first proposed, had evoked a strong Japanese protest in Washington. Hoshi Toru, whose career exemplified the opportunism of those party men who were most impatient for power, had even advocated naval intervention by Japan to contest it. Sensitivity on behalf of Japanese emigrants to Hawaii had been stimulated by knowledge of the measures taken to restrict Chinese immigration into the United States.

Nevertheless, Japan's relations with the United States in the last decade of the nineteenth century were generally correct, even cordial. The Japanese leaders remained well disposed towards Washington. They were able formally to welcome the United States' annexation of the Philippines. At the same time, and with the annexation also of Guam and other islands of strategic significance, they noted that the United States had strengthened its position as a Power in the Pacific. It is sometimes forgotten that the image of the white man's burden was expressed by Kipling in reference to the American assumption of Spain's former colonial responsibilities in the Philippines.

The opposition parties in the Diet had supported the Japanese government during the war with China, and they did so again during the operations against the Boxers, for the relief of the legations in Peking, where Chancellor Sugiyama had been one of the first to be murdered. Japan's contingent, at 8,000 men, was the largest in the combined force as eventually constituted, and by all accounts among the best disciplined. Although the British were appreciative of this performance, British sponsorship, as it was called, of Japan's participation was criticized by some of the Powers. The appointment, at a late stage in the proceedings, of von Waldersee to command the combined forces was seen as a snub to the Japanese, and was no doubt intended as such by the German Emperor, whose view of the yellow peril, to use the phrase attributed personally to him, was already well known. By August 1900 it was equally clear that, of all the Powers, Japan was the most solidly represented in Peking, the Russians having chosen to intrigue for the extension of their position in Manchuria rather than exert themselves to show solidarity with the international community.

Readiness to put down the Boxers was not incompatible with concern for China's best interests, but it meant joining a group of non-Asian Powers. It prejudiced Japan's claim to be the special representative, in world politics, of the Asian countries and peoples. Japan was becoming a Power like other Powers of the period, tending to put the accumulation of national strength and prestige above all other considerations, if to a large extent for reasons of self-defence. Any prospect of a new and improved relationship with China receded; was indefinitely deferred. Those who pressed for an Asian bias in foreign policy, such as Prince Konoe Atsumaro and his followers, now tended to be drawn into the anti-Russian campaign, which amounted in the longer term to demanding that the Japanese government take a strong line over Manchuria. The secret societies of the right showed the same tendency. Even the principal opposition parties, when transformed into the rulers, for the first brief spell in 1898 backed Okuma in a notably assertive set of claims to rights in China; that is to say, to rights of the same character as those whose termination had so recently been secured by Japan in respect of her own territory, after the long struggle for revision of the unequal treaties. It was hard to see beyond the weakness of the Qing dynasty. Ito may have tried to do so. The delay in his return from a visit to China not long before the decision was taken to intervene against the Boxers remains unexplained.

Meanwhile, in domestic politics Ito had handed over to Matsukata in 1896, after his longest term as Prime Minister. Matsukata, whose cabinet included both Okuma and Itagaki, was uniquely well qualified to deal with the financial problems resulting from the war with China; and to find funds for the rearmament programme adopted after the Triple Intervention. The indemnity from China also enabled him to see to Japan's adoption of the gold standard, thus satisfying another of the criteria for status in international affairs. In addition, Matsukata arranged for Japan to return to the London money market for the first of a series of new loans, the first from abroad for twenty-five years: the dignity of independence was no longer at stake. This arrangement was negotiated on the basis of yet another of those personal connections with the British establishment which were becoming increasingly noticeable and significant. But even Matsukata, with the former opposition leaders among his ministers, could not carry the lower House with him in making proposals for an increase in the Land Tax. The imposition of new restrictions on the freedom of speech, combined with the impasse over taxation, proved fatal to the government.

When Ito resumed the premiership, in 1898, he was also unable to obtain approval for his similar fiscal proposals; and so the former opposition parties, with Okuma as Prime Minister, had an opportunity to exercise the authority of government. They failed to sustain their unity, falling out, in effect, over the spoils of office. Consequently, Yamagata once more became Prime Minister in November 1898.

Yamagata was responsible for the introduction, in 1900, of the Peace Police Law, a repressive measure which caused serious problems for the nascent trade union movement and for the early Japanese socialists. It also purported to outlaw secret societies: the intention is noteworthy, even if it was not fulfilled. When, later in the same year, Yamagata gave way once again to Ito, it was in the hope that a government of party politicians would disintegrate for a second time. For Ito, having concluded that it would be right to assist the development of reputable party government, rather than continue to frustrate it, had now formed and assumed the presidency of the Rikken Seiyukai, a party based, with his assent, on Itagaki's old Jiyuto.

In studying the mutual relationship of Ito and Yamagata, it is never clear where the border lay between rivalry and subtle collaboration. Both believed in the necessity for Meiji Japan of strong central government. Yamagata was convinced that the political parties were beyond redemption. Ito apparently came to the view that government, certainly government by consent, could not long continue successfully without their participation.

21

The House of Peers would have supported transcendental government until the end of time. The House of Representatives would never willingly settle for the role of rubber stamp; and the financial powers given them under the Constitution would ensure that the members never had to do so.

The gradual strengthening, in the 1890s, of the institution of the Genro, so inconspicuously introduced that its exact origins remain obscure, may be seen as a last attempt by the united Meiji leadership to insulate major decisions of policy from the hazards of interference and eventual control by the House of Representatives; to interpose yet one more layer of prestigious authority between the Emperor and the unanointed politicians.

Various other mechanisms were put in place with the same broad purpose of restricting the scope and efficacy of the lower House, mostly by Yamagata. It was he, soon after the war with China, who initiated the ordinance which laid down that the posts of War Minister and Minister of the Navy were reserved to senior officers on the active list, in order to protect the administration of the armed services, and defence policy itself, from the politicians. His creation of the Supreme Military Advisory Council, in 1898, strengthened the point. He also entrenched the position of the bureaucracy, by the introduction of an examination system, and by means of ordinances on appointment to and retirement from the civil and government services. These were all measures which would reduce party politicians' access to the levers of power.

It is sometimes suggested that Ito was driven to work with the political parties by his fear of forfeiting his own pre-eminent position to Yamagata. He may simply have thought it was right. Quite apart from considerations of personality, Ito may well have perceived a need for a stronger political counterweight to the influence of the military, who had, after all, reached Peking and found it not to be the summit of their aspirations; or of the bureaucracy, or of the combination of the two. Conclusive evidence is lacking.

The intellectual ferment precipitated by the Meiji Restoration lasted to the end of the century, and beyond. The pressure of events at the international level was such that much of the debate within Japan had to do with the concepts of modernization and Westernization, including the ideas of resistance to both these processes. The impact of Fukuzawa Yukichi, to take the most distinguished example, on social and political thought, or of Hara Kei and others through the media of information, was essentially educational. The publicists and communicators, for all their brilliance, tended to fall behind the pace of events. The direction of government by the Meiji leadership was as pragmatic as it was purposeful. They were men of very great capability. Their successors were already active; they included Komura and Kato, in foreign affairs, and in politics, with Saionji; Shibusawa, Yasuda and Okura in industry; Takahashi with his experience of the bureaucracy and his pre-eminence in finance; Oyama, Nogi, Yamamoto and Togo in the armed services.

Both generations reflected the temper of Meiji Japan at the turn of the century. Meiji Japan, in turn, reflected the predominant characteristics of the world of the Powers and the march of progress. A highly distinguished Japanese statesman said to the Anglican Bishop of South Tokyo in the 1890s, 'Other Eastern nations have cared chiefly to adopt from you your guns and means of defence. We have honestly tried also to understand your thought.' In return, Bishop Edward Bickersteth understood, as many Westerners did not, that Japan was 'a land where independence is a passion'. He remarked, reflecting once again the temper of both East and West in late Victorian and Meiji times, that in Japan patriotism was 'so nearly universal as scarcely to be counted a virtue'.

2

Expansion on the Asian Continent, 1900–12

Ito's fourth term as Prime Minister lasted only from the autumn of 1900 until early June 1901. Failure to obtain approval for the budget was once again fatal to the government. An appeal to the Emperor's authority was a recourse which now proved damaging to Ito's personal prestige. There were difficulties over the control and administration of the city of Tokyo itself. Moreover, Ito's health was poor, and Saionji had to act for him during two absences of several weeks each. At the same time, relations with the Russians deteriorated, and there was open talk of war. By the spring of 1901, indeed, Yamagata had concluded that a collision with Russia was unavoidable, and might have to be faced sooner rather than later. It was Yamagata's protégé, General Katsura, who succeeded Ito as Prime Minister, having served briefly in Ito's cabinet as War Minister. Komura was designated Foreign Minister, but remained at the legation in Peking until the peace agreement between the Allies and China was signed, on 7 September 1901. On his way back to Tokyo, he visited Korea.

Prevarication by the Russians over the withdrawal of their troops from Manchuria, coupled with the completion of the Trans-Siberian Railway, and the implications of these developments for continuing competition and rivalry in and around Korea, was by this time widely considered to present a grave strategic threat to Japan. The gradual intensification of this threat had stimulated increasingly serious study in Tokyo of the possibility of an agreement with Great Britain. Komura had been aware of this before he left Peking. Hayashi, the Minister in London, was now instructed to explore this possibility directly.

The idea of a treaty of alliance, first mooted tentatively in Japan in the mid-1890s, and separately and independently by Joseph Chamberlain in 1897, appealed strongly to those in both countries who gave a high priority, in their respective national interests, to the containment of Russian expansion. The British saw it also as a means of escaping from the continuing

24

growth in their commitment of resources to keeping the peace, and ensuring the free flow of trade, in the Far Eastern region as a whole. The Japanese valued the assurance it would give them that, in the event of war with Russia, they would not have also to face hostilities with other European Powers. A second major advantage to Tokyo lay in the formal recognition they were able to obtain from Great Britain of the 'peculiar degree' of Japan's political, as well as her commercial and industrial, interest in Korea.

Though the concept of such a treaty had been widely supported in the Japanese leadership, there were those who expressed doubts as to the wisdom of entering into alliance with a Power already perceived to be beyond the summit of its achievement and tending towards decline. This point of view, taken, for example, by Yamaza Enjiro, who followed Komura at the Japanese legation in Peking, deserves to be recalled not because it came near to prevailing in Japanese counsels, still less because it may have reflected some sophisticated contemporary opinion elsewhere, but rather as an illustration of a Japanese capacity for thinking in the long term. The most weighty resistance in Japan to the expediency of alliance with Britain came from Ito himself, who remained determined that every possible effort should be exerted to reach an accommodation with the Russians before recourse was had to London, for insurance. Indeed, the knowledge that Ito was still at work in St Petersburg while the negotiations for the Anglo-Japanese Treaty drew towards a satisfactory consummation caused some surprise in London. Equally, the news that a treaty of such bold scope and unusual balance had been concluded in London, following so closely upon Ito's conversations in St Petersburg, caused something of a shock to the Russians and contributed to the building up of a sense of suspicion and antagonism between Russia and Japan.

The news was well received by the public in Japan, where it was regarded as providing confirmation of the country's status among the leading Powers and strengthening national prestige. It carried a vivid symbolical signifi-cance, with racial as well as political, industrial, commercial, regional and immediate strategic implications. The British were, after all, indisputably the world's leading Power. For some time, they had regarded their own freedom from foreign entanglements with evident satisfaction. But the splendour of their isolation had lain in its confident basis of global power and influence. That isolation had nothing in common with the deep seclu-sion from which Japan had emerged so recently, though both experiences had served to promote the sense of national pride. That the British should choose to enter into this compact with an Asian country might seem to suggest a recognition that the era of Eurocentric civilization was ending. Such perceptions, however, were not in vogue. The dominant mode was that of empire. This was the context in which the impact of the Anglo-Japanese Treaty was felt. It gave Japan, as it were, a licence to think in imperial terms. The containment of Russia was the end in view; the extension of Japan's influence, even of Japan's authority, on the continental mainland of North-East Asia, and in the North Pacific, would be the means of its achievement. No limits had been established for imperial ambition.

The conclusion of the Anglo-Japanese Alliance must also be seen as a setback for Ito's approach to foreign policy, as compared with Yamagata's; for an approach which was inclined to give political and diplomatic considerations the greatest weight, as compared with one in which strategic and military factors were usually paramount. From the turn of the century in 1901, such differences were expressed through proxies, initially Saionji and Katsura. Any weakness from which Yamagata's partisans might have suffered as a consequence of their leader's continuing hostility to the political parties, now themselves enjoying benefits from Ito's abandonment of the transcendental way, were compensated for partly by Yamagata's cultivation of influential peers and bureaucrats, and even more substantially by his close association with the military, whose role in the determination of national policy was growing. Nevertheless, Ito had gained in London an assurance from Lansdowne that the British government would not object to Japan's seeking an agreement with Russia over Korea, provided that any such agreement was compatible with the Anglo-Japanese Treaty. In principle, therefore, diplomatic options were retained (by Britain as much as by Japan).

But this achievement did not suffice fully to restore Ito's declining influence. His reputation suffered from his deliberate association with lower House politicians, who were themselves mistrusted even by many of those acknowledging, like Ito, the inevitability of their increasing access to power. Hoshi Toru had been forced to resign from Ito's last cabinet because of charges of corruption. He was assassinated in 1901, while president of Tokyo City Council. His replacement in the Cabinet by Hara Kei had provided evidence of the vitality of the political system, of its capacity to produce forceful and original contenders for office, and incidentally of the influence of the press, in his work with which Hara had first begun to develop a wide base to support his career. Though both were the targets of assassins, it would be misleading to suggest that Hoshi and Hara had much in common beyond membership of the Seiyukai, for Hara was by far the more significant, both in personality and in achievement. Neither was especially close personally to Ito. Hara was linked rather with Inoue Kaoru and with Mutsu Munemitsu. Ito's closest associate, from before the turn of the century, was Saionji Kinmochi. Descended from a family long prominent at Court in Kyoto, Saionji was a liberal, cosmopolitan aristocrat, who had considered it his duty to interest himself in the welfare of the mass of the people, and in their civic and political rights. He represented the statesmanlike magnanimity of educated privilege, and was also capable of analysing the national interest dispassionately, against the background of a broad understanding of international affairs. Hara was more thrusting, acquisitive and assertive by nature; and he had the instincts of a political dealer.

From June 1901, however, power was predominantly in the hands of Katsura. He, with Yamagata's other associates, acted firmly against any threats of organized opposition to the authority of the administration, and against any interest groups not sponsored by the bureaucrats or the military which might aspire to exert undue influence at the national level. Discipline was maintained in industry, and in the rural communities, by a combination of equally strict proprietorial supervision, prefectural government and police control. Freedom of religion had been granted under the Constitution. Freedom of expression, however, had been subject to somewhat arbitrary limitation from the early years of the Meiji period. All the same, there was an active intellectual ferment, with lively and open criticism of political corruption, bureaucratic rigidity, moral decay, and the adoption of materialistic values, much as there would be in any more unequivocally open society. Philosophies of individualism were popular in academic, literary and artistic circles. The authorities worked hard and unceasingly to propagate and sustain a spirit of patriotic orthodoxy, in schools and in society at large. Their simple messages were much more easily disseminated than were the reflections of a small intelligentsia, little more than a series of coteries, of unorthodox thinkers.

In truth, the limits of official tolerance were easily reached. The authorities would have defended their practice in this regard on the grounds of pragmatism. They were the guardians. In so far as they grounded their policies on ideological foundations, those foundations were constructed of liberal sentiment. They would be tolerant of dissent up to the point at which its expression might be judged to pose a threat to the established polity. When it reached that point, they would suppress it instinctively. And at this time, when ideas seen as subversive of established government throughout the civilized world were causing growing unease, in the capitals of Powers long accustomed to dealing with dissenting opinion, the authorities in Japan became increasingly suspicious of movements even lightly tinged with revolutionary fervour. Since the inspiration of such movements most often came from within the territory of their principal potential adversary, their suspicions were easily justified. Thus the Social Democratic Party was no sooner formally constituted, in 1901, than it was banned. Socialism was a sinister concept in the civilized world of the day, not only in the minds of the controllers and supporters of authoritarian regimes, but even among moderate conservatives. In Japan, it was not only those regarded as dangerous extremists solely on account of their political philosophies or programmes who came under close scrutiny. The prospects of the Christian Churches

27

also suffered from their adherents' association with potentially unsettling theories of social reform. The suspicion that the representatives of faiths of alien origin, and their converts, might tend, or even intend, to subvert the civil power, probably in the interest of eventual foreign domination, lingered on as a legacy of Hideyoshi's proscription of Christianity three centuries before. This smouldering suspicion was fuelled by inflammatory rumours out of China, baseless but readily assimilated, and not extinguished by Japan's recent experience of working with European contingents for the relief of the legations in Peking.

Renewed threats to the country's independence, and status, were taken with the utmost seriousness by those who had done most to establish them. For the poorer people, rumours of such threats could provide a welcome spice in the daily gruel. For workers in the new factories, where the labour force doubled in the first decade of the century, this gruel was very thin; as it was for tenant farmers and landlords' peasant labourers in the paddyfields, who still accounted for more than half the total working population of Japan. It was their duty to put patriotism before personal interest or prosperity, and the authorities viewed with concern any movement which might disturb this sense of values. The founding of the *Heimin Shimbun* (*The People's News*) in 1903 was in part an attempt by Kotoku Shusui, Sakai Toshihiko and others to promote awareness of social conditions and problems, and of ways to improve or overcome them. The authorities closed it down within a year. Resistance to harsh and repressive conditions in manufacturing industry was still mostly local in scale, and ineffectual, the organization of labour unions on a nationwide basis remaining illegal. Resistance to the rate of tax on land, and to the exploitation of those who worked it, continued. Country people were also the victims in 1903 of a serious famine in the Tohoku region.

Hardship, though it would not be forgotten, did not noticeably reduce the general level of patriotic sentiment at this time, nor the shared pride in overcoming obstacles to the successful construction of the modern state. The endurance of hardship was accepted as a necessary sacrifice in the building not only of a new nation but also, now, of an empire. The authorities had no need to shirk a confrontation with Russia for lack of confidence in the national temper. Indeed they might hope, without cynicism, that a challenge would further reduce the level of dissent, certainly in the Diet, as it had at the time of the war with China. They were confident that the popular response to national emergency would be robust. But it was Plehve, not Yamagata, who was to say that what his country needed was a short, victorious war.

Soon after the conclusion of the Anglo-Japanese Treaty in 1902, the Russians had agreed with China terms for the withdrawal of their troops from Manchuria, by stages. This was welcomed in Tokyo. Further temporary signs of improvement in Russo-Japanese relations followed. The Russians made some attempts to conciliate all three leading Open Door Powers, the United States and Britain as well as Japan, over their intentions in Manchuria. But their troops were not withdrawn on schedule. Moreover, early in 1903 they showed renewed interest in the exploitation of timber in Korea. An alarming interpretation was put upon their activity in this enterprise in a report by a team of Japanese general staff officers, which included Major Tanaka Giichi, of Choshu, formerly military attaché in St Petersburg at the time of Ito's visit there in 1901, currently connected with the Kogetsukai group of ambitious and chauvinist army officers, and later Prime Minister. The army attached to the integrity of Japan's position in Korea a degree of importance which the navy considered excessive.

At this stage, Ito persisted in advocating a more conciliatory line towards Russia than was favoured by Katsura, who also resisted a British suggestion that he might consult Washington with a view to the consolidation of an agreed position by the leading Open Door Powers. Katsura and Yamagata sought to reduce Ito's public influence by contriving to have him appointed president of the Privy Council, thus securing his formal surrender of the leadership of the Seiyukai.

Nevertheless, negotiations with Russia were pursued. Although military planning was also put in hand in the autumn of 1903, under General Kodama Gentaro, former Governor-General of Taiwan and War Minister, it was only among comparatively junior army officers, rather than in government circles, that there was any settled opinion in favour of war. Yamagata and General Oyama were both highly sensitive to the threat, but were equally cautious when it came to planning the response. The navy, for which Admiral Yamamoto spoke, was even sceptical enough to impose delay on the implementation of certain preparatory plans. Kurino, at the legation in St Petersburg, was an associate of Ito, and not likely to become an advocate of war.

Nor was Russian policy in the hands of those favouring war. Alexeyev was inexperienced, and over-confident of his deterrent strength, judging that Japan would not dare to challenge Russia directly. Initially this also seems to have been the view of Rosen's legation in Tokyo. Kuropatkin, whose visit to Japan at a delicate stage in the developing crisis left him with respect for Japanese organization and drive, was loyal to the Tsar's desire that hostilities should be avoided.

Other Powers were easily influenced by those on both sides who persisted in playing down the likelihood of conflict. MacDonald, the British Minister in Tokyo, attached significance to Ito's clear concern to avoid war with Russia. Lansdowne, having suggested in vain that the Japanese should approach Washington in favour of a move by the Open Door Powers acting together, found that his colleagues were unable to offer their support to a

29

British initiative to this end. British and French attitudes were influenced by preoccupation with the construction of their own bilateral *entente*. Both governments made some efforts to avert war in the Far East, but they may have underestimated the urgency, or extent, of the danger. The Germans were hoping to profit, as suppliers, from Russian activity in Manchuria, and were also inclined to welcome the prospect that Russia might impose some restraint on Japanese ambitions in the wider region of North-East Asia. In Washington, there was a feeling that the Japanese could look after themselves. A growing association with Tokyo in financial matters may have served to induce complacency.

The collision of interests arose in Korea, and in Chinese territory. The Japanese, however, wished to avoid direct Chinese involvement in the dispute, for essentially the same reason as that for which they preferred to do without mediation by third parties: it would only complicate and delay their own negotiations with the Russians, in which the time factor was already pressing, because of strategic considerations. This left the Russians with their argument that what went on in Manchuria was of concern exclusively to the Chinese and themselves. But this argument was weakened by the fact that Prince Ching, while accepting that this might seem illogical, adopted an attitude of neutrality towards the dispute.

The Japanese leaders' conviction that Russian prevarication in the negotiations covered a continuing build-up of naval and military forces in the Far East resulted in their imposing deadlines, first upon themselves and then on their adversaries. They sought to conclude a secret agreement with Korea, to legitimize in advance the execution of their plan of action against Russia. An agreement was indeed signed, in late January 1904, but the Koreans withheld ratification on the grounds that the guarantee of respect for Korea's neutrality, which they required from the Japanese, was not forthcoming. By the beginning of the year there had evidently been a genuinely collegiate decision among the Genro, including Ito, that it would be dangerous to allow the Russians further time in which to build up their forces in the region, and to develop the operational capacity of their strategic railways. An ultimatum was accordingly delivered in St Petersburg on 16 January; and on 6 February the Japanese informed the Russian government that they were breaking off negotiations and severing diplomatic relations.

Although war was not declared formally until 10 February, Admiral Togo attacked the Russian fleet at Port Arthur on 8 February, thus ensuring for Japan immediate command of the Yellow Sea; and Japanese troops landed at Chemulpo (Inchon) the following day, to secure early control of the Korean capital. It was much debated in the world at large whether the rupture of relations constituted sufficient warning of active hostilities. The Japanese doctrine of supreme command (*dokudan senko*) has sometimes been invoked in justification of Togo's striking at his own discretion, but it is clear that operations went exactly as planned at headquarters. The existence and invocation of the doctrine of supreme command are of interest as illustrations of the readiness of the Japanese military to arrogate to themselves responsibilities which would usually be thought to lie with the central government. As for Korea, it had from the start been the Japanese plan to strike first, and strike through Korea. Arrangements for a prior agreement with Korea having been frustrated, the violation of Korean neutrality was covered retrospectively by an agreement of 23 February under which Japan, acting in effect as occupying power, assumed responsibility for Korea's independence and territorial integrity.

The Japanese Army had no difficulty in bringing the whole of Korea under their control. Having asserted its claim to command of the Yellow Sea, the Japanese government was able to extend the strength of the expeditionary forces rapidly and substantially. In April the Imperial Navy inflicted further losses on the Russian fleet, in another engagement outside Port Arthur. By early May the army had succeeded in pushing across the Yalu into Manchuria. Their objectives were to occupy the Liaotung peninsula, and to press northwards to Liaoyang and Mukden in order to achieve control of as great a length as possible of the south Manchurian branch line of the Chinese Eastern Railway. From the Yalu crossing, the First and Fourth Armies moved on Liaoyang, while General Nogi's Third Army turned down the coast of the peninsula, to link up with General Oku's Second Army, which had been landed 50 miles north of Port Arthur.

Both sides sustained losses at sea in engagements in April and May, but the Russians were not inclined to risk a main fleet action; and after the capture by the Japanese Army of hills round Port Arthur the Russian warships could be shelled where they lay at anchor. Port Arthur was invested by the end of August, the Russians having desisted from attempts to prevent its encirclement after battles which were otherwise inconclusive. The besieging armies were 90,000 strong, the defending garrison rather less than half that strength, with an equal artillery force of about 500 guns on each side. The siege came to involve slaughter on a scale faintly foreshadowing that of the First World War. General Nogi's army, for example, lost 15,000 men in the assault on 174 Metre Hill alone, and 10,000 at 203 Metre Hill, which was not taken until early December, by which time heavier guns had been brought into action in support of the attack. General Stoessel surrendered Port Arthur in early January 1905. For this he was later court-martialled, and briefly jailed. The capture of the port had cost the Japanese 60,000 casualties in all.

Russian resistance to the Japanese advance further north was equally stubborn, in the main battle south of Liaoyang, which began at the end of August, and in the battle of Sha Ho in October. After two weeks of fighting there, the Russians withdrew, but it was a true strategic withdrawal, not the retreat of a defeated army. At this time, the decision was taken in St Petersburg to send the Baltic Squadron half-way round the world, to redress the naval balance of power in the Far East. It was to be the virtual annihilation of this ill-fated and ill-found squadron by the deadly efficiency of Admiral Togo's fleet at the battle of Tsushima, on 27 May 1905, which would give the Japanese government the opportunity to suggest to President Theodore Roosevelt that 'entirely of his own motion and initiative' he might invite Japan and Russia to enter into direct negotiations for peace.

Meanwhile, under General Oyama's supreme command, the Japanese armies in Manchuria, with a combined strength of some 320,000, had brought superior Russian forces to battle before Mukden, had inflicted heavy casualties on them, and had entered the city. Before the peace conference opened at Portsmouth, on 9 August, a separate, small Japanese expeditionary force had been dispatched in July to take the sparsely defended island of Sakhalin.

Although the Japanese government appeared, especially to their own people, to be in a strong position, victorious on every front, the reality was otherwise. Their resources of trained men, of material, and above all of finance, were strained to the limit. The ability or willingness of London or Washington to extend further loans was doubtful. The lines of supply and communications for their large force in Manchuria were expensive to maintain, and could prove to be dangerously extended. For although there was rioting and bloody repression in Russia, the threat of massive reinforcement against Japan was not affected. The capacity of the Russians, with time more than ever on their side, to train new armies if necessary and to transport them by trainloads to the eastern provinces was hardly impaired. General Kuropatkin was fully aware that he had the resources to win a prolonged war, if it came to that.

The consciousness of reserves on which they would be able to draw in any renewed conflict, together with a readiness to take pains over the public presentation of their position, gave the Russians formidable advantages in the negotiations for peace, even though they were seen to have been defeated in the war. In particular, Witte made it plain that he would sooner see the talks fail than offer the Japanese any indemnity at all, let alone the substantial sum they demanded. However, the Russians were prepared formally to acknowledge, in the Treaty of Portsmouth of 5 September 1905, Japan's superior position in Korea. They also yielded to Japan the leasehold of the Liaotung peninsula, though this had to be made subject to China's acceptance. In addition, they finally agreed to cede the southern half of Sakhalin (Karafuto). Their readiness to make this latter concession was apparently at first concealed from the Japanese government by Roosevelt, to whose ambassador in St Petersburg it had been confided. So, though there was genuine gratitude on the part of Japan's leaders for the President's good offices, they were left with a suspicion that his motives in exercising them might not have been as straightforward as they had supposed.

The terms of the treaty of peace, immediately they were announced, were received by the public in Japan with incredulous rage. Such was the outcry that Komura had to return home very quietly from the United States. The Anti-Peace Movement fomented immediate, widespread riots, centred on the Hibiya district of Tokyo but involving attacks on the police and on other manifestations of authority throughout the capital, as well as disorders in many other parts of Japan. These riots were remembered to the end of their days by all who saw them. Although the left naturally took advantage of the opportunity to make strident demands for domestic reform, essentially these violent protests were an expression of mass chauvinism, and of resentment that sacrifices, not only in the war but also in the construction of the modern state, should have been so inadequately rewarded.

The strength of feeling at this time, which was so vigorously demonstrated, and so widely, had a major influence on the direction of policy thereafter. Successive Japanese governments felt obliged to try to ensure that benefits were seen to accrue to the people from the position won for the Empire on the Asian mainland. Though the Russo-Japanese War was fought primarily for reasons of strategic rivalry, and in order to dispel a perceived threat to Japan's security and independence, its justification had to be conjured out of imperial policies founded upon its conclusion.

The Japanese government therefore moved at once to consolidate their position in Korea. This had already been endorsed unequivocally by Great Britain in the revised Anglo-Japanese Treaty of August 1905; secretly by the United States, which obtained in return, in the agreement signed by Taft and Katsura the previous month, an assurance that Japan would not attack the Philippines; and by the Russians in the Treaty of Portsmouth itself. Now, in negotiations with Ito in November, the Koreans were prevailed upon to accept the continuing status of a Japanese protectorate. Early in 1906 Ito was appointed Resident-General in Seoul. He had insisted that this appointment must not be liable to the interference of any independent army commander. He himself was endowed with extensive powers; but he was against annexation, believing that he could secure Korean collaboration with his own administration, and that Japan could come to enjoy Korean goodwill.

Ito's appointment was not made until after Saionji had succeeded Katsura as Prime Minister. For, although both the Chinese and the Korean authorities had been brought to accept by that time the implications of the terms of the Treaty of Portsmouth for the advance of Japan's interests at the expense of their own, and the support of the Diet had been obtained for its ratification, the treaty's unpopularity in Japan remained so great as to require the continuing imposition of martial law; and finally to bring down the government in the New Year of 1906. The mood in the Diet, and in the country, was to insist above all upon the consolidation of such gains on the continent of Asia as the wartime leadership claimed to have assured in the aftermath of victory; and at the same time to scotch any subversive response at home to dangerous developments such as could be observed abroad, especially those surrounding the events of Bloody Sunday in Russia.

This was not a mood likely to sustain Saionji's premiership for long. His short-lived licensing of the Japan Socialist Party in 1906 was strongly criticized. Socialism was widely regarded as a form of treason. It was not forgotten that Katayama Sen had shaken the hand of his Russian counterpart at the Second International in Amsterdam during the late war. There was little inclination to bother with distinctions between those on the left, like Katayama, who advocated parliamentary reform, and those, like Kotoku Shusui and Sakai Toshihiko, who supported direct action. Even at the end of the first decade of the twentieth century, the actual vote was restricted to some 3 per cent of the population. Among bureaucrats, landlords and industrialists, who constituted the bulk of the electorate, there was little enthusiasm for any loosening of social discipline, especially not after the Hibiya riots. The police felt themselves to be on their mettle. The army and the navy were for empire.

With the exception of the Seiyukai, itself cohesive only to the extent of its response to unmistakable trends in popular sentiment, parties in the lower House were small and ill-organized. The reputation of lower House politicians was still clouded by evidence of their venality. The philosophy of Hoshi Toru, who, in response to Theodore Roosevelt's more worthy dictum, was said to have favoured talking loudly and carrying a bag of gold, had apparently survived his own departure. The House of Peers remained overwhelmingly conservative in outlook. This outlook was reinforced in the country by the end of the decade, by the formation of the Imperial Reserve Association. Ito may have hoped to order public administration differently in Seoul.

But Korean resistance to increasing Japanese encroachment on what remained of their independence was immediately expressed in non-cooperation, and in violence. Under pressure also from his own government to secure fuller compliance by the Koreans with their policies, and anxious to avoid the imposition of military control, Ito presented the Korean king with demands which the latter was unable to accept, and in protest against which he abdicated. The former Crown Prince Yi, who succeeded him, effectively surrendered; but this did not extinguish the spirit of Korean independence. The prospect of continued resistance served, in turn, to harden the determination of those in Tokyo who considered that the complete subordination of Korea was an essential Japanese interest. Ito remained opposed to annexation. But Saionji's government fell, in July 1908, as the result of his having taken what was regarded in the Diet as an insufficiently hard line

34

against socialists and other leftist demonstrators, in the Red Flag incident. It was succeeded by a second Katsura government; and within a year Ito resigned. In October 1909, while on a tour of inspection in Manchuria, Ito was assassinated, on the station platform at Mukden. When told, as he lay dying, that his assailant was a Korean, Ito said, 'The fellow's a fool.'

This was the end not only of the greatest of all the brilliant men of the Meiji period, but also of the capacity for domination in the national counsels of a certain style, combining ambition for Japan with a sense of its proper limits, which others shared but lacked the ability to assert, at any rate for a full generation. Saionji had the presence, but never acquired the full authority in his own person, and enjoyed too little forceful support. On behalf of some of those who were later murdered on account of their probity or balance, this might be considered a harsh judgement. There can, however, be little doubt but that Ito's combined qualities of statesmanship and leadership were of rare distinction. That his murder was to become the pretext for annexation of the country over whose destiny he had so recently aspired to preside in the capacity, as it were, of temporary guardian, was an irony no doubt greatly to the taste of his detractors and critics at home. At the outset of the Russo-Japanese War he had told the Korean king that he believed it was necessary for Japan, China and Korea to work together, but co-operating also with Europe and America, not antagonizing the Western Powers.

The belief of Yamagata, and of army leaders, in the necessity of the outright annexation of Korea sprang in part from their consciousness of persisting Russian strength, in part also from their determination to validate Japan's status as victor in the war, despite the initial bitter unpopularity of the peace in the estimation of the Japanese people. This meant getting on with profitable business in the newly acquired territories, as well as safeguarding the new frontiers. As an example of work to be done, the narrow-gauge military railway which their engineers had constructed to support the Japanese armies in the war had to be replaced by a line of broader gauge, to increase its serviceableness, with a view especially to its utility in international trade. In order to exploit it, the South Manchurian Railway Company, destined to grow into an empire of a kind itself, was constituted in 1906. The achievement of any degree of development and prosperity in the new territories in Manchuria depended to a great extent on some reconciliation with Russia. Just as Ito had been forced to accept the need for war, so the former war party had now to explore the possibility of a new relationship with Russia, much more like that which Ito had originally advocated. The first, secret agreement involving railway collaboration was reached as early as 1907.

Meanwhile, the Harriman initiative – to build up a global network of communications which would take in both the South Manchurian Railway and the bulk of the Trans-Siberian Railway, potentially the greatest capitalist enterprise of the century and perhaps the greatest enterprise for peace – had foundered in Tokyo. Katsura found the Harriman plan attractive, but he was then persuaded by Komura that they could not risk appearing to abandon any of the gains made in the much-reviled Treaty of Portsmouth, or to be handing them over to others to exploit. Harriman himself had been caught in Tokyo by the Hibiya riots, and had been advised to visit Nikko and Chuzenji instead of continuing his negotiations. Even today, contemplation of the scale of this abortive enterprise and its capacity to have converted a web of strategic rivalries into a chain of international collaboration, even to have averted the First World War itself, leaves a monumental sadness. The pursuit of much the same objective, but at the political level, notably by Secretary Knox in 1909, merely aroused the suspicions of both the Japanese and the Russian governments. They drew closer together in a further agreement concluded in 1910, a secret component of which provided for common action against any threat to their interests in the Far East, by implication from the United States.

Japanese relations with the United States had already entered what was to become a prolonged period of intermittent deterioration. This may be regarded as having begun with the opposition of the Californian state legislature to unrestricted immigration from Asian countries, followed by discriminatory measures on the part of the city authorities of San Francisco. The situation was improved, after lengthy discussion, by the so-called gentlemen's agreement reached in early 1908, under which the Japanese themselves undertook to impose limits on emigration to the United States. The subject, however, remained highly sensitive. It gave rise to President Roosevelt's decision to send 'the Great White Fleet' on a world tour in 1908, starting in the Pacific. Since the Panama Canal was not yet in operation, this involved sending sixteen battleships and their escorting vessels from the Atlantic ports of the east coast of the United States round Cape Horn. By the time the fleet arrived to visit Japanese ports, in the summer of 1908, Katsura was once again Prime Minister. The visit, designed to convey an impression of awesome power, was received with cheerful hospitality by the Japanese public. But from about this time, on the basis of calculations of national interest and of strategic balance in the Pacific, and taking the Anglo-Japanese Treaty fully into account, the Imperial Japanese Navy came to regard the United States Navy as its principal potential enemy, for the purposes of defence planning and fleet exercises. The Root-Takahira Agreement of November 1908 brought about no substantive improvement in the bilateral relationship even though it reaffirmed the mutual respect of the United States and Japanese governments for each other's position in the Pacific (by clear implication, in the Philippines and Korea respectively), and the continued support of both parties for the Open

Door in China; and it had some value in reassuring public opinion. When the Anglo-Japanese Treaty came up for renewal in 1911 it was revised to accommodate Japan's annexation of Korea; also, at British request, to exclude the United States from its sphere of application.

Although the Japanese leaders had room for manoeuvre in adjusting relations with the other Powers in the first decade of the century, and could calculate with some confidence the probable consequences of such adjustments as they made, dealing with China was altogether a more uncertain business. The instincts of the Meiji statesmen, by this time, were generally cautious and conservative. But the late war with China itself, and its consequences, still fresh in memories, their part in putting down the Boxers and imposing the Boxer Protocol with its long-term indemnities, their insistence on taking over the lease and rights in the Liaotung peninsula after the Russo-Japanese War, their obvious further ambitions in Manchuria, their domination of Korea, and the vigour of their commercial activity in the Treaty Ports, and generally, put them at a disadvantage in any attempt to develop relationships of trust with any part of the decaying machinery of government in China.

The Japanese leaders, given their own conservatism, were not naturally inclined to sponsor Chinese dissidents, but they were often content that such people should be afforded refuge in Japan, since this helped them to keep closely in touch with developments in China. Leading exponents of reform in the Hundred Days had been received at the turn of the century; and later, when some of their ideas had been taken up by the Dowager Empress, many more Chinese students were given hospitality in Japan and facilities for the study of contemporary social, political and scientific developments. These students participated in academic and public debate in Japan, and gave it new stimulus. Some of the resulting intellectual ferment was welcome; some of it was tolerated for the insight it provided; and some of it was regarded as subversive. Thus, Sun Yat-sen, as a socialist and republican revolutionary of peasant origin and Christian background, was expelled from Japan in 1907, having spent considerable periods in the country as a visitor. Some Japanese groups, including some of the most notorious secret societies, enjoyed a kind of licence to keep in touch with otherwise unacceptable Chinese factions, for intelligence purposes and because they might prove to be influential in the future.

Such was the confusion in the administration of China, and in the intellectual climate during the last years of the Manchus, that no single tendency seemed appropriate for the Japanese government to sponsor or befriend. If elements which favoured Pan-Asian thinking, for example, might seem attractive, the likelihood was that they would also advocate socialism or republicanism, which were anathema. Similarly in Japan itself, where Kita Ikki's *Theory of the Kokutai and Pure Socialism*, published in

1906, was an immediate success, but a book which the authorities very soon found it necessary to ban. Here was the beginning of a kind of national socialism, though not of course under that name. The thesis represented a new brand of dangerous speculation, verging on the fringe of that which must be eliminated totally, yet half tolerated partly because of the author's Chinese connections, partly because, for all its otherwise threatening short-comings, it seemed to propagate belief in an imperial mystique which might indeed be considered pure.

Soon after the Dowager Empress turned towards reform, the example of Japanese constitutionalism was for a time espoused as the approved model for China. But by that time the hold of the Qing dynasty on power was tenuous. For practical purposes, the Japanese leaders made as much as they could of a strictly pragmatic relationship with Yuan Shih-k'ai, and with powerful or respectable provincial figures in China. The Chinese tradition of scholarly bureaucracy, which had produced hard-headed administrators with drive and determination, such as Li Hung-chang, and other provincial governors-general capable of withstanding adversity, was giving way to military science. The decline and eventual breakdown of the central author-ity of the Empire led to the emergence of local and regional warlords. The Japanese were able, through Yuan Shih-k'ai, to take advantage of the demand for military training in China, competing successfully on price with the Germans, long established in this sector. The Japanese were also to profit later from chance encounters made during this period, notably that, in the course of the war against Russia, between the then Colonel Tanaka Giichi and the future warlord Chang Tso-lin, whose career Tanaka effec-tively sponsored – instead of ending it summarily, as he well might have done on capturing a Chinese guerrilla operating strictly outside the rules of war. It was significant later that Chiang Kai-shek was one of the many Chinese students who came to Japan in the years leading up to the Chinese Revolution of 1911.

The spreading confusion in China, together with the continuing atmos-phere of revolutionary conspiracy in Russia and beyond, served to underline once again the importance of discipline and orthodoxy for the Japanese leaders, and the need to defend and consolidate their territorial gains. The heavy expenditure incurred in the war against Russia, and popular demand for evidence of worthwhile returns, as expressed in the Hibiya riots and persistently thereafter, stimulated them actively to exploit these gains. There were legitimate expectations of imperial expansion. But the disorders were regarded as symptomatic of a decline in social discipline and in respect for traditional values. A wide and lively interest in new ideas was balanced by a heavy disapproval, by the authorities, of nonconformity and softening of the work ethic. The influence in rural areas of soldiers demobilized after the war was not uniformly satisfactory from this point of view. It was found necessary to rally the people, in the Emperor's name, to a renewal of the dedicated patriotism of early Meiji years, in the Boshin Rescript of October 1908. Both the Convention of National Youth and the foundation of the Imperial Reserve Association in 1910 had similar purposes.

These post-war years saw changes in the atmosphere of political life rather than in the political structure. The Seiyukai remained by far the strongest force in the lower House, but was variable in its direction, depending on the interests of sub-groups within its membership, which would be willing to offer support to Katsura when circumstances seemed to require this, not taking the view that Saionji had any exclusive claim to their allegiance. The Genro functioned as arbitrator between the Seiyukai and Katsura, or between Katsura and Saionji. It might have been expected that Ito's death would leave Yamagata indisputably dominant, both among the Genro and in the Privy Council. In reality, however, this period saw the beginning of the decline of the Genro as an institution; and although Yamagata was to remain President of the Privy Council for many years, his support both in the upper House and in the bureaucracy was tending to fragment, while factionalism, often connected with the influence of secret societies such as the Kokuryukai on activity in Manchuria and policy towards China, was also restricting his prospects of continuing to enjoy the full confidence of the army. Below the surface of perceived political currents, the most significant development was the consolidation of support for the Seiyukai, in the regions, in local government, in the construction industry, and among the newly influential industrialists and businessmen generally, for which Hara Kei was working, greatly extending his personal influence as he did so. Until the death of the Emperor Meiji, however, and for a little thereafter, the rationale and the style of political leadership remained set in the pattern which was predominantly of Ito's design. Politicians' paternalistic attitude towards the people was for the most part insufficiently sensitive or sophisticated to comprehend the connection between popular unrest and the failure of wages to keep up with rising prices.

Immediately after the war with Russia, although the economic and financial position was difficult, there was a prospect of successful expansion, and Japan's international credit recovered from the setback originally incurred by the decision to fight. Annual expenditure had greatly increased, as had the national debt. Levels of taxation had had to be raised, with some harsh consequences, especially in agriculture. There were problems of the allocation of strained resources, arising especially from the insistent demands of the army for greatly increased strength, to meet enlarged commitments. On the other hand, the central government had come to enjoy new sources of revenue, including the higher productivity of industry, the innovation of tobacco and camphor monopolies and, from 1911, at last, full tariff autonomy. The specialized institutions under the supervision of the Ministry of Finance and the Bank of Japan, including those newly established, were playing effective roles in the strengthening of the economy. The Industrial Bank of Japan, for example, which was given responsibility for financing development in the Kwantung (Liaotung) peninsula, was successful in raising funds in London for the South Manchurian Railway Company, continuously from 1907. Following a period during which the Dai Ichi Bank had looked after all Japanese interests in Korea, the Bank of Chosen was set up in Seoul, after annexation, on the same lines as those applied to the Bank of Taiwan a decade earlier. The Oriental Development Company was entrusted from 1908 with the promotion of industrial activity in both Korea and Manchuria. The Yokohama Specie Bank, retaining its special position with regard to foreign exchange, was active in the stimulation of foreign trade.

So were the increasingly powerful zaibatsu groups. The planning and financing of their expansion were carried out largely by their respective commercial banks. These were enjoying a period of rapid growth, with the notable multiplication of small private accounts. The public sector was also benefiting substantially from the volume of savings being placed with the Deposits Bureau of the Ministry of Finance. Private investment in manufacturing industry was effected to a large extent indirectly, through both these channels. The influence of the authorities on the scale and direction of the industrial effort was greatly facilitated as a result, given the relationship of close co-operation they were at pains to foster with the conglomerates. As for the scope of the latter at this period, the Mitsui group's acquisition of major or controlling interests in Oji Paper, Kanegafuchi Spinning and the nucleus of what was later to become the Toshiba Corporation may give some indication of it, bearing in mind the group's already existing financial and mining activities and the simultaneous dramatic extension of their participation in foreign trade.

In industrial production, silk and, increasingly, cotton textiles were still easily the leading performers, with the additional output of woollen cloth being sharply stimulated by the requirements of the armed forces. Cotton spindleage roughly doubled in the first decade of the century. The iron and steel industry was much slower to develop. Much of Japan's coal was of inferior quality. Most iron ore had to be imported from China and Korea. Shipbuilding remained on a modest scale, though heavily subsidized. Japan was achieving self-sufficiency in naval shipbuilding in the years leading up to the First World War, after the outbreak of which there was no choice but to depend confidently on the country's own resources. The engineering industries and the development of electrical machinery also progressed slowly, and greatly relied on collaborative agreements with foreign firms. The supply of hydro-electric power built up rapidly, with the support of foreign capital. It was found expedient to take foreign oil companies into partnership, and to allocate to them more than half of the domestic market.

Industrial development was largely now in private hands, the nationalization of the main railway network in 1906 being an exceptional move in the contrary direction. Nevertheless, the influence of government was everywhere in evidence. The subsidies provided to shipping, as well as to shipbuilding, constituted the essential stimulus to growth. The skill of the bureaucracy in guiding industry in the interests of efficiency and harmony was a key factor in its steady, if unsensational, advance. The small silk producers, for example, were encouraged to adopt measures of quality control and standardization in order to ensure continued success in export markets, and crucially in the United States. The conflicting interests of sugar importers and refiners, similarly, were reconciled as the result of official intervention with the zaibatsu corporations involved. The benefits to the Japanese economy of the sugar cane now available in Taiwan were maximized accordingly.

Although colonial policy as such could scarcely be said to have existed at this time, both the officials in government departments at home and the military overseas were conscious of the importance of economic factors in the administration of the newly acquired territories, and especially in planning for their future contribution to the national interest. In cultural terms, the idea, however vaguely expressed or dimly perceived, was assimilation. At the same time, there was a deep and enduring respect for Chinese culture. This had some influence on the conduct of the administration in Taiwan, but did not of course apply in Korea. The people in Taiwan, equally, though early resistance movements had been dealt with harshly by Kodama Gentaro and others, were able to see some advantages in being spared the growing lawlessness to which the provinces of mainland China were subject. There was no such restraint upon the Koreans' desire to recover their independence. If assimilation was one side of the coin current in Japanese policy, repression was the other. The Japanese governors-general in both Taiwan and Korea were always senior military officers. Their brief was to maintain law and order; to foster agricultural and industrial productivity and trade; and to protect the legitimate interests of merchants and settlers from Japan, allowing the participation of foreigners in the economic activity of the territory where this was consistent with the requirements of the security of the Empire. In south Manchuria this latter consideration became closely bound up, from an early stage, with the policy of maximizing immigration from Japan itself, for both economic and demographic reasons.

Rice, sugar and tea from Taiwan were significant imports to Japan from the earliest years of empire, as iron ore from Korea was soon to become. But, to put colonial trade at this stage into perspective, it is only necessary to note that Japan's annual trade with the United States was no less than ten times the value of the trade with Taiwan, in the years leading up to the First World War. Perhaps equally significantly, Japan's share of China's foreign trade was smaller than Britain's, and Japan's share of foreign investment in China was only a fraction, perhaps one eighth, of Britain's. Japan had no base upon which to build up its interests in China comparable with Britain's position in the Shanghai Municipal Council, and in the trade and development of the Yangtse basin generally. In the interests of correcting this situation, there were doubts in Tokyo about the wisdom of applying Open Door principles in Manchuria. There, as further south in China despite the putative disadvantages noticed above, Japanese merchants and entrepreneurs were active from the start. The number of Japanese civilians in Manchuria, including both traders and settlers, was nearly 100,000 by 1910. There was already widely believed to be an explosive pressure of population in the islands of Japan itself. This belief marched in step with the belief in an imperial destiny.

The idea of empire was chiefly propagated, and realized, by the joint endeavours of civil servants and military officers, many of them also active in political life, but the opportunities it promised to the private sector of the economy were eagerly grasped. The power of the zaibatsu was in any case expanding, both at home and overseas. Their trading companies soon came to dominate the handling of bulk exports and raw material imports. Half Japan's total exports towards the end of the Meiji period were textiles: raw silk (easily the most important single commodity) and silk piece-goods, cotton yarn and piece-goods. Raw cotton accounted for nearly a third of Japan's total imports, the shipping of the longer staple cotton from Bombay ushering in decades of competition with the Lancashire industry. Japanese merchant houses obtained a large share in this trade, with the result that the nineteenth-century predominance of foreign merchants in Japan's overseas trade as a whole was ended. Japanese merchants and shippers achieved a commanding position in the handling of the bilateral trade with China. In general, imports of iron and steel products, machinery and machine tools were of growing significance. Foreign merchants retained a strong position in the handling of technically advanced manufactured imports, but the zaibatsu groups, with their integrated ranges of interests, were increasingly formidable competitors in every trade. By 1913, moreover, half of all imports and exports were carried in ships flying the Japanese flag.

By that time, the leading zaibatsu families had long been held in great respect, and to be connected with names such as Mitsui and Mitsubishi (Iwasaki), Sumitomo, Yasuda or Okura was to be privileged indeed; in another kind of peerage, as it were. The Viscount Shibusawa, who came from a rich farming family, but not from one of the great Daimyo houses, may be taken as the personification of the evolution of the upper stratum of society which had been brought about during the Meiji period. Starting as a banker, and going on to found and lead a vast range of multifarious businesses, of which the Toyo Spinning Company was perhaps the most famous, he came to epitomize the prestigious, industrial patriotism of the day. His example and his influence in social and public affairs were to remain effective subsequent to his retirement in 1909 from direct management of business enterprises. Long after its destruction, the great novelist Tanizaki was to recall seeing, in his own childhood, 'the fantastic Shibusawa mansion rising like a fairy-tale palace on the banks of Kabutocho . . . the Gothic-style mansion with its Venetian galleries and pillars'.

For those whose role was to support the achievements of the period without a voice in its direction, life in Japan remained harsh. Factory workers were afforded no statutory protection from the common threat of cruel exploitation until the passing of the controversial Factory Act of 1911, and even that inadequate measure was not to come into full effect for some years, most of its provisions even then limited to the prohibition of outright inhumanity to women and children. In 1909 the men at the copper mine at Ashio rose in revolt against their conditions of work, and troops had to be sent to put them down. (It was the same place whose effluent, poisoning the rivers below, had caused the first environmental emergency of its kind, some years before. The mines have long been closed, but to this day a bitter malevolence seems to linger over the site if you look down towards it, say, from Half-Moon Hill). That there was a continuing drift of population from rural to urban districts, not wholly attributable to the provisions of the new Civil Code in favour of primogeniture, suggests that the living conditions of the poor were as severe on the farm as they were in the factory. Nagatsuka's novel *Tsuchi*, in which he describes his own village community, gives ample confirmation of this.

By the standards of the time, as established by other Powers elsewhere, Japanese social, industrial and colonial policies at the end of the Meiji period were unexceptional, even unexceptionable. What distinguished Japanese officials, administrators and political leaders was their zeal and ambition to promote the national interest, and their pride in achievements which put them on an equal footing with the most prestigious of the older Powers. Excesses were not avoided, however, and the period closed in the shadow of the worst of these. The leaders were consistently anxious to avert softening or subversive movements of opinion. Even the most liberal among them had to guard against lax or complacent tendencies in their own jurisdiction, as Saionji had been made aware in 1908.

In the summer of 1910, under Katsura's second cabinet, socialists and anarchists were rounded up by the police, and 26 were charged with plotting to assassinate the Emperor. They were brought to trial in secret at the end of the year, and 24 of them were sentenced to death, of whom 12

43

were executed, in January 1911, including Kotoku Shusui. A newspaper editor at the time went so far as specifically to commend the decision to hold the trial in secret, and the severity of the proceedings was certainly not regarded as excessive by a public which venerated the Emperor both as a person and as the embodiment of the national polity and its spirit. The so-called High Treason incident has, however, long been regarded in Japan as having almost certainly involved the abuse of power by the authorities and the connivance of government at the highest level with this abuse. The intimidation of the extreme left for some years was assured. Many in Japan may have been thankful for this when, in October of 1911, the Qing dynasty was overthrown.

Given also the unsettled relations between the European Powers by that time, the death of the Emperor Meiji in July 1912 seemed to the people of Japan to expose them once again to all the threats and uncertainties from which he had relieved them by the magnificence of his personal example. What he had personified was confidence. His personal appearance at the ceremonial parade held to welcome Admiral Togo and the sailors on their return to Tokyo after the destruction of the Russian fleet in the battle of Tsushima symbolized the achievements of his whole reign.

3

World Crisis and Reconstruction, 1912–22

The Emperor Meiji's majestic funeral procession marked the maturity of the polity founded upon the Meiji Restoration, and the full achievement both of national independence and of equality with the other Powers. Yet the Emperor's death came at a time of deep uncertainty and precarious instability both at home and abroad. Immediately after the imperial funeral, the ritual suicides of General Nogi and his wife seemed to some of the older generation to be a kind of lament for the passing not only of the leader, but also of the spirit of an age.

Japanese society, so far from settling obediently and unanimously into a new order, contained uneasy and fractious elements. The so-called High Treason incident of 1910 had cowed some of the exponents of active subversion, but it had not served to extinguish civil dissent, nor to suppress altogether manifestations of concern by and on behalf of those who lived and worked in squalid or servile conditions. The tramway drivers' strike over the New Year of 1912, in particular, left a deep impression on the public, whether of sympathy or outrage. The formation of the Yuaikai by Suzuki Bunji soon afterwards served notice on the authorities that the passing of the Factory Act of 1911 would not suffice as official recognition of the need to control the exploitation of labour.

There were deeper domestic anxieties. On the one hand, people were allegedly being allowed to lose sight of the Confucian virtues. On the other, the prominence which had come to be accorded to State Shinto, especially within the educational system, seemed in danger of breeding an excessive nationalism. As Minister for Home Affairs in Saionji's second cabinet, Hara Kei called a meeting of leaders of the Shinto, Buddhist and Christian faiths in 1912. His intention was to give reassurance of even-handed toleration. The effect was weak and transient. The gesture was not repeated in the lifetime of the Meiji Constitution.

The two principal issues dominating the last years of the Meiji period and

45

the early years of the reign of the Emperor Taisho were the scale of defence expenditure and the response to events in China surrounding and following the collapse of the Qing dynasty. These persistent and related issues, often linked with yet broader considerations of Asian, Pacific or global scope, and influenced by social and economic developments, were to overshadow Japan's political life for decades.

The dangers and opportunities apparent in the aftermath of the Chinese Revolution of October 1911 (the Double Tenth) had the effect in Japan of sharpening a debate which had already preoccupied military and political leaders for some time, the climax of which came to be known as the Taisho crisis. Saionji had returned to power in 1911 because Katsura was able to obtain neither the agreement of the Diet nor even the endorsement of the Finance Ministry to the provision of funds for an extra two divisions, to enable the army to ensure the security of Korea and south Manchuria. When Saionji's cabinet proposed measures of retrenchment which would reduce defence expenditure all round, the army refused to nominate a replacement for the deceased War Minister. Saionji was forced to resign, and Yamagata insisted that the Genro should designate Katsura to form a new government, the assumption being that he would give the army the reinforcement it was demanding. Now, however, it was the navy's turn to decline to participate in government. Katsura sought the cover of imperial sanction, with the object of forcing the navy to co-operate, but succeeded only in alienating both the public and the Genro. Yamagata himself felt obliged to oppose his protégé over this move. Their relationship was finally severed when Katsura abandoned the transcendental way, to form a new political alliance, the Rikken Doshikai, in early 1913, with Kato Komei (Takaaki) as his principal partner. Already widely experienced as politician and diplomat, Kato was opposed to the domination of public affairs either by the Satcho clansmen or by the Genro. His own connections with the world of the zaibatsu, and with Mitsubishi interests in particular, through his marriage with Iwasaki's daughter, made him an exceptionally influential figure.

Following demonstrations of public dissatisfaction, however, and a speech of rare cogency, in the lower House, by Ozaki Yukio, the veteran champion of constitutional and personal political integrity, who castigated the practice of sheltering behind imperial authority, the government fell; and Yamagata and his fellow Genro were, perhaps for the last time, decisively instrumental in the appointment as Katsura's successor of Admiral Count Yamamoto Gonnohyoe (Gonbei). Katsura was to die within a few months. Yamamoto succeeded in obtaining the backing of the Seiyukai for necessary measures of retrenchment and reform. He saw to it that not only serving officers but also those on the retired lists should be regarded as eligible for appointment as ministers for war or for the navy (though this achievement was not to outlast the next great debate, less than twenty years later, about the structure and size of the armed services). His cabinet, with Baron Makino Nobuaki (second son of Okubo Toshimichi, and father-in-law of Yoshida Shigeru) as Minister for Foreign Affairs, Hara responsible for Home Affairs, and Baron Takahashi Korekiyo at the Ministry of Finance, was well qualified to bring to an end a period of bitter instability in domestic politics. Successive scandals over naval procurement foreclosed this opportunity. Given especially his well-known concern to ensure that naval strength was sustained at an adequate level, Yamamoto felt obliged to accept responsibility for the exposure of corruption directly affecting this objective. He resigned in April 1914.

Meanwhile, the further revision of the Anglo-Japanese Treaty in 1911 had provided the Japanese leaders with a continuing assurance that the country need not approach the business of international affairs from a position of isolation. Nevertheless, the British government, in agreeing that the alliance should continue for at least a further ten years, had stipulated that its provisions should not be regarded as having any scope for application to matters involving the United States. This had the effect of adding to the pressure for sustained Japanese naval expenditure, especially given the new flexibility from which United States naval deployment would benefit within a few years with the expected coming into operation of the Panama Canal. The Japanese had also made concessions about emigration, in the treaty negotiations, in order to enable the British government to be seen to respond to growing apprehensions in Australia and New Zealand. A certain wary ambivalence which might be said to have characterized relations with Great Britain from the earliest days was evident in these developments. So far as the building of a more solid underlying foundation of trust was concerned, much must depend upon the interaction of the two countries' interests and policies in China, where it was rivalry at one turn of events and mutual support at the next, competition in one area and common interests in another.

After the Revolution of 1911 in China, the Powers were soon in general agreement that the best hope for stability and progress lay in supporting Yuan Shih-k'ai, who had so skilfully outmanoeuvred Sun Yat-sen's more naive and idealistic Republicans, and who seemed capable of dealing in a godfatherly way with provincial warlords. Japanese banks joined British, French, German and Russian banks in the five-power consortium with which Yuan negotiated his Reorganization Loan. The withdrawal of United States participation from this consortium, on the grounds that the Powers, through their banks, were imposing an unwarrantable degree of control over Chinese administration as a condition of the loan, was the first major demonstration of President Woodrow Wilson's approach to international affairs. It was partly in recognition of the character of this approach that the

British government pursued the idea of a Treaty of General Arbitration with the United States, in 1914. Japanese governments preferred to avoid accepting such additional limitations on their freedom of action as might be involved in instruments of this kind, and to concentrate their attention on the consolidation of their position in North-East Asia, especially such opportunities as might be presented by the evolution of the situation in China as a whole, and in Manchuria.

As ambassador in London from 1909 to 1913, covering the whole period of negotiation of the revision of the treaty and with the great advantage of having served before as Minister there from 1895 to 1899, Baron Kato Komei had had every opportunity to reach a full understanding of Great Britain's interests in East Asia, and of British attitudes towards Japanese aspirations in the region. He knew that the British Foreign Secretary himself accepted the likelihood, even the inevitability, of some further Japanese expansion; and that, on the basis of equal access to markets through the Open Door, subtly coupled with mutual respect for spheres of special interest, Grey was not dismayed by this prospect. There was a recognition in London that the promotion of stability in China was a shared objective, and that Japanese discipline could make a substantial contribution to the realization of satisfactory conditions for trade. At the same time, there was evidently also some concern lest the vigour of Japanese enterprise might sometimes unsettle things. When Kato told Sir Edward Grey that the Japanese drive to develop the leased territories in the Kwantung peninsula and around the South Manchurian Railway involved afforestation and agricultural colonization, the British Foreign Secretary commented, 'You have planted blood there!' It was a remark to be treasured, but not necessarily one to be heeded. It was a warning which might well be overlooked, on either side, as the growing instability of the balance of power in Europe diverted attention from the chronic unsettled condition of China.

Though out of sympathy with Katsura's personality, and with his associations both with the Genro and with the Choshu clan, Kato had been appointed Foreign Minister in Katsura's last cabinet, and had joined his Rikken Doshikai after Katsura's resignation. When Yamamoto's government fell, and the veteran Count Okuma was brought back from years of political retirement to form his own second cabinet, Kato was invited once again to become Foreign Minister. He had been back in office for less than four months when the First World War started.

Kato's voice was already dominant in Okuma's cabinet, and the policies which he now advocated, and which were adopted, have to be seen against the background of a general expectation that the conflict would be short. The British government sought Japan's help in protecting Hong Kong and Weihaiwei, and in suppressing German naval raiders operating against merchant shipping in the Pacific. They were unable to conceal their fears of possible Japanese plans to provoke China's hostility, when Kato persuaded his colleagues, acting with due regard to their obligations under the treaty with Britain, to send an ultimatum to Berlin on 15 August, demanding not only that the Germans withdraw or disarm their vessels in Far Eastern waters, but also that they surrender the leased territory of Kiaochow in the Shantung peninsula, including the naval base at Tsingtao. The outcome was that a British and Indian brigade came under Japanese command for the assault on Tsingtao, which was successful, though the allied combination was in itself no better than a qualified success. By early November, before the first battle of Ypres was over in the West, not only the German leased territory and other German installations in China were in Japanese hands, but so also were the German Pacific islands north of the equator, both the Carolines and the Marshalls. It soon became clear that the conflict was not going to be short. Japanese naval co-operation with Allied, and especially with British naval commands, on escort and convoy work, intensified in later stages of the war; and the remains of a number of Japanese sailors lost in these operations rested in the Commonwealth war graves cemetery in Malta. Japanese governments were, however, not willing to contemplate the dispatch of military formations to the Western Front. In the Japanese army, where connections with German military method and doctrine were strong, there was persistent scepticism about the prospect of Allied victory. The Japanese people were too distant from it to grasp the scale of the conflict fully, or the devastation it caused. They did not experience the war as it was experienced by the peoples of the principal combatant countries. The reflection, for example, that the British alone lost more men both in the Somme campaign of the summer of 1916 and in the Passchendaele campaign of the following year than were serving in the combined armies of the entire Japanese expeditionary force before Mukden in 1905 would not have been likely to occur to them; nor, if it had done so, would it have seemed wholly credible. This distance of Japan from the main battlefields of the war was profoundly significant, above all because it also represented a distance from the great change in outlook which the war brought about in the nations most heavily engaged.

For Japan, the immediate business of taking over German possessions in China and the north Pacific having been accomplished, the war opened up far-reaching questions about policy towards China. Indeed, given the pre-occupations of the European Powers with the struggle on their own continent, the Japanese government was almost bound to assume a progressively greater share of responsibility for the shaping of the future of East Asia. Japan, of course, also faced greatly enlarged opportunities for commercial and industrial development, and for the consolidation and expansion of empire. The proposal that a comprehensive settlement should be attempted with China was not Kato's alone; various ideas were put forward by both diplomatic and military experts. These ideas were shaped by Kato into a coherent agenda; and Okuma and his other senior cabinet colleagues were persuaded by Kato that this was the programme they should adopt. Yamagata urged caution, reminding the government that the attention of the European Powers would return before long to focus on the region once again. All could see that there was new scope for the promotion of Japanese interests and influence on the continent, and for successfully containing competition from other Powers in Manchuria, but it was Yamagata's view that they should not take undue advantage of China's weakness. Instead they should seek to work with China, and should also seek the prior understanding of the other Powers, not press forward unilaterally, as they were already tending to do in the Shantung peninsula, following the expulsion of the Germans from Tsingtao.

Kato had his way nevertheless, and the proposals which came to be known as the Twenty-One Demands were presented in strict confidence and, contrary to normal practice, directly to Yuan Shih-k'ai, in mid-January 1915. The advantages which Kato set out to obtain for Japan in this way were for the most part such as might have been conceded by Yuan in exchange for Japanese support for his own regime, and perhaps for his supreme ambition to assume the title and enjoy the prestige of Emperor. On a strictly literal interpretation, it could have been argued that the pursuit of these advantages was also compatible with respect for the principles of the Open Door. But the document setting out the Japanese proposals also contained a section expressed as 'wishes', which went so far – especially in suggesting the appointment of Japanese advisers in the central departments of government and administration in Peking – as to amount to a take-over bid. The privileges and facilities requested for Japanese institutions and individuals throughout China would have been appropriate in circumstances of the country's outright colonization by Japan. Given that the Chinese had already shown their clear displeasure at developments in the Shantung peninsula, it must have been obvious to Kato that they would not accede fully to his demands. Yuan shrewdly rejected the confidentiality of the approach, and appealed to Washington and London for help. Kato was careful that the section of 'wishes' should not be disclosed in discussions with the British, but a full account of the Japanese demands was given in an Osaka newspaper.

The British government's reaction to Kato's extraordinary initiative amounted to no more than a caution. Washington took occasion to remind both Tokyo and Peking of their international responsibilities. In China itself, however, there was an outcry as the result of which Kato came under public criticism in Japan, on the grounds that he had handled the matter clumsily, not because his objective had been mistaken. Following the dispatch by Yuan of an emissary carrying a personal appeal for Yamagata's help in resisting the Japanese government's pressure, the Cabinet in Tokyo withdrew the 'wishes' originally put forward on its behalf. The remaining demands were, however, sustained and, after an ultimatum, accepted in modified form, and embodied in two treaties which, with other formal instruments, were signed on 25 May 1915. Japan had obtained valuable advantages: in the transfer to Japanese control of German interests in Shantung; in the assured management of certain mining installations and related facilities in the Yangtse basin, which were essential to their iron and steel industry; and even more substantially in additional privileges in south Manchuria and eastern Inner Mongolia. Misgivings on the part of some Western Powers had been brushed aside, and various later agreements were to confirm the specific acceptance, before the end of the First World War, by the United States, Britain, France and Russia of many of the gains made for Japan by Kato's move towards a definitive settlement with China.

There had, however, also been some substantially disadvantageous consequences of this move. It left suspicion, even resentment, in the capitals of the Western Powers, but much the most serious of the unfavourable repercussions were in China itself. Here the spirit of the new nationalism, itself ironically owing so much to the Japanese example, was strongly provoked and stimulated, 25 May being designated for the remembrance of humiliation. In the United States too, public opinion was alienated from Japan. It was primarily because of the outcry in China itself, and the nationwide demonstrations there of hostility towards Japan, that Yamagata worked successfully for Kato's resignation, forthcoming as soon as the outcome of the Twenty-One Demands was formally concluded in the summer. At the time of Okuma's resignation the following year, it was again Yamagata who insisted that there could be no question of bringing Kato back to succeed him as Prime Minister, as Okuma proposed. Exerting his supreme authority among the Genro and in the Privy Council, and his influence with the Imperial Household, Yamagata secured the premiership for his last grand protégé and nominee, General Count Terauchi Masatake, who had been serving as Governor-General of Korea since its annexation. In that capacity, responsible directly to the Emperor, Terauchi had not hesitated harshly to repress any attempts by Korean nationalists to re-establish their country's independence. It was under his administration that Dr Syngman Rhee had been forced to take refuge in the United States, in 1912. Now, in the shadow of Yamagata's tutelage, Terauchi sought to pursue towards China a policy which would make amends for Kato's and Okuma's high-handedness.

The domestic political situation in China was further transformed with Yuan's death, after his bid to secure imperial status for his own rule, in the summer of 1916. The season of the provincial warlord was setting in, to frustrate the flowering of republican reform. In effect, Terauchi's policy was, by subsidizing Tuan's fragile authority, indirectly to cultivate the Peiyang militarists. He arranged the Nishihara loans, through the distinguished banker of that name, in the hope that the beneficiaries would protect and foster Japanese interests, while consolidating their own power and bringing stability to China. There was a body of opinion in Japan which held that it would have been preferable, on Yuan's demise, to have supported the reformist cause in China. In the same line of thought, at an earlier stage, there had been elements in Japanese military and naval circles, and in secret societies such as the Genyosha, which prided themselves on their capacity to provide intelligence for the armed services, in favour of siding with the reformists and republicans immediately after the collapse of the Qing dynasty. It was possible in Japan for groups of markedly reactionary outlook to support republicanism abroad, often in the pursuit of a larger Pan-Asian objective, itself to be revealed ultimately as the realization of their own Emperor's destiny of continental or even global leadership. Apparent contradictions might in such schemes seem to find mystical resolution. Neither Yamagata nor Terauchi, for all the ardour of their patriotism and devotion to the Imperial House, was a dreamer. Neither would have supposed it likely that reformists in China would prove reliable partners. Terauchi secured the necessary support from the Seiyukai and followed his hard-headed policies, confident that he could hold his ground in the Diet.

Terauchi also succeeded in obtaining further acknowledgements by the other Powers of Japan's principal interests in North-East Asia. The British were willing to pay in this coin for Japanese naval co-operation in the Mediterranean. The French and the Italians were compliant allies. The Lansing-Ishii agreement, however, proved illusory, the United States administration making it clear later that a key phrase was never intended on their side to apply to parts of China not strictly contiguous with Japanese territory, as it had been alleged to do by the Japanese. Agreement reached with the Russians as recently as the summer of 1916, by Okuma, was repudiated, along with all earlier agreements, after the Russian Revolution of autumn 1917. Terauchi found himself facing the projection eastward of Bolshevik power. There was already a lively debate within the Japanese government about the implications for the country of the Russian Revolution, even before the possibility of intervention in Siberia was taken up between the Allies. From Washington, by now the capital of the leading belligerent country with interests in North-East Asia, its resources for action in that region being greater than those of the British government, came the suggestion that Tokyo might wish to contribute a modest force, perhaps of 7,000 or 10,000 men, to the Allied expedition to Siberia. A hard internal debate, in which the expansionists did not easily prevail, eventually resulted in the dispatch of almost 75,000 men of the Japanese Army, with naval support. No sooner had the decision to join the Allied expeditionary force been taken than Terauchi's government fell, carried away by the rice riots of 1918, by far the most serious of all purely civil disturbances to have been experienced since the Meiji Constitution came into force.

The shock caused by these disturbances was all the greater because they followed a period of apparently unprecedented national prosperity. The great loans to China and the great expeditionary force for the Siberian operations had been made possible by wartime benefits which exceeded the capacity of economic management to handle them. The outbreak of war had disrupted patterns of trade and finance, especially through its impact on the City of London, to an extent that was for a time alarming. By the spring of 1915, however, it was already clear that both the terms of trade and the opportunities for growth were favourable to Japan as never before. Competition in Asian markets diminished. Allied governments not only surrendered mercantile advantages in various third countries to Japan; they also placed contracts for munitions with Japanese factories, and were responsible for a heavy and constantly increasing demand for Japanese shipping.

Japan's exports trebled in value during the war years, though increasing by no more than half as much again as pre-war in annual volume. The tonnage of Japanese merchant shipping doubled, while income from freight rose to no less than ten times its pre-war level. A huge current surplus on international account replaced a chronic deficit. Gold reserves rose steeply, especially foreign holdings. Foreign investment, however, if unfairly typified by the Nishihara loans to China, was neither well considered in general nor notably successful in particular applications. Nor, when boom conditions gave out in 1920, was the sophistication of financial administration sufficient to deal smoothly with the consequences. The Bank of Japan had neither the muscle nor the machinery to exert effective control over the chief ordinary banks, whose allegiance was naturally given to the various, only too independent, zaibatsu groups which owned them.

Textiles continued to dominate Japan's export trade during the First World War, though there was also the beginning of a rather greater diversification, for example into exports of engineering products, by no means confined to items of war material. Employment in manufacturing industry increased sharply, by more than 60 per cent in the war years themselves. Production of finished steel more than doubled in volume, and new iron and steel plants were brought into operation in Korea and Manchuria as well as in Japan. In 1917, measures were taken to exempt new plants in this sector from taxation for ten years, and to permit them to import ores and construction materials free of duty. The production of coal rose by 50 per cent during the war, and electric power capacity was doubled.

Wartime industrial growth, and the prosperity both of the established zaibatsu groups and of powerful specialized manufacturing companies, was accompanied by levels of price inflation which bore especially heavily on the poorer sections of the working population. The price of rice itself, the indispensable staff of life, trebled; and it was this which finally provoked the rice riots of August and September 1918. These violent disturbances began with raids on rice dealers' stocks in the fishing villages of Toyama, on the Japan Sea coast, and spread rapidly, right across and up and down the country, and into all the major cities. The police were unable to maintain control in some areas. The army was brought in to intervene drastically, discipline revealing no frailty in the ranks when soldiers had to put down their fellow-citizens. While the newly enlarged urban populations posed a greater problem for the restoration of law and order, the peasant farmer had suffered at least as badly as his sons in the city, from the rocketing of prices. At the end of it all, the power of the landlord was seen to have increased in relation to that of the tenant farmer, just as the distance had grown between the industrial leader, the entrepreneur, or the *nouveau riche* war profiteer (the *narikin*), and the worker on the factory floor.

In these circumstances, the need for organized combinations in self-defence, whether of groups of factory hands or of tenant farmers, became more obvious and more pressing. The ideals of socialism, temporarily set aside after the shock of the High Treason Incident, began to reassert their appeal. A generation of students sceptical of the limits of routine morality as prescribed in the Imperial Rescript on Education, and of the tenets of conventional society, listened attentively to teachers such as Yoshino Sakuzo at Tokyo Imperial University and Kawakami Hajime at Kyoto. Interest grew strong in the aim of universal manhood suffrage. There was a renewed undercurrent of murmuring about the problems of the disadvantaged, the destitute, and the outcaste *burakumin*; and there was the beginning of a serious movement in favour of the recognition of women's rights.

These tendencies were not, for the most part, to take organizational shape for a few more years. The movement for universal male suffrage was, however, endorsed by the Kenseikai, in 1919. This party, having absorbed the Rikken Doshikai of Katsura's foundation, and having accepted Kato Komei as its leader, was now established as the principal party in opposition to the Seiyukai. Hara Kei, as the first Prime Minister to depend essentially upon the support of his party in the Diet, and in the lower House at that, being also the first commoner to lead a government in Japan, might have been expected to accommodate the growing desire that all men should have the vote; but he found himself unable to do so. In the aftermath of the rice riots, such a move would have been difficult to carry through the somewhat frightened higher echelons of the Seiyukai. There was no strong or concerted demand for it from within the civil service. Despite the strength of his position not only in the Diet but also throughout the country, built up over many patient years, Hara did not bring about major change in the political life of the nation. It could nevertheless be said that his own career was an exemplar of change, influenced by the great process of change in the outside world, associated with the First World War, and coinciding by chance with the ageing of the Genro and the felt need to move beyond the achievements of the Meiji period.

Hara had, accordingly, to recognize the need to re-establish domestic harmony and tranquillity after the shock of the rice riots. For some consolidation of his cabinet's position, he also had to allow the people, long accustomed to seeing power rest effectively in the safe hands of the Genro, to accept the implications, and the practical operation, of a system of party politics which had at last evolved to form the basis of governmental authority. Such acceptance was the harder to obtain, and the more necessary, because politicians as a class, never highly regarded, had recently sunk to a new low point in popular esteem. The general elections of 1915 had been widely considered the most blatantly corrupt yet conducted, not as violent as those of 1892, but with money and place and the intrigue of special or local group advantage wholly overshadowing the debate between policies putatively competing for selection on grounds of national interest. Okuma himself had been a lifelong enthusiast for parliamentary government, and he had appointed men of principle, such as Ozaki Yukio and Wakatsuki Reijiro to his cabinet; but he had never thrown off a reputation (dating back to the scandal of the Hokkaido Colonization Board in 1881 when he had, ironically, appeared to be contesting a piece of questionable patronage) for association with the shabbier and more unsavoury manifestations of democratic practice. A sort of tradition, as it could now be regarded, of unscrupulous politicking, had flourished, not with Okuma's approval, but under the cloak of a certain complacency on his part. Hara personally was under suspicion, not of direct malpractice but of conniving with the manipulation of provincial affairs and appointments, to his party's advantage.

In such matters, it must be said that the most highly respected and upright of the great figures of the Meiji period, such as the Princes Ito and Yamagata themselves, had inherited a tradition of political fighting in which victory mattered much more than compliance with the rules of war, if any, and in which the highest mark of honour was a spirit of single-minded determination. Neither had shrunk from use of the dark smear as a political weapon. In its purest form, the style may be studied in Kurosawa's great films of strife in the Tokugawa period.

A more compelling reason for the comparative modesty of Hara's domestic programme than the desirability of taking things at a gentle pace for a time at home, was the pressure of international events. The First World War was stumbling to its end as Hara came to power. For Japan, the Conference of Paris was the climax of the war, not a post-war anti-climax. Everything Japan hoped to have gained from active collaboration as one of the Allied Powers, in the Pacific and more especially in China, since China was also a belligerent in the Allied cause, was now at stake. Saionji was appointed to lead Japan's delegation to the Conference in Paris, with the experience of Baron Makino in support, and Yoshida Shigeru among their subordinates (in his case perhaps also the most insubordinate by nature). Saionji took his place as the representative of the Power which ranked next after the United States, Great Britain and France. With the addition of Italy to these, Japan was one of only five countries represented on the dominant Council of Ten, which began discussion of the terms of peace in January 1919. Japan was not represented, however, on the Council of Four. Furthermore the enjoyment of great prestige did not always facilitate frank communication, or full understanding. Despite Saionji's having known Clemenceau from his own days as a student in Paris, despite the experience of the treaty relationship with Britain, and the availability of those such as Viscount Chinda, from his embassy in London, who were closely aware of European thinking, the Japanese delegation found themselves at times out of sympathy with the detailed proceedings of the conference. To make the conduct of their own diplomacy more difficult, they had to cope with a Chinese delegation which included representation of Nationalist opinion from Canton and the south, as strong as that from Peking and even less well disposed towards any proposal involving concessions to Japanese ambition.

Japan's objectives in Paris were to gain the former German possessions in the Pacific, north of the equator; to secure the current position in Shantung, which amounted to more than the succession to Germany in Tsingtao; and to promote formal international condemnation of racial discrimination. The first of these aims was attained in substance, through the grant by the newly established League of Nations of a mandate to govern the Mariana, Caroline and Marshall Islands. The second aim looked likely to be assured on the strength of the agreements which were now disclosed to have been made in secret during the First World War, with Britain, France and Italy, even though Washington would not otherwise have contemplated this outcome. The achievement was frustrated by the refusal of the Chinese delegates to sign a peace treaty which would in effect have incorporated new derogations from China's sovereign rights in its own territory: it was not fitting that one member of a victorious alliance should be required to make a sacrifice in order to satisfy the pretensions of another. Disagreement over Shantung not only led to the premature departure from Paris of the Chinese delegation; it was the primary cause of the failure of the United States either to ratify the Treaty of Versailles or to participate in the work of the League of Nations, whose very foundation had owed so much to President Wilson. It was also the failure to settle Far Eastern territorial issues in Paris which, together with the perception of a need to seek agreement on the limitation of naval armaments, led the Powers to favour the convening of the Washington Conference in 1921, at the invitation of the United States.

As to their third objective in Paris, the Japanese delegation was obliged to acknowledge that the conflicting desire of the British government to conciliate apprehensions in the Dominions about immigration was too strong to permit London to acquiesce even in a statement of principle. The United States administration, though deeply committed under President Wilson to the pursuit of ideal standards in international relations, was also mindful of experience with public opinion in states on the Pacific coast, and was content to let consideration of this issue be abandoned. The importance originally attached by the Japanese government to recognition of the principle of non-discrimination was not correctly appreciated by the other Powers, which preferred to regard racial problems as being susceptible of pragmatic solution, as and when they might arise. In seeking to have a reference to this subject inserted into the Covenant of the League, the Japanese government was acting primarily in self-defence. The rejection of their initiative was used only later as a stimulus in the propagation of Pan-Asian sentiment, against the West.

In making their proposal that racial discrimination should be renounced formally, the Japanese government may have been ahead of the times. In respect of colonial issues, and the treatment of subject or backward communities or nations, and of the principle of self-determination, however, they had not kept pace with the admittedly rapid evolution of thought among certain of the Allied Powers. Shidehara Kijuro, ambassador in Washington from 1919 until 1922, and in later years always regarded in the United States and in Britain as the leading exponent in Japan of a liberal international and political philosophy, could describe the whole concept of the League of Nations as 'an extremely annoying thing for Japan'. Even when he was in the Washington embassy, exceptionally perceptive observer as he was, Shidehara – not surprisingly, given the sharp change in emphasis between the administrations of Presidents Wilson and Harding – found it difficult accurately to gauge the implications of American attitudes to the post-war reconstruction of world order. He was not alone in this; and in Tokyo, although there were some visionaries with international range, they were not in the ascendant. From the London embassy, Chinda did not always report the full force or the precise drift of representations made to him by Curzon, no doubt fearing to overdraw on his own credit in Tokyo, or to risk arousing misunderstanding on matters not essential to the conduct of current business. Curzon was sometimes patronizing (no less so to his own countrymen, as was well known) but he made a considerable effort to develop, in effect, the argument that the manner of Japanese expansion in East Asia was just as important, when it came to its international acceptability, as its confinement within reasonable limits, which themselves required to be satisfactorily defined. Leaving principle aside, there was much to be done in the regulation of practical matters, especially in arrangements for the control of the Tsingtao–Tsinan railway, which might have the effect of allaying both Chinese fears and the suspicions of British and other foreign competitors for business in China.

Successive Japanese governments were already suffering from their inability to control the outposts of an undefined and fluid empire. Before the Russian Revolution, they already had 50,000 troops in Shantung and Manchuria combined, as well as a large garrison in Korea. The dispatch of the expeditionary force of some 75,000 men to Siberia, and their retention there contrary to inter-Allied agreement, exacerbated both the problem of exercising control and the penalties of failure to do so effectively. So did the notorious barbarity of the marauding bands and irregular forces which were ravaging post-revolutionary Russia and extending a baneful stimulus to the recruiting officers of warlords in north China. Following the massacre of Japanese nationals at Nikolaevsk in 1920, reprisals were taken. The standards of discipline for which the Japanese army had been admired in both the Sino-Japanese and the Russo-Japanese wars were not maintained in Siberia, Manchuria or Shantung. In Korea, mass demonstrations in favour of independence, in early 1919, were suppressed with deliberate harshness and widespread incidental brutality, thousands of demonstrators being killed and tens of thousands arrested. The actions of the Japanese army there became the object of strong and sustained protests from Allied governments. These problems were not caused by mere bad judgement on the part of subordinate local commanders. Neither on the scale nor on the duration of the intervention in Siberia had the generals themselves been prepared to accept the spirit or the letter of moderate instructions, and they would no longer listen even to advice from Yamagata. The occupation of North Sakhalin was a gratuitous extension of the Siberian expedition; in such matters it was sometimes unclear whether the government in Tokyo had given ill-conceived instructions or was covering up its inability to deal with insubordination on the part of commanders in the field, by supporting their errors or excesses *ex post facto*.

Taken together with the continuing political disagreements over Shantung, themselves serving to keep alive, in Washington especially, the bitterness surviving from the whole episode of the Twenty-One Demands, these developments formed an unpromising background to the Washington Conference, when it was proposed in the summer of 1921. Japan's reputation in China itself continued to deteriorate after the demonstrations and boycotts against Japan and Japanese goods which had followed the withdrawal from Versailles of the Chinese delegation, and which came to give 4 May 1919 a continuing significance in China, as a date to be commemorated. Hara cancelled the outstanding business of the Nishihara loans, writing off some losses. Japan's willingness to join the new post-war consortium to co-ordinate the international handling of China's needs for foreign funding earned some goodwill, but this was offset by resentment of the Japanese government's resistance to proposals for any application of international financial co-operation in respect of Manchuria.

Hara was well aware of the need to counter criticism which might come to damage Japan's standing among the Powers. In late 1920 he published an article in the *Diplomatic Review* (*Gwaiko Jiho*) in which he set out to defend his government and his country against some of the defamatory charges which he believed to be current in foreign circles, formerly better disposed. He admitted that there had been some defects in the recent past, in the co-ordination of national policy, but claimed that 'it certainly cannot be maintained to-day that the army controls politics and compels the Government's China policy'. It was noticed, however, that in the same article the Japanese Prime Minister referred to the control of Korea, Sakhalin, Manchuria and some other areas as if it was legitimate to regard all these as being on the same footing, and their control as a matter more or less exclusively of concern to Japan, if not indeed exclusively within Japan's competence to exercise. On the domestic situation, the Seiyukai having triumphed in the general elections of summer 1920, Hara wrote with undisputed authority, emphasizing his earlier point about civilian control by asserting that 'party politics have developed, and the Government is organised in accordance with the wishes of the majority of the people'. If this was true, it was also the case that the Japanese people continued to believe in their imperial destiny. The public was not particular how expansion was brought about, so long as it promised to deliver economic benefits. Nearly everyone by now believed that greater relief must be found in North-East Asia for the pressure of overpopulation in the home islands; and this became an even more insistent theme as the wartime boom vanished, in 1920.

By the summer of 1921 nothing had been devised that could decisively appease American critics of the methods whereby Japanese expansion was being achieved. As the British government made its preparations for the Imperial Conference the same summer, Sir Auckland Geddes reported in a telegram to Lord Curzon on the state of American opinion: 'It has to be remembered that American people think of Japan in same way as many British thought of Germany in 1913, as inevitable enemy of next war, and view a British association with Japan now as we should have viewed an American association with Germany at that time.' If the Japanese delegation to the Washington Conference were to be out of favour with their hosts, it must be desirable that they should be on the best possible terms with the British.

Hara was emphatically in favour of renewing the Anglo-Japanese Alliance, which was due for review that summer. This was highly relevant to the decision that Crown Prince Hirohito, soon to be Regent, and later Showa

Emperor, should make the visit to Britain a principal object of his first tour abroad, on which he embarked in the spring of 1921. The visit was highly successful. Apart from his evident enjoyment, the Crown Prince showed himself keenly interested in the British monarchy and its relationship with the people of Britain and of the Dominions and Empire. Hara regarded the visit with great satisfaction, as did Lloyd George. The Crown Prince came to understand vividly the point of Bagehot's doctrine that a constitutional monarch, in a system such as that obtaining in Britain, had a right to be consulted, to encourage and to warn; but equally that he should not interfere in his government's conduct of public and official business. It was not King George V who would decide the future of the Anglo-Japanese Treaty, nor would the Crown Prince's visit decisively influence the approach to it of either party. Yet the visit did exemplify and even embody a separate relationship, which could be of benefit to both countries. The Prince of Wales was invited to return the visit the following year.

In the summer of 1921 the Imperial Conference in London held a well advertised, if formally private, debate on the future of the Anglo-Japanese Treaty. Strong Canadian opposition to its renewal contrasted, contrary to Churchill's expectation, with keen Australian and New Zealand support for its maintenance in force. Tension was relieved by the arrival of invitations to the proposed Washington Conference. For this, a further survey of the treaty's advantages and demerits, looked at from every angle, was commissioned in Whitehall. This examination went into great depth (and may still be regarded as a model of its kind, combining a broad outlook with careful attention to detail). It was well known to the Japanese government that Sir John Jordan, from Peking, would be urging the British government to take full account of the unpopularity of the treaty in China, and the consequent penalties for British interests there of its continuation. They were also confident that Sir Charles Eliot would not fail to counter these arguments, from Tokyo. They may have expected Foreign Office views, as expressed by Wellesley for example, to put the future of British relations with the United States above all other considerations, not least because the Americans could be relied upon to keep a heavy boot in the Open Door; but they also counted on Lloyd George, Balfour and Curzon to place a fair estimate on the value of the alliance with Japan. Japanese officials, however, understood, when the time approached for decision in Washington, the attraction which must inevitably be felt in British circles for an arrangement designed to subsume the Anglo-Japanese Treaty within broader instruments of more general application, thus averting any necessity for an open choice by Britain between Japan and the United States.

Before that stage was reached, Hara was stabbed to death on Tokyo station by a young extremist of the right. The public reaction to this outrage, as to the murder of a prominent banker some months previously, was subdued, and tinged with a curious ambivalence. Corruption and profiteering, even simply riches, if newly acquired, were currently the objects of particularly strong public distaste. Hara was recognized as a champion of parliamentary democracy through genuine party government, an enemy of faction based on the traditional allegiances of clansmen, and of deference to mere seniority. But his extensive network of support was alleged to be based on financial and other considerations of doubtful propriety. He was said to have arranged for the Seiyukai to receive support from the South Manchuria Railway Company for which it ought not to have been eligible. He tended to be surrounded closely by followers whose appearance was that of the bullies and thugs (*soshi*) customarily employed by local political bosses (*oyabun*), but kept away from the centre of government. His great qualities as a party politician did not endear him to the remaining transcendentalists, any more than to Satcho traditionalists. Neither was he a promoter of what were considered liberal or progressive causes. Hesitant advances by the proponents of such causes, such as the foundation of the New Women's Association in 1919 or the organization of the Japan Socialist Union the following year, owed nothing to favour or even to toleration on Hara's part. Indeed, during his premiership a Tokyo University professor was dismissed and imprisoned for giving a lecture on Kropotkin. He was as anxious as any colleague in the Seiyukai to keep Bolshevism away from East Asia. It is worth noting that it was his cabinet towards the end of his time, which approved a proposal for co-operation with Chang Tso-lin in Manchuria. He had Tanaka Giichi as his War Minister until the summer of 1921. Then continuing disagreement about the Siberian expedition caused a dangerous split within the leadership of his party, so that the advantage gained in the general elections of 1920 was lost to the Seiyukai.

So Hara's power had been greatly weakened some months before his assassination. Unavoidable preoccupations with foreign and economic policy, with the post-war recession and the approach of the Washington Conference, had in any case restrained his capacity further to shape and influence the evolution of the domestic political system, the field of action in which his talents were most effective. As it was, he had done a good deal to strengthen the machinery of local government. It is an irony that the introduction of the single-member House of Representatives constituency, for which he was responsible, might, if maintained, have helped others to avoid the taint of money politics from which he himself suffered. The failure of Japanese society to express outright condemnation of such a man's assassination was an indication of the limits reached at that time in the process of political evolution which he had promoted. It was also ironical that divisions within his own party should have brought that process to a halt immediately after his death, in favour of a temporary return to transcendental government. Hara was succeeded by his Minister of Finance,

Takahashi Korekiyo. Kato Komei returned to a prominent position, in the leadership of Japan's delegation to the Washington Conference.

Convened in the year in which the Nazis began to operate in Germany, and the Communist Party in China, the Washington Conference tackled some of the unfinished business of Versailles, and represented an attempt to harmonize the approach of the Powers to the problems of East Asia and the Pacific. Political stability, which meant the Open Door in China together with an agreed framework for the containment of Japanese expansion; and disarmament, which meant agreement on the limitation of the major naval shipbuilding programmes, were its objectives. Japan's participation signified willingness in principle to work with the other Powers, but without abandoning the ambitions of what could still be thought of as legitimate imperialism. The divisions of domestic opinion which had plagued Hara were directly relevant to the decisions that had to be made in Washington, and gave a lowering background to the work of the Japanese delegation. The Japanese government, though aware of intense strain in relations between London and Washington, was also apprehensive lest Japan be exposed to concerted pressure from the Anglo-Saxon Powers. The threat to the Anglo-Japanese Treaty was obvious. Unlike the British, however, Japanese leaders were not generally concerned at the implication of the conference's venue for a shift in the centre of gravity, in Western power, away from London and Europe and towards the United States. They saw this as an accurate reflection of the significance of North American resources.

Despite all the difficult circumstances, the Washington Conference made good progress in its work. The failures of the United States legislature to ratify the Versailles Peace Treaty and to endorse the foundation of the League of Nations had the momentarily beneficial effect of stimulating co-operative endeavour among the nations sharing this attempt to do for twentieth-century Asia what the Congress of Vienna had done for nineteenth-century Europe. In mid-December 1921 the conclusion was announced of the Four Power Pact, in which France joined the United States, Britain and Japan in agreeing mutual respect for each other's rights in East Asia and undertaking to consult together in the event of any crisis in the region. This instrument actually provided for the termination of the Anglo-Japanese Treaty, which accordingly lapsed finally in 1923. The same Powers, together with Belgium, Italy, the Netherlands and Portugal, as well as China itself, subsequently negotiated the Nine Power Treaty, concluded in February 1922, in which undertakings were given to respect China's independence and integrity, and some practical measures agreed, most significantly in connection with the control of customs revenues, which would enhance China's prospects of developing a unified, efficient and permanent machinery of administration and government.

Meanwhile, the United States, Britain and Japan, with France and Italy, had also reached agreement on a ratio of capital ship tonnage of 5:5: 3:1.75:1.75 respectively, with provision for the scrapping of some existing older warships, a ten-year holiday from new building, and a maximum limit of 35,000 tons displacement on capital ships. The Japanese delegation made concessions here, having held out at first for a ratio of 10:10:7 as between the United States, Britain and Japan. But Japan gained, in exchange, a prohibition on the fortification of islands in the Pacific, and assurances that first-class naval bases would not be constructed at Hong Kong or in the Philippines. Japan's overall security should have been judged to benefit from these arrangements; but Japanese naval opinion was from the outset bitterly divided as to their merits. It was all very well to argue that Japanese naval power would be concentrated, while the United States fleets would be divided between the Atlantic and the Pacific, even if they did not also come to match the responsibilities of the British in the Mediterranean, the Gulf, and the Indian Ocean as well. It was another matter to have accepted a position so far short of parity.

The political achievements of the Washington Conference could have been regarded, for the most part, as no more than the recording of pious generalities, previously acknowledged but never fully honoured. Such a view would have done far less than justice to those involved in the negotiations, experienced and distinguished statesmen, who believed themselves to have been formulating a basis of trust on which a sounder international order could be constructed. They could not have been expected to foresee the destructive impact of the ideologies of communism and national socialism, nor the nature of the totalitarian regimes by which those ideologies were to be promoted. As things were, the Japanese government was criticized at home for having shown weakness, by those who believed that the country must depend solely upon its own strength and determination. Those in circles where there was belief in the value of international co-operation knew that it could be developed only on the basis of mutual trust. It was relevant that those in both countries who most keenly regretted the abandonment of the Anglo-Japanese Treaty did so not on account of the value of any of its specific provisions, in circumstances which had altered radically even since the treaty's last revision, so much as because it, too, had signified a shared intention to build on a foundation of trust.

The charges of weakness levelled at home against the performance of the Japanese delegation were stimulated partly by the acceptance of allegedly disadvantageous limitations on naval armaments, which was to cause continual dissension in Japan; but they also arose out of an agreement reached with China outside the main conference, with the encouragement of Secretary Hughes and of Balfour. Under this agreement, the Shantung Treaty of 4 February 1922, Japan restored Shantung to China, on the understanding that the whole province would remain open to foreign trade and residence;

and handed over the Tsinan–Tsingtao Railway in exchange for financial compensation. This development was widely judged to be the prelude to a period of greatly improved international understanding and co-operation in East Asia. It gave rise to a genuine feeling of hope that the Anglo-Japanese Treaty had been sacrificed in the cause of wider interests, from which both parties would benefit. There was no irony intended in Kato's expression to Balfour, at the conclusion of the Washington Conference, of satisfaction with the success of their collaboration. The concept of international co-operation, however, remained suspect in some circles in Japan.

4

Earthquake, Economic Tremors, Violent Indiscipline, 1922–31

It was the persistence of the split existing in Hara's time within the Seiyukai which brought down Takahashi's government in the summer of 1922. Friction had been exacerbated by the commitment to withdraw from Siberia, made at the Washington Conference. There was a widespread sense that the United States and Britain had colluded in Washington to restrain or frustrate Japan's reasonable ambitions. This was balanced uneasily by some recognition of the need to take account of the views and interests of the other Powers, arising as much from awareness of the limits of national resources as from belief in the efficacy of international co-operation. What came to be known as the Washington Treaty System was, like the principle of naval arms limitation, treated with scepticism from the start in those circles where competition between the Powers was still regarded as the permanently dominant factor in international affairs. Realism was tempered with sentiment. A popular visit to Japan by the Prince of Wales went some way temporarily to counter chagrin caused by the impending lapse of the Anglo-Japanese Treaty.

In an uncertain climate of opinion, Takahashi was succeeded as Prime Minister by Admiral Baron Kato Tomosaburo, whose personal prestige as former Chief of Staff to Admiral Togo and Navy Minister in the expansive days of Okuma, Terauchi and Hara, had secured credibility for the pursuit of naval arms limitation. As Japan's chief delegate at the talks in Washington earlier in the year, his support for the validity of this concept had been decisive. Its acceptance was bitterly opposed by Vice-Admiral Kato Kanji, who had withdrawn in sickness and discontent from the talks in Washington and returned to Tokyo to lead the so-called fleet faction of the navy in direct defiance of his service chief, now also his political master. Kato Tomosaburo's leadership of what came to be known as the treaty faction of his service signified a moderation born of prudence rather than tinged with pusillanimity. He saw the need for some immediate retrenchment to consolidate recovery after the collapse of the wartime boom. He may have lacked his predecessor's understanding of the detail of economic policy, for his period as Prime Minister saw a continuing worsening in Japan's balance of payments. Prices had not fallen in Japan to the same extent as they had in Britain and the United States. The value of the yen on the international exchanges was too high: exports were falling off, and imports rising fast.

Kato Tomosaburo was not a party man. His outlook on international affairs was not unlike that of Prince Yamagata. In 1922, Yamagata died. Born thirty years before the Meiji Restoration, he had exercised a major influence on national policy, and indeed on the character of the modern state and its whole machinery of administration, both in central and in local government, for more than fifty years after 1868. Towards the end of his life this influence had declined as the result rather of his unfortunate decision to advise against the marriage proposed for the Crown Prince than of any weakening of purpose. Whether he really believed that colour-blindness should disqualify a future empress, or whether he was so zealous a Choshu man that he could not bring himself to accept without protest a princess from Choshu's Satsuma partner and rival fief, remained unclear. He never abandoned the view that government should transcend party politics, and, although the cause of transcendentalism did not long survive him in its original form, the idea that a public servant owed his duty to the state as personified by the Emperor, rather than to the government of the day as representative of the Emperor's subjects, certainly did survive (as something like it survived in other monarchies). If some of Yamagata's attitudes became old-fashioned, he never lost his capacity to assess the national interest dispassionately. His belief in the necessity for secure boundaries did not lead him to countenance excessively ambitious nationalism. He did not trust the older Powers, least of all Russia, nor did he think it prudent to antagonize them needlessly. Conscious of his own country's limited resources, and of cultural affinity with the continent, he preferred to work for partnership between Japan and China rather than simply to maximize territorial acquisition on the mainland of Asia. He has been accorded the reputation of a great military and civil administrator and far-sighted strategist; but there has been a tendency to emphasize the character of the Satcho autocrat at the expense of that of the canny statesman.

Like Yamagata, Okuma was born in 1838 and died in 1922. His career, however, was markedly more erratic in terms of success and failure, primarily because of his open and sustained hostility to the dominance of Satcho interests, ideas and men. His understanding of and sympathy with liberal Western political thought were deeper than those of most of his contemporaries; and he negotiated skilfully with the Powers both over the treatment of Christians in Japan and for treaty revision. His first term as Prime Minister was cut short by political in-fighting which it was probably beyond his power to control. In his second, any prospect of exerting a lasting influence on the evolution of parliamentary government in Japan was sacrificed in favour of the response to opportunities seemingly opened up in China in consequence of the outbreak of the First World War. Okuma's political career was ultimately disappointing. His lasting achievement was the founding of Waseda University.

If the deaths of these two elder statesmen in 1922 might have seemed to mark the passing of an era, the recall of Admiral Baron Yamamoto Gonbei to succeed Kato Tomosaburo as Prime Minister on the latter's death towards the end of August 1923 might equally have looked like an attempt by surviving veterans of Meiji traditions to revive those old days. It was the Great Kanto Earthquake of 1 September 1923 which determined that things would never be the same again. This was one of the worst natural disasters of recorded history. The people of Japan were familiar with earthquakes, but not with calamities on this huge scale. Nearly 100,000 lost their lives, and some 2 million were left homeless. The first shock came when the midday meal was in preparation, mostly on open, charcoal braziers (*hibachi*) so that the conflagration was instantaneous and devastating. The firestorm and the tidal wave which followed the shocks utterly destroyed most of Yokohama and much of central Tokyo. Vast areas of wooden housing were reduced to ashes, the inhabitants suffocated and incinerated. Survivors were so badly affected that many were temporarily out of their minds. Some hundreds of Koreans resident in Greater Tokyo were the victims of an irrational desire for vengeance, and some known socialists were also attacked on the strength of rumours that they, too, had engaged in an imaginary plot against their fellow-citizens. A group of police officers took the opportunity to arrest and, hoping to escape detection, to murder Osugi Sakae, his companion anarchist, Ito Noe, who was also a leading proponent of women's rights, and a nephew of Osugi.

The disturbance and aftershocks were also deeply felt in financial circles, not only in Japan but round the world, and especially in the London insurance and reinsurance markets. Aid, too, was forthcoming from worldwide sources, particularly generous support being given by the United States. The Japanese government sought to alleviate the disaster by making funds available through the banks, to sustain both private individuals who had suffered losses, and also corporations. The necessary subsidies were provided to the banks without regard to their capacity to offer collateral security. Industrial concerns were thus enabled to recover, and even to increase their competitive strength in overseas markets. Overall, some consciousness of international interdependence was newly promoted, but some old fears of dependence were revived at the same time.

The Great Kanto Earthquake further unsettled a social climate in Japan which was already sharing something of the post-war volatility evident in

Western societies. The modern boy and modern girl, known as *mobo* and *moga*, were conspicuously harmless figures, but their more easygoing manners seemed to symbolize the weakening of traditional relationships and the loosening of conventional standards of behaviour. Experiments in the arts invited a similar reaction.

Concern about more openly subversive tendencies focused on the threat of Bolshevism. A new Japan Communist Party had constituted itself in 1921. Its existence remained secret for a time. But the menace of contamination and intrigue from Soviet Russia seemed to grow, and to come closer, when it became known that the Chinese supporters of Dr Sun Yat-sen, the Kuomintang (KMT), shortly to adopt the simple title of Nationalists for use in the outside world, were obtaining from Moscow not only arms but also advice and training, in particular from the sinister Michael Borodin, who arrived in Canton in 1923, and General Galen (or Blucher). The future of relationships between the Kuomintang, the Chinese Communist Party (CCP) and the Soviets, and between each of them and each of the leading warlords in the north of China, was now, and remained for some years, impenetrably obscure.

Japanese secret societies active in China were involved from this time in an extremely complex web: they sought to manipulate and deal with forces which posed threats to Japanese interests or even to national security, as well as with those (sometimes under the same management) holding out the promise of extended influence or power. Relations with the Japanese military intelligence services and, when available, with central government, were liable to come under strain. The careers of Toyama Mitsuru and Uchida Ryohei, as leaders of the Genyosha and Kokuryukai, are paradigms of ambiguity. Although Uchida was charged in 1925 with plotting the assassination of Prime Minister Kato Komei, he and his associates were generally able to claim some indirect influence with politicians, including elements of the government of the day, as with military and industrial groups and, to a lesser extent perhaps, with senior civil servants.

Kita Ikki and Okawa Shumei, of the Yuzonsha, had similar objectives in foreign policy, involving Pan-Asianism as a vehicle both for the expulsion of Western and for the extension of Japanese influence. But they propagated a form of radical nationalism at home, designed as a philosophy capable of standing up against communism, which, though taking account of developments of interest in Italy and Germany, was essentially irreconcilable with the established polity, the *kokutai*. Later, Kita and Okawa parted company, each exerting some influence on revolutionary right-wing ideology especially in army circles. In the early 1920s, Kita (originally a socialist) was regarded as a considerable expert on the revolution in China, on which he had published a book, drawing on first-hand experience. In 1923 he published his thesis on the reconstruction of Japan. This revolutionary tract achieved a popularity never attainable by much less extreme formulations of leftward political philosophy. There would always be applause for attacks on politicians or the zaibatsu, but the sanctity of the imperial line could not be questioned by any person or party with political aspirations. Kita and other shadowy figures knew this. More respectable persons of the right and centre knew it as a weakness of even the moderate left. Besides the secret societies of the extreme right, there were so-called patriotic societies dedicated to the defence of the state against socialism.

In the aftermath of the Great Earthquake, any threat to the stability of the state aroused passion. An attempt on the life of the Prince Regent, early in 1924, brought about the resignation of Prime Minister Yamamoto. The elders, anxious to restore public morale, made a last avowedly transcendental appointment, choosing as his successor Kiyoura Keigo, an ageing former protégé of Yamagata, and currently president of the Privy Council. This was a misjudgement. It became a disaster when Kiyoura appointed his cabinet exclusively from the House of Peers. A second Movement for the Protection of Constitutional Government was formed, based on a loose organization which had played a central part in forcing Katsura from office in 1913. Members of the lower House collectively were naturally affronted. Moderate public opinion was shocked. The cause of universal manhood suffrage was sharply stimulated in response to what was perceived as a timorous kind of reactionary politics, out of touch with the times. By mid-June, Kiyoura was obliged to resign.

This led to the appointment of Viscount Kato Komei (Takaaki) as Prime Minister, at the head of a coalition government. It was a strong team, with Wakatsuki Reijiro as Minister for Home Affairs; Hamaguchi Osachi as Finance Minister; Shidehara Kijuro at the Foreign Ministry, with every intention of pursuing a moderate policy in China and of working with the other Powers on the lines envisaged at Washington; and General Ugaki Kazushige as War Minister. Ugaki accepted the need for retrenchment, and reduced the army's strength by four divisions, while also achieving some useful measures of modernization, both of organization and of equipment, including the introduction of air and tank forces. He was on good terms with General Tanaka Giichi. Tanaka was the outstanding soldier of his generation, but he retired from the army in 1925 to pursue his political career. Ugaki was not therefore shielded by his patronage from the criticism of certain less senior but conspicuously ambitious officers, such as Araki Sadao, who sneered at him as a political general.

The great achievement of Kato's first cabinet was to secure the passage through the Diet of a bill giving the vote to all males over twenty-five years of age. Kato's own party, the Kenseikai, had long been in favour of universal male suffrage, and in early 1925 they were also able to enlist support for it from their partners in the Seiyukai. The enactment of this measure increased the electorate at a stroke from 3 million to 12.5 million. It gave encouragement to the development and expression of moderate opinion. There was, however, great nervousness lest it might risk allowing what were known as the proletarian parties – that is not only communists, anarchists and socialists but also the labour and farmers' movement – to undermine or even overwhelm established political interests and organizations. The government therefore introduced the notorious Peace Preservation Law, also of 1925, whose provisions were so widely and loosely drafted as to facilitate the suppression even of ideas, if deemed hostile to the state as constituted at the time. It was not long before tens of thousands of suspects were to be arrested under this ill-defined measure.

A few months before these legislative milestones were reached, the Japanese government and public had been shocked and affronted by the passage through the United States Congress of the Immigration Act of 1924. This measure, also known as the Exclusion Act, which seemed to foreclose the possibility of future Japanese emigration to the United States, was regarded as combining racial discrimination with bad faith, since it amounted to a unilateral repudiation of the gentlemen's agreement so painstakingly negotiated in 1907. It was opposed by Secretary of State Hughes, and signed only with reluctance by President Coolidge; but the damaging consequences could not be averted. Racial discrimination on one side of the Pacific would inflame xenophobia on the other. This was the worst possible introduction to the conduct of Japan's foreign policy by a minister of Shidehara's style and disposition. It contributed towards a renewed public sense of threat to Japan's independence and security, and provided some apparent justification for the views of extreme nationalists, in the armed forces and the patriotic societies. Among politicians and bureaucrats, it caused deep resentment and again aroused suspicions of hostile Anglo-Saxon conspiracy. For example, before the end of 1924 the British ambassador in Tokyo was told by a senior Japanese official that the proposed fortification of Singapore would be an unfriendly act; this no more than a year after the formal lapse of the Anglo-Japanese Treaty (and despite the probability that the proposal would be deferred, largely on the grounds that hostilities with Japan were regarded by the British government at that time as a remote contingency).

Nevertheless, Shidehara's handling of foreign affairs at first proceeded with some success. Recognition was accorded to the Soviet government, with which a convention was signed in Peking in 1925. Japan undertook to withdraw from North Sakhalin in return for some oil and coal concessions there. The agreement on fisheries made with the Tsar's government in 1907 was revived and usefully revised. The situation in China, however, was so uncertain as to frustrate any attempt by the Powers, whether acting singly or in concert, to make any decisive move. The Treaty Port system was being undermined gradually, with no agreed practical interpretation, let alone effective application, of the Washington system to take its place. In 1925 the British-trained police in the international settlement at Shanghai found themselves in the position of having to open fire on demonstrators, as did the Anglo-French detachment of marines in Canton. There were widespread allegations that communist agents were actively seeking to provoke outbreaks of violence between the Chinese population and their foreign communities. What remained of central government in Peking lacked authority. Warlords proliferated. In the republican area of the south, Sun Yat-sen's death, also in 1925, drew Chiang Kai-shek, previously known exclusively for his military competence and responsibilities, on to the centre of the political stage; but no one could foretell how he would decide to play his new leading role.

At this time, Shidehara was less disturbed by the possibility of a period of dominant communist influence in China than was the British government. Japanese officials were also less favourably inclined towards or optimistic for the prospects of the republican cause, whose leaders were beginning to claim the title of Nationalists exclusively for themselves, than were some Americans. A strong central administration in China was what the Powers all professed to desire, but the means were not available to promote this. The British for a time, the Japanese more consistently, were dependent in practice, for the securing of their interests, on dealings with local authorities. This meant, in the crucial case of Japanese interests in Manchuria, dealing with a warlord whose writ ran throughout a region variable in extent, but never small, and whose aspirations were unlimited. While the Japanese already placed considerable reliance on Chang Tso-lin, however, Shidehara was personally committed to a policy of co-operation with the other Powers. The Tariff Conference convened in Peking in 1925 was intended by the participants to demonstrate the usefulness of such co-operation. But it soon broke down. Positions had not been concerted in advance: the Powers proved to be divided among themselves, while the authority of the Chinese officials in Peking was, at the best estimate, of doubtful validity. Meanwhile, throughout China the clamour against the unequal treaties became ever more strident, while the nature and location of the institutions through which it might find its authentic expression remained obscure. The Powers were sometimes inclined to defend their interests by force, singly or in varying combinations; sometimes, at the other extreme, to continue the search for a valid Chinese interlocutor with whom they might discuss the modalities of the surrender of their extraterritorial rights.

Shidehara rejected the general idea of concerted military operations to protect the positions of the Powers in China, and refused at least one specific invitation to join a combined defensive action. The British for a time replaced the Japanese as the principal objects of Chinese anti-imperialist zeal. Japan's trade with China, which now took about a quarter of Japan's total exports, was briefly stabilized. To this extent Shidehara's policy began to earn a reward. But non-intervention was scarcely a sustainable option at this disordered time for foreign countries engaged in commerce through the Chinese ports. Furthermore, the Japanese commanders and administrators on the continent had by now developed and thickened relations with Chang Tso-lin. Indeed, the fact that his considerable warlord's power was based in Manchuria made this inevitable. The Japanese position in the Kwantung leased territories was clear-cut: by contrast, their further rights to control and police the extended operations of the South Manchurian Railway were never likely to be defined to the practical satisfaction of all concerned. Chang Tso-lin's ambitions for the extension of his own power in China were equally lacking in well-defined limits. His fortunes went up and down.

While Shidehara might express some complacency about the threat of communist influence in China, the Japanese government was not going to risk acquiring the taint of actual association with it. Meanwhile, it was the Kwantung Army, not the government in Tokyo, which enjoyed the closest contact with Chang. The responsibilities of the Kwantung Army were already formidable. Its size was still modest at this time. Policing the railway zone beyond the leased territories was bound to involve political complications, even if staff officers who entertained far-reaching schemes of national aggrandizement, and who welcomed opportunities to display enterprise, had not been posted to the frontiers of empire. The military police in the railway zone were no better qualified to make distinctions between the legitimate activities of patriots and the depredations of bandits than were their opposite numbers in the Treaty Ports. The notions of imperial expansion and consolidation seemed much more practicable in sparsely populated Manchuria than along the teeming China coast. Chiang Kai-shek's Northern Expedition, and his decision to confront Chang Tso-lin, became the catalyst for further developments.

Before Chiang's march north, and before he moved against the communists within his own jurisdiction, the political scene changed again in Tokyo. Kato Komei had reconstituted his govenment in August 1925 to depend exclusively on the Kenseikai, thus narrowing the base of its support in the lower House. It was unpopular in the House of Peers, which had opposed the introduction of universal male suffrage, and had resisted the modest reforms in its own composition for which Kato had also been responsible. Accordingly, Kato's death in January 1926, following months of ill-health, left his successor, Wakatsuki, in a somewhat vulnerable position.

The death of Kato Komei (Takaaki) in his mid-sixties was another serious loss to the vitality of Japanese politics. His deepest interest was in international affairs, and his two periods in London had given him an understanding of the outlook of the older Powers. This understanding had been acquired, however, before that outlook itself was transformed by the experience of the major combatants in the First World War. His handling of the Twenty-One Demands suggests that Kato did not sense the onset of this transformation. By the time he became Prime Minister, the combination of economic problems at home, rendered critical by the consequences of the Great Earthquake, with chronic disorder in China, was to restrict his scope for practical interpretation of Japan's role under the Washington Treaty system. His contribution to domestic political development was, on the other hand, substantial. His opposition both to the Satcho *hanbatsu* and to the authority of the Genro as an institution was effective, in the latter case possibly even decisive: following the death of Matsukata in 1924, Saionji was and remained the sole representative of the Genro, embodying in his person the prestige accorded to the collective wisdom of the elders, but permitted to exercise progressively less of their original discretionary power. Kato's support for universal male suffrage was conclusive, and gives him a unique monument. He left the Kenseikai well prepared for involvement in the further development of a two-party system in the lower House. His own close connection with the Mitsubishi interest was passed on to this party.

Though Kato's legacy to Wakatsuki, his successor as Prime Minister, was less enduring, it included some progress in economic recovery from the effects of the Great Earthquake. It soon became apparent, however, that this had been achieved at the cost of a temporary weakening in the domestic banking system as a whole. Some of the smaller banks had overextended their resources, in lending beyond prudent limits on the strength of government subsidies for reconstruction in industries suffering from earthquake damage. Publicity for the results of an investigation into the distribution of outstanding earthquake relief bills led to a run on many banking institutions, temporarily halted by the intervention of the Bank of Japan but damaging to confidence and potentially prejudicial to the country's reputation in foreign financial centres, now as important and sensitive as it had ever been. The most substantial and dramatic failure was that of the Bank of Taiwan, itself overexposed in its incautious support of various smaller institutions and in its dealings with the hitherto highly regarded Suzuki group of Kobe. The closure of the Bank of Taiwan in April 1927 caused renewed panic for a time. The general effect of this so-called crisis, apart from its being the proximate cause of the fall of Wakatsuki's government itself, was to concentrate financial power yet more closely in the hands of the banks at the centre of each of the zaibatsu groups, and thus also to increase the industrial influence and range of these groups. The Suzuki interests, themselves very substantial, were mostly absorbed into the Mitsui group.

It is a question whether the atmosphere of crisis was produced by any sense of serious threat to the economy, or whether it was artificially stimulated by those who wished to bring down the Kenseikai government primarily because of the alleged weakness of its policy in China. For by March 1927 Chiang Kai-shek's Northern Expedition had assumed the character of a threat to Japanese interests in China, and of a direct challenge to the position of Chang Tso-lin. Japan's interests in north China had developed since the Washington Conference, quite substantially, but sporadically and uncertainly owing to the disorderly conditions prevailing throughout the country.

Indeed, in the early 1920s Japan's exports to the United States were growing faster than exports to China. Above all, the silk industry was able to benefit from the boom conditions in the United States, which were inducing worldwide prosperity and optimism. The concentration of industrial power within Japan was already proceeding at this time, even before the acceleration, noted above, which was a result of the financial crisis of 1927. The zaibatsu came to participate on a major scale in every economic activity of significance. Collectively, they assumed an increasingly dominant position in manufacturing as well as in mining and foreign trade, and in the overseas territories of the Empire. They were not confined or hampered by regulation, merely supervised, if even that is not too strong a term, lightly and at a benevolent distance. Government intervention, other than in reconstruction after the earthquake disaster, was most apparent in measures to ensure standards of quality in the manufacture of goods for export. Guilds were formed for this purpose, which also facilitated communication between government and industry. It was understood, in the discussion of industrial policy, that the outcome should not be dictated, neither by politicians nor by the most exalted officials.

Growth in industrial production was most notable in the silk and cotton industries. In the latter, spindleage rose from 3.8 million in 1920 to 6.6 million in 1929. Corporate businesses grew dramatically in size. The sector, still equipped with hand-looms, which provided for the domestic consumption of traditional materials and made-up goods, was diminishing in importance. With growing demand both for uniforms and for civilian dress of Western style, the output of woollen cloth rose sharply. Of all factory workers in 1930, half were employed in textiles. Pottery was another sector in which the production of traditional wares continued in small enterprises, while plants were brought into operation on a large scale for the manufacture of china and porcelain in the Western taste, much of it for export.

In the iron and steel sector, although output increased substantially, that of finished steel exceeding 2 million tons in 1929, Japan remained dependent upon imports for about a third of the country's overall requirements, and imports of scrap became a significant necessity. In engineering, there was a similar strengthening of the domestic industry combined with a continuing reliance on imported technology and components in certain areas, including the motor industry. Shipbuilding was in relative decline throughout the 1920s, mercantile construction launched in 1929 reaching only 165,000 tons, and that in what was considered quite a good year. Naval building was, of course, constrained by the Washington Treaty.

Working conditions in the modern manufacturing industries remained hard. There was a continuing evolution in labour relations, but based always on the inherited traditions of paternalism, such as survived almost unchanged in the strong, separate, traditional sector of craft production, rather than on the recognition of newly claimed standards or rights. In the early 1920s there were some famous strike actions, such as that at the Kawasaki dockyards in Kobe, led by the Christian Socialist Kagawa Toyohiko. These strikes amounted to a series of defeats for militant workers; but they were defeats for labour from which management also learned some lessons. The Japan Federation of Labour (Sodomei) had been permitted to come into operation after the First World War. It had difficulty with its own left-wing extremists. These were expelled from positions of influence in the organization by 1925, when leadership passed to the right wing, represented by Nishio Suehiro, Suzuki Bunji, founder of the earlier Yuaikai, and Matsuoka Komakichi (all of whom, as it happens, survived to resume activity after the Pacific War, if only for one post-war year in Suzuki's case). Of some 6 million workers employed in manufacturing industries, including building, by 1930, fewer than half a million were members of trade unions, and the right of collective bargaining had been accorded formally to few trades. All the same, real wages had risen substantially in the years leading up to the worldwide depression.

If standards of living tended to improve steadily, but slowly, for factory workers in these years, they depended as ever on harvests, for the peasant farmer, and on market conditions, both of which were beyond his control. The 1920s saw little change in the factors affecting land tenure. There was an extension in the range of agricultural products, while a growing reliance on imports of rice, especially, from the Empire, from Taiwan and Korea, provided for the continued increase of population. The chemical industry was able to supply improved fertilizers, thanks in part to the availability of a growing volume of soya bean imports from Manchuria. Tenant farmers were engaged in a constant fight against the burden of rent, and were progressively better organized to defend their interests, though, as with the workers in manufacturing industry, the bodies set up to represent them came under close scrutiny by the authorities, and constant suspicion. It was not, however, until the collapse of rice prices, following a good harvest in 1930, and of the silk industry, following the slump, that conditions for agriculture and for rural communities generally became desperate. Meanwhile, throughout the 1920s, the fishing industry prospered, drawing advantage not only from the rise in living standards of the urban population, but also from technological advances, notably the development of floating canneries and oil-burning marine engines.

Leading industrialists of the mid-1920s gained some encouragement from Shidehara's express intention to concentrate on economic diplomacy, and from the knowledge of business affairs which he could be presumed to have derived from his close personal link with the Mitsubishi interests. The extreme difficulty of developing stable trading exchanges with China at this time (as throughout the period of greatest disorder and uncertainty in that country for two decades after the Revolution of 1911) nevertheless rendered the concept of economic diplomacy attractive as an aspiration rather than as a practical policy. The development of the Empire was a more rewarding task than trying to expand beyond the Treaty Ports on the China coast, and seemed to gain in urgency because of China's very weakness. Some of the most distinguished industrialists, however, such as the veteran Shibusawa, made it a principal concern to cultivate better relations with the United States, both in order to offset the effects of the Exclusion Act and in recognition of the inevitable growth in importance to the Japanese economy of exchanges of goods and services between the two countries. There was at the same time a continuing expansion of financial relationships with the Western Powers generally, and of professional competence in this field, as signified by careers such as that of Ikeda Seihin at the Mitsui Bank and, later, the Mitsui Gomei.

The zaibatsu companies were prominent in developing empire trade with Taiwan and Korea, and increasingly with Manchuria. From the two former territories there was very substantial business to be had in shipping rice and other foodstuffs into Japan. Textiles, above all, and a wide range of consumer goods, were exported in great volume to those colonies. The government saw to it that the export surpluses earned by the colonial territories were put into the development of their infrastructures; but the predominant industrial participation in this development was in Japanese hands. Immigrants from Japan were given favourable treatment in the colonies, in order to boost production and facilitate administration, and progressively as a means of coping with the increase in the population of Japan itself, which was running at about a million a year by the end of the 1920s. This was regarded as an explosive rate of increase; yet the total Japanese civilian immigrant populations of Taiwan, Korea and Manchuria combined never rose substantially above one year's current increment in the population of the Japanese Islands themselves. Better educational facilities were provided for the children of immigrant Japanese families than for Taiwanese or Koreans, the level of whose participation in the administration was strictly controlled. There were prominent advocates in Japan of political devolution for the colonies, including notably Professor Yanaihara Tadao; but after Hara's death no political voice of equal weight with his. Nor was Hara's appointment of Den Kenjiro as the first civilian Governor-General of Taiwan looked upon with favour in Tokyo. The colonial governments retained an authoritarian character and a philosophy of assimilation.

Imperial expansion was strongly criticized on economic grounds by Ishibashi Tanzan, of the *Oriental Economic Journal*, but his ideas for a market economy, though politely received, were not in keeping with the times. The great world depression which began in 1929 added to pressures in favour of maximizing self-sufficiency within the Empire, and later within East Asia. The concentration of industrial power which was one of the consequences of the financial crisis of 1927 gave the economy a flexibility of great value, especially in assisting the process of recovery from the depression. The advantages flowing from this disguised blessing of 1927 far outweighed the disadvantages resulting from the ill-timed attempt of 1928 to return to the gold standard.

As already noted, what has always been known as the financial crisis of 1927 was caused as much by political as by economic considerations. For dissatisfaction with Shidehara's policy in China reached a first crescendo in March 1927. In that month, Chinese Nationalist forces attacked foreign concessions in Hankow and pillaged the United States, British and Japanese consulates in Nanking. The Powers shared a determination to avoid playing into the hands of communist elements bent on provoking hostilities between the Nationalists and the foreign imperialist presence in China. Disaster was narrowly averted in Hankow. In Nanking, British and United States warships were in action to save the lives of their expatriate communities; and the British government announced the dispatch of 12,000 troops to protect British interests in the international settlement in Shanghai. By contrast, though he had authorized the employment of Japanese marines to protect Japanese lives and property, Shidehara's restraint earned the condemnation of much of public opinion in Japan, where it was characterized as 'weak-kneed (*nanjaku*) diplomacy'. It was not immediately apparent, either in Japan or elsewhere, that Chiang Kai-shek was determined to repudiate the Chinese Communist Party and their Soviet advisers, nor even that he was capable of doing so effectively, and of substituting negotiation with the Powers for provocation against them. In any case, such developments, however welcome in principle, did not relieve the Japanese authorities of concern about the consequences for their position in Manchuria of a confrontation between Chiang Kai-shek and Chang Tso-lin. The strength of the position acquired by the latter in Peking made conflict almost inevitable.

This was the threat to which General Baron Tanaka Giichi immediately turned his attention on coming into power in April 1927, as Prime Minister of the new Seiyukai government. He authorized the dispatch of two successive contingents of troops to Shantung, ostensibly for the protection of Japanese citizens resident in that province. Tanaka was his own Foreign

Minister. He also established for the first time a Ministry for Colonization, and assumed charge of it. Ignoring protests from Nanking, and resisting international criticism of the Shantung expedition, he summoned a conference of senior Japanese officials near the end of June, to discuss policy towards China and on the Asian continent. The scale of this conference was unprecedented, Japan's interests having expanded, but the same title of Eastern Conference (*Toho Kaigi*) is given to a meeting held by Hara in 1921, at which the decision was taken to back Chang Tso-lin. It seems doubtful whether any such far-reaching decisions were made at the 1927 conference, but the occasion was taken to issue a firm statement of the Japanese government's intention to protect Japan's interests in China, and to intervene as might become necessary in Manchuria and Mongolia. The move of the headquarters of the Kwantung Army from Port Arthur to Mukden, which took place the following year, was no doubt foreshadowed at the conference.

For Japan, more even than for the other Powers with substantial interests in China, Chiang Kai-shek's Northern Expedition was a decisive development. Chang Tso-lin had certainly overreached the limits of his capability, in assuming a dominant position in and around Peking; but he was Japan's protégé, and Japan's prospects in Manchuria evidently depended on relations with him and his successors. In 1927, benign neglect did not seem a sensible option to the authorities in Tokyo any more than to the commander of the Kwantung Army. Tanaka's intention in dispatching troops to Shantung had been to protect the relationship with Chang Tso-lin, not directly to challenge the Nationalists. He was able to withdraw these troops in the autumn, the Northern Expedition having petered out, temporarily. Chiang Kai-shek actually spent some time in Japan that same autumn, with what result in terms of negotiation is unclear. Tanaka judged it necessary to send a further expeditionary force to Shantung in the spring of 1928, and there was a fairly major clash with Nationalist forces at Tsinan in May. By this time the Japanese government was seeking to prevail upon Chang Tso-lin to abandon his pretensions in Peking in exchange for some guarantee on their part of his base in Manchuria.

This plan was frustrated by Colonel Komoto Daisaku, a staff officer who believed that his superiors wished for a pretext to justify the assertion of more extensive authority in Manchuria, that they had finally lost confidence in Chang Tso-lin, and perhaps that they would have better prospects of enjoying satisfactory collaboration with his son, Chang Hsueh-liang. Colonel Komoto arranged Chang Tso-lin's assassination, having the railway carriage in which he was retreating to Mukden blown up just outside the city. If Komoto and his associates were hoping to provoke further incidents involving the expansion of the Kwantung Army's jurisdiction, they were disappointed. The Japanese authorities attributed the incident to Nationalist agents, but the truth of it (though not confirmed until the hearing of evidence at the International Military Tribunal for the Far East) was widely suspected. The Kwantung Army refused both to publish their report of the incident and to contemplate charging Komoto and his accomplices before a court martial. The Emperor's anger at this failure of military discipline is believed to have been a major factor in bringing about the resignation of Tanaka and the fall of his government early in July 1929. As for Chang Hsueh-liang, by the close of 1928 he was committed to the support of the Nationalist Government of Chiang Kai-shek, whose regime was by then also recognized by the other Powers, and came to be recognized by Japan early in 1929. At that time, after a widespread boycott of Japanese goods in China, and appeals to the League of Nations by the Nationalist government against Japan's intervention, a bilateral agreement was reached under which Japanese troops were withdrawn from Shantung.

The circumstances leading to this intervention were often overlooked in subsequent assessments of the contrast between the policies towards China of Tanaka on the one hand and Shidehara on the other. While it is true that Tanaka took stronger measures than Shidehara had been willing to contemplate, it would be wrong to attribute to Tanaka any tendency to delegate the proper role of the central government in decision-making to Kwantung Army headquarters. On the contrary, his resignation appears to have been prompted primarily by awareness of the need to retain control in Tokyo, and a sense of frustration over his inability to assert this control fully, after the assassination of Chang Tso-lin. The so-called Tanaka Memorial, a document setting out a 'strong' China policy for Japan, allegedly prepared for submission to the Emperor after Tanaka's Eastern Conference of 1927, is no longer regarded as authentic.

Tanaka died soon after his resignation. His foreign policy has sometimes been made to look harsher than it was in reality, not only for reasons suggested above, but also because this was a period in international affairs in which the expression of good intentions was sometimes confused with the actual settlement of problems. The Washington Treaty system was itself deficient in the provision of devices for the monitoring of developments as they occurred. The League of Nations was crippled by the failure of the United States to participate in its work. The Kellogg–Briand Pact of Paris was a fine statement of moral principle, but it did not go far towards creating international security. It was, however, concluded precisely at the time, in 1928, when Japanese policy seemed to diverge sharply from the spirit, and the process, of pacification by pacts. In 1929 the Japanese government opposed the attempt by the British and French governments to make the sanctions envisaged by Article 16 of the Covenant of the League applicable to all wars prohibited by the Pact of Paris. The economic crisis then supervened, to preoccupy the attention of statesmen.

But if Japanese foreign policy retained a pragmatic character up to this time, the domestic political atmosphere was becoming increasingly stuffy, partly as a precautionary reaction to the achievement of universal male suffrage and partly from growing apprehensions about the threat of international communism. The reconstituted Japan Communist Party itself, after a brief break from the guidance of the Comintern, returned to an obedient ideological orthodoxy in 1927. It began publication of its own newspaper, *Akahata*, in the following year. In March 1928, and again in April 1929, mass arrests were carried out, followed by prosecutions which showed that the authorities were determined to smash the party, destroy its organization and eliminate its influence. A good few prominent members of the party sent to prison at this time were to remain in detention until 1945. Some were to undergo a process of conversion (*tenko*) or recantation during the 1930s. As a threat to the security of the state, the party ceased for the time being to count. From among moderate members of the socialist movement, the Shakai Taishuto was formed in 1932, and permitted to operate openly until 1940. The leftist elements which had been expelled from Sodomei formed an association (Hyogikai) lasting until 1928. It played a considerable role in industrial disputes for a few years, but it, too, was repressed by the police and other authorities. Sodomei restricted its activities to the promotion of legislation favourable to labour, avoided anti-government agitation, and adopted a strongly anti-communist line in political propaganda.

While oppression by the authorities was partly responsible for the failure of the left to make headway during the 1920s, internal divisions also weakened it. Among Marxists, there were disagreements about the nature of capitalism in Japan and the consequent requirements in revolutionary activity. The Labour Farmer Party (Ronoto) became for a time a front through which the Japan Communist Party obtained cover for the pursuit of extra-parliamentary tactics. Although a few of its members were elected to the lower House of the Diet, many were among those arrested under the Peace Preservation Law, and the organization was dissolved in the spring of 1928.

None of these organizations achieved much to benefit the poorest or the most disadvantaged in Japanese society, or to relieve the monotony of poverty, toil and conformity. Some improvement in the standards of living of urban workers resulted from the mere growth of the economy, though this was not fast in the 1920s; but this was not matched in the country, where tenancy disputes proliferated and rents kept pace with gains in productivity. In village society, the traditional guiding hands of the elders were as heavy as those of the landlords or the police. Throughout the country, military training had been made a compulsory addition to the curriculum in 1925, for all students of middle-school age and above. The primary motive for this legislation had been to offset military unemployment following the retrenchment in defence expenditure made under

Kato's government. In conservative circles there was hope that it might also serve to counteract any tendency for social discipline to suffer from racy, modern influences. In truth, if society suffered, it was from rigidity rather than from decadence.

In 1929, with the slump, economic suffering set in with unprecedented severity, especially in the countryside, and most destructively in the principal silk-producing areas, where the sudden, often complete loss of orders for the American market is still remembered as vividly as the dole queues are in the United States, or the hunger marches in Britain. With the subsequent fall in rice prices, felt most acutely and most bitterly after the deceptively abundant harvest of 1930, starvation became a real threat to millions of country people. There was bound to be dangerous political fall-out. The extreme left having been decimated and disarmed, opportunities for agitation, propaganda and recruitment were available to the extreme right as never before. Not only was it easy to make a case for some version of national or imperial socialism, on economic grounds. It was already clear that there was a strong trend in Europe towards the adoption of a parallel political philosophy. There were other considerations seemingly pointing in the same direction. There was much vague talk of a New Order (*shin chitsujo*) and some thrusting middle-ranking officials became known as the new bureaucracy (*shin kanryo*). In the armed services, there was a consciousness that staff planning had assumed a political character. Officers involved with the secret and patriotic societies, where politicians, civil servants and industrialists were also to be encountered, heard, and themselves made, increasingly frequent references to the supposed need of a Showa Restoration (Showa Isshin). The programmes put forward varied, as did the philosophies on which they were based. The assassination of Chang Tso-lin had shown that there were bold spirits among the talkers, ruthless and prepared to take high risks.

With Tanaka's resignation at the beginning of July 1929, Inukai Tsuyoshi became president of the Seiyukai. Hamaguchi Osachi, under whom the principal opposition parties had come together, in 1927, to form the Minseito, came to power as Prime Minister. Shidehara returned to the Foreign Ministry, Ugaki to the War Ministry, and Inoue Junnosuke to Finance. Even if it had not been hampered by the initial adoption of an uniquely ill-timed deflationary policy, which exacerbated all the worst effects of the slump and which reached its objective, the return to the gold standard, only to see it abandoned again in 1931, this experienced team would have been powerless to avert economic disaster, worldwide as it was. Inoue, who had seen Japan through the economic aftermath of the Great Earthquake, as Minister of Finance, and through that of the financial crisis of 1927, as Governor of the Bank of Japan, was deservedly respected in international financial circles.

The onset of the great depression closely coincided with the further review of naval arms control and disarmament which had been provided for under the Washington Treaty. Preparations for the London Naval Conference, which took place between January and April 1930, were among the most urgent calls on the attention of Hamaguchi's government. The former Prime Minister, Wakatsuki Reijiro, was appointed chief delegate, and was accompanied to the conference by the Navy Minister, Takarabe Takeshi, whose responsibilities in Tokyo were assumed by Hamaguchi himself, throughout the minister's absence.

The Japanese government was prepared to make clear once again in London its dissatisfaction with the status accorded to its navy in Washington. There was an abiding suspicion that Britain and the United States (if not also the other participants) were in collusion against Japan, and were attempting to use the talks on naval limitation effectively to impose a brake on the progress of Japan's imperial ambitions. The failure of Japan during the previous year both to support the British over sanctions under the Covenant of the League, and to fall in with the United States Secretary of State Stimson's proposals for the settlement of a dangerous dispute between China and the Soviet Union over the Chinese Eastern Railway (a dispute in which Chang Hsueh-liang was deeply involved) were examples of what threatened to be an increasing divergence of Japan from its Anglo-Saxon partners in the Washington Treaty system. Japan was now frequently accused of following a 'spheres of influence' rather than an Open Door policy in Manchuria. You grant me a sphere of influence and I will show you an open door, was what Western statesmen thought the Japanese often seemed to be saying. Hamaguchi's government desired to restore confidence in relations with London and Washington. Equally, they were determined to stick out for better terms than those obtained in 1921. The delegation was successful in securing a slightly improved ratio, for Japan as compared with the other Powers, for application to smaller warships, than that which had been applied to capital ships in the earlier agreement. This was not good enough for the naval general staff, who fought bitterly against acceptance, with the support of the Privy Council. They argued that it was constitutionally contrary to the navy's prerogative of supreme command, and right of direct access to the Emperor, for the Cabinet to determine levels of armament, with their operational implications, as opposed to matters of administration. Hamaguchi and his colleagues stuck to their butter, and signed a new agreement. The naval Chief of Staff stuck to his guns, and resigned.

There was once again great bitterness. Talk of insubordination, and mutterings of coups and violence were rife. Nevertheless, the Minseito did well in general elections, which confirmed Hamaguchi's government in power. Some shrewd moves were made to this end by the Minister for Home Affairs, Adachi Kenzo. Adachi had been implicated, all those years before, in the murder of Queen Min of Korea. It seems surprising that he was included in Hamaguchi's team. His reputation may indeed have contributed to the disaster which now befell the government, though the immediate motive of Hamaguchi's assassin seems to have been resentment at naval limitation. Like Hara nine years before, Hamaguchi was shot on Tokyo station. Though very badly wounded in this attack, in November 1930, Hamaguchi was determined to resume charge of the government. His wound proved fatal, however, and he died the following April. Shidehara had acted for him, but it was Wakatsuki who formally succeeded him. This appointment might even have seemed, in normal times, an unnecessary provocation to extremists in the armed services. But it was already clear that the times were not normal, and that the continuation of party government was in doubt.

In March 1931 plans came to light for a coup. The leading conspirator was Colonel Hashimoto Kingoro. He had been detected earlier in subversive activity with a secret society known as Kinkikai. He was influenced by the ideas of Kita Ikki and Okawa Shumei. His plot depended upon the willingness of General Ugaki to assume a leading position after the overthrow of the Cabinet in which he held office as War Minister. Instead, Ugaki blew the whistle on the conspirators. Partly because of the embarrassment of his involvement, the incident was kept from public knowledge for long enough for the conspirators to regroup and plan a second coup, in which it was their intention to eliminate the Cabinet by bombing it from the air, and to kill some of the Emperor's principal advisers. General Araki Sadao was chosen this time to take power after the coup. Like Ugaki, he turned down the conspirators' approach, and shopped them. But he also contrived to turn the incident to his own advantage, and, unlike Ugaki, he was himself in favour of what was now known as the reform movement.

The main purpose of this second abortive coup was to reinforce and follow up the action of the Kwantung Army, in the Manchurian Incident, which itself became, in the event, a far more significant development. Certain staff officers at army headquarters outside Mukden, notably Colonels Ishiwara Kanji, Itagaki Seishiro and Doihara Kenji, with accomplices in the War Ministry in Tokyo, arranged that an explosion on the South Manchurian Railway line, on the night of 18 September 1931, falsely attributed to Chinese troops, would be used as justification for the occupation of Mukden itself, and for the subsequent taking over of all Manchurian territory by Japanese troops, including substantial reinforcements from the garrison army in Korea, whose participation was authorized locally, and improperly. Operations, supposedly put in hand in self-defence, went ahead rapidly. The government in Tokyo, faced with a *fait accompli*, made statements about containing the conflict. Government spokesmen soon became in effect the apologists for a very large-scale act of insubordination.

That something of this kind was in contemplation had been suspected for some time in Tokyo. A message directly instructing compliance with prudent standing orders was entrusted to a messenger who was himself privy to the conspiracy, and delayed its delivery deliberately. Whether the commander of the Kwantung Army was also an accomplice remains uncertain. His was not the decisive role.

The international repercussions of this so-called incident were of course substantial and prolonged, and centred on Washington and Geneva. The League of Nations resolved to take action, in response to Chinese protests, but the composition of the Lytton Commission was not agreed until towards the end of the year, and its work took most of the first half of 1932. The United States made clear its position that no change brought about by violence would be recognized. The Japanese government began to develop its thesis that China was not an organized state and could not be regarded as such. Shidehara's position was discredited among his own people, and Wakatsuki's government resigned in December 1931, giving way to a Seiyukai cabinet with Inukai Tsuyoshi as Prime Minister. The change was brought about in part by Adachi Kenzo, who refused to give Wakatsuki his continued collaboration unless a coalition was formed embracing both main parties, the Minseito and the Seiyukai: an interesting might-have-been as footnote to a disastrous year.

Things were to get even worse early in 1932. Operations continued in Manchuria, but were extended to Shanghai in January, when the Japanese Navy landed a strong force in support of their consul-general's demand for reparations, following an attack by Chinese, close to the boundary of the international settlement, on a small party of Japanese which included two Buddhist priests. The navy may have welcomed the opportunity to prove that they were as effective as the army was already seen to be, in Manchuria. But the fighting which developed in and around Shanghai was bitter and prolonged. Army reinforcements were sent in, but the Chinese 19th Route Army put up an unexpectedly stiff resistance. Hostilities deteriorated into brutalities and atrocities. The international community in Shanghai, which at first had tended to welcome the prospect of a firm imposition of law and order by the Japanese forces, was shocked by the flood of hundreds of thousands of destitute Chinese refugees, and by the scale and ferocity of the conflict. World opinion was disturbed by the reports of correspondents, who were able to observe the operations closely from the international settlement. Nanking itself was bombarded, and this stimulated growing criticism of Japan's conduct.

Meanwhile, having completed the conquest of Manchuria, the Kwantung Army acclaimed in mid-February the allegedly spontaneous establishment of the 'independent' state of Manchukuo, in reality the army's puppet, whose Regent, Pu-yi, was formally installed in March 1932. Renewed concern was expressed in Washington and Geneva. In Japan itself, on 9 February Inoue Junnosuke, Minseito statesman and former Minister of Finance and Governor of the Bank of Japan, was assassinated. He was a known opponent of the Kwantung Army's unauthorized initiatives. These were not, however, repudiated by the Japanese government. In response to an appeal from the League of Nations to cease its attacks on China, Tokyo claimed to be the aggrieved party, in effect denying China's right to be regarded as a recognizable state. This was immediately followed by the publication of Secretary of State Stimson's letter to Senator Borah, underlining the importance of the Nine Power Treaty and the Pact of Paris, and the illegality of changes to the existing situation brought about by the use of force.

When the members of the Lytton Commission reached Yokohama in late February 1932, they received a critical press; but hopes were expressed in the Japanese newspapers that the League might still reach a favourable appraisal of Japan's case. In March the same terrorist organization which had struck down Inoue assassinated Dan Takuma, who was greatly distinguished as a leading figure both in the Mitsui group and in the economic life of the country. This was the Ketsumeidan, a terrorist society led by Inoue Nissho. The society accused its victims of having enriched themselves at the expense of the farmers and peasants. Inoue Nissho was punished with life imprisonment; others got off more lightly.

The situation seemed at last to show improvement when, in early May, owing in large part to the persistent mediatory efforts of Lampson, the British Minister in Peking (later Lord Killearn), a truce ended the fighting round Shanghai, and temporarily restored peace between Japan and China. Tension, however, was not to be relaxed in Tokyo. On 15 May 1932 Prime Minister Inukai Tsuyoshi was shot dead by a gang of young officers, from both the army and the navy, who attacked other targets before all were apprehended. They were court-martialled in public, afforded the opportunity to pose as patriots, and given rather light sentences.

5

National Dreams, International Nightmares, 1931–41

According to the later testimony of his son, Inukai was murdered primarily because he was believed to be recommending the issue of an Imperial Rescript which would confine the future operations of the Kwantung Army to the South Manchurian Railway zone. Certainly, he was in favour of discipline and restraint. It was equally clear that he would not be given the support of his own party in the Diet if he sought to rely on parliamentary authority to inhibit the further pursuit of a forward policy in Manchuria. Too many Seiyukai Diet members, while in opposition, had endorsed unequivocally the need for the country to take a firm line there. The truce accepted around Shanghai had not affected their attitude. By now, public opinion was also inflamed. Among the chief factors influencing the public to call insistently for strong policies were foreign criticism of the Manchurian campaign and of the conduct of operations in the Shanghai area, the renewed and effective Chinese trade boycott linked with the beginnings of foreign moves towards protection against Japan's new drive for export markets, chagrin over the terms of naval arms limitation, and the loss of the main outlet for silk goods, the United States, with its devastating impact on employment and livelihood throughout whole regions of the country.

There was also a fairly widespread sense that the Kwantung Army had after all done well for the country in striking while China was in political turmoil, and still toiling towards recovery from the disastrous floods of 1931, while the other Powers had serious economic as well as political preoccupations elsewhere; and at a time, again owing to the worldwide recession, when Japan was in need of the stimulus which imperial expansion should provide. Industrialists who might have criticized the army's forward strategy, especially for having damaged or even ruined their businesses in China, often came to tolerate or support it because of the scope it seemed to offer them, in an enlarged empire, in compensation for any such losses. Those sections of society which had suffered most severely from the recession were encouraged to think of Manchuria as their salvation, whether directly, if they were potential settlers there, or indirectly, simply on account of its rich resources. A range of political and economic argument could be and was deployed to give expansion the glamour and urgency of a national crusade, or to make it seem a necessity rather than merely a challenging option.

There were endless opportunities for activists to bully and cajole, as well as to offer inducements. The small, uncoordinated groups of fanatics, whose deeds, even when gruesome, often commanded some sympathy because of the purity ascribed to their patriotic fervour, made only a limited appeal on the basis of their ideologies; though where it was effective it was a strong appeal, well calculated to reach the disadvantaged and the unemployed, and even to impress moderate army officers, genuinely concerned about social conditions. The European doctrines of Fascism began to exert some influence in Japan early in the 1930s, but it was the idea of the total mobilization of national resources which commanded the greatest attention among the officers and civil servants intent upon a 'Showa Restoration', rather than the political creeds themselves.

After Inukai's assassination, the responsibility for advising upon the appointment of his successor was primarily for Saionji to bear, as sole Genro. The Emperor had expressed to Inukai certain key desiderata, implying the need to reimpose a full sense of discipline, and of the proper limits of their own responsibilities, upon the armed services. The Emperor's advisers, Saionji himself and others such as Count Makino, were in favour of moderation and restraint, and were now indeed the principal representatives of moderate opinion, the political parties being divided among themselves and lacking in leaders capable of asserting immediate authority over the direction of the country's affairs. It fell to the veteran Admiral Viscount Saito Makoto to form a 'Cabinet of National Unity'.

In the army itself, unity was not achieved. In particular, intense rivalry was developing between the Kodoha, the Imperial Way faction, and the Toseiha or Control faction, the more radical of the two in terms of ambition for reform of the national polity. In their strategic outlooks, the former envisaged that national policy should concentrate on preparing for an inevitable war with the Soviet Union, while the latter advocated a sweeping programme of expansion in China, and further south. Both were represented actively at Imperial Army headquarters, in the War Ministry, and in the Kwantung Army, whose current operations continued. The acquisition of influence or territory in Inner Mongolia, in Jehol, or in other provinces of northern China was seen variously as being designed to lead to the establishment either of buffer zones or of bridgeheads. Officers involved in serious disputes about future strategy, and the objectives for which national resources should be mobilized, were impatient with the Lytton Commission, and increasingly contemptuous of the League of Nations as a whole. The sometimes wild ambitions of comparatively junior officers were treated with indulgence by their superiors, so that the old Tokugawa period expression *gekokujo*, denoting a situation in which subordinates have effectively usurped the leadership, was given new currency.

As the representatives of moderate opinion close to the centre of affairs, Saionji and his associates at Court were inhibited by considerations both of constitutional propriety and of concern for the Emperor's personal position. There was a need, as they saw it, in knowledge of the Emperor's own views, to consolidate the establishment of the constitutional monarchy as such. A constitutional role meant that encouragement or warning would always be followed in the end by consent; and that their Commander-in-Chief would deal directly with the Chiefs of Staff of the Imperial Army and Navy on substantive matters only when these were matters of defence such as did not fall within the purview of the Cabinet.

Such definitions have a limited utility. Saionji's partly self-imposed, partly institutional task was bound to be extremely delicate at a time when euphoria had taken the place of common sense, and intimidation that of discipline. It seemed necessary, for the most obvious reasons, to ensure that the Emperor himself was not involved in public controversy. It followed that the Emperor's views must be revealed only to those both entitled to know them and who could be relied upon not to abuse either the constitutional conventions or their sovereign's confidence. This might protect the Emperor's name from any embroilment which could not be disavowed convincingly by the court officials. Unfortunately, it could not prevent, and might even facilitate, claims by unscrupulous elements that the Emperor supported actions or plans of which he had no knowledge, or even of which in reality he wholly disapproved. Equally, if the Emperor's views could not be made known in those circles where they would be treated with proper respect and accorded their full weight, his personal authority and influence would be circumscribed and diminished. Some of these considerations were not immediately apparent to the Japanese public, let alone to the outside world.

It was, however, apparent in Tokyo, to those who wished to restore discipline to the armed services no less than to those inclined to applaud what the Kwantung Army had done, that condemnation by the other Powers of Japan's actions and policies in Manchuria and towards China was neither unqualified nor universal; and that it was unlikely to find expression in the imposition of effective sanctions. The Hoover administration was consistent in its criticism, but Stimson's doctrine of non-recognition was evidently not leading towards the adoption of measures to enforce Japan's withdrawal. The participation of the United States in the work of the Lytton Commission even assumed a reassuring aspect, from

Tokyo's point of view, when coupled with the Americans' lack of commitment to the Covenant of the League of Nations. It began to look like a substitute for the independent exertion of national effort and the deployment of national resources.

The British, though keen supporters of the efficient operation of the machinery of the League, were clearly still inclined to recognize that Japan was equipped to play a crucial stabilizing role in North-East Asia, and indeed to regard Japan as an ally in the promotion of law and order as well as a competitor in trade and investment in China. There were also wider reasons why a reluctance to alienate Japan might be expected to persist as a strand in the thread of British policy. Cecil might be an outstanding advocate of the need to assert the principles of collective security under the Covenant of the League: Simon was essentially pragmatic in his assessment of the Manchurian situation, seeing it primarily as an incident of regional significance rather than as a critical development in world affairs. Drummond, the international civil servant, took a view perhaps closer to Simon's than to Cecil's. As for Lytton and his colleagues, they had a clear duty to reach an accurately balanced judgement such as would carry conviction with the membership of the League, as a whole. Other considerations affecting the Powers tended to cancel each other out. The French, for example, though they wished to prevent the Japanese from encroaching on privileges and concessions granted to others, both in the Treaty Ports and in the interior of China, saw in the toleration of a degree of Japanese expansion a form of insurance against the emergence of a powerful central government, in a unified China, which would have had unwelcome consequences for French interests in Indo-China. The Germans, though increasingly deeply involved in the provision of military training and advice to the Nationalists in China, were also beginning, with the Italians, to champion and propagate doctrines which harmonized with the aspirations of radical nationalists and renovationists in Japan.

To the latter, their ambitions for empire stimulated by a newer but no less urgent desire for economic self-sufficiency, it seemed that policy in Manchuria and China could safely be conducted without constant or over-scrupulous consultation with international opinion. Many, of course, had always taken a more extreme, self-confident and assertive position, but they had not previously enjoyed much support outside their own more or less private organizations. Public opinion, however, suspicious of ignorant foreigners in Geneva, was now enthusiastic for expansion, seeing gains of territory rich in natural resources as giving some assurance of economic recovery. The press, though wary of the danger of alienating world opinion, was happy to popularize the idea that prosperity might be founded on a constructive imperial adventure. An increasingly repressive atmosphere, provoked by the activities of extremists on the right and justified by apprehensions about those on the left, stimulated the growth of a conformist jingoism and stifled public debate. In this atmosphere, it was immediately taken for granted in Japan that indignant rejection was the appropriate reaction to the Lytton Commission's report, on its publication in October 1932.

The most important recommendation of this report was for the establishment of an autonomous government in Manchuria, over which China would retain sovereignty, but which would pledge its recognition of Japan's rights and interests. This conclusion was widely regarded by other members of the League as conciliatory towards Japan; but it was based on findings that Japan's actions in Manchuria had not been taken in self-defence, and that the creation of Manchukuo had not been the outcome of a spontaneous movement for independence. The Japanese government dissented strongly from these conclusions, and during the diplomatic exchanges which followed publication of the report the Delegation of Japan at Geneva was led by Matsuoka Yosuke, whose reputation at this time was that of an exceptionally well qualified and eloquent advocate of the Japanese case. A native of Yamaguchi Prefecture, Matsuoka had been to school and university in the United States before entering his diplomatic career. He had been a member of the Japanese delegation to the Paris Peace Conference. He had cultivated the acquaintance of those in civil, military and political circles who believed in the prospects for expansion on the mainland of Asia, and had secured a transfer from the Japanese Foreign Office to serve almost throughout the 1920s first as a director and later as Vice-President of the South Manchurian Railway Company (SMR). In 1930 he had been elected to the Diet, where he had been prominent among the Seiyukai critics of Shidehara's foreign policy. He knew what was at stake for Japan in Manchuria, as did Saito's Foreign Minister, Uchida Kosai, himself a former President of the SMR.

The report of the Lytton Commission was approved almost unanimously by the General Assembly of the League on 24 February 1933, Japan alone voting against its adoption, with Thailand abstaining and Chile deliberately absent. Matsuoka then led his delegation out of the assembly. He had let it be known that he expected this to signify not simply Japan's dissociation from the assembly's adoption of the Lytton recommendations, but Japan's intention to withdraw from the League of Nations itself. Saito's cabinet took the decision to do this, after discussion in the Privy Council and with the Emperor's advisers. It was agreed that the decision warranted the issue of an Imperial Rescript. Meanwhile, military operations continued in Manchuria and were extended into Jehol. The Emperor himself reportedly enquired why, if things were going according to plan, it should be necessary to break away from the League. His advisers succeeded in securing the inclusion in the Rescript of an affirmation of Japan's intention to promote relations of mutual confidence with 'all the other Powers'. This was not the kind of double-talk with which the world of the later 1930s was to become so familiar; it was evidence of divided counsels. The Rescript also contained a coded rebuke of the indiscipline shown by the army and those civilians who connived with it. No doubt, the Emperor's advisers thought it prudent, in order both to protect and to respect the Emperor's constitutional position (perhaps also in order to protect his person), not to insist on the use of plainer language in this passage.

This may be judged a lost opportunity. The League of Nations might well have recovered its authority, though it failed to do so. The Emperor's advisers, as established at that time, were to find the scope for the exercise of their discretion ever more closely circumscribed. No sooner was the Manchurian Incident effectively accomplished than General Honjo Shigeru, having completed his eventful tour of duty as Commander-in-Chief of the Kwantung Army, was appointed chief aide to the Emperor.

With General Araki Sadao, the most senior avowed supporter of the military reformists, as War Minister, Saito's cabinet never set out in earnest to assert its own authority over the army. Hatoyama Ichiro, the Minister of Education until the spring of 1934, was perhaps the only politician at that level who might have been minded to insist that the effort be made, but his friends in the Seiyukai would scarcely have supported such a stand. By far the most considerable figure in the government was Takahashi Korekiyo, and he, though remaining staunchly correct in his constitutional judgement, had embarked on new financial policies designed to effect recovery from the slump, and was single-minded in the pursuit of that objective. The success of these policies was to enable others to insist on providing the army and the expansionists with the resources they required. Takahashi's judgement that the government could borrow and spend its way out of the great depression has its place in economic history, anticipating as it did in practice the influential theory shortly to be formulated by Keynes. His success meant that the Kwantung Army could be doubled in strength between 1931 and 1936, so that, at nearly 200,000 men, it was roughly the same size as the peacetime British Army; that Japan could afford to reject proposals for continuing limits on naval strengths at the London talks in 1934, and thereafter; and that industries essential to the building up of an economy capable of sustaining a major war could be developed in Japan itself, and in Korea and Manchuria, both of which were to absorb investment on a massive scale. Takahashi was fully prepared to reimpose stricter controls on public expenditure whenever this might be necessary. Meanwhile, his policies were beneficial to Japan.

On the basis of Takahashi's financial management, and the sound foundations put in place earlier by industrialists, including the board of directors of the SMR, great progress was made by the Japanese economy in the years immediately following the initial shock of the world depression. Success in handling the devaluation of the yen, and deficit-financing as a tool of policy, led to vastly increased exports and strong investment, without provoking severe inflation.

Despite widespread continuing hardship in the agricultural sector, tenancy disputes declined in the early 1930s and some help was given to farmers by means of subsidized prices. The drift of population to urban, industrialized centres accelerated. While incomes of households relying exclusively on farming remained static, wages and standards of living improved for factory workers, and in the cities generally. The range and quality as well as the volume of industrial output grew steadily, especially in engineering, machinery and chemicals. By 1936, exports of finished steel exceeded imports in volume. Advances in efficiency extended to mining, as well as throughout manufacturing industry. Improved technology benefited established sectors, including notably both textiles and pottery, as well as new enterprises. By 1937, for example, Japan's production of rayon was the largest in the world. At the same time, the volume of exports of keenly priced cotton piece-goods was causing anxiety and distress in Lancashire.

Japan's economy was enjoying a period of sustained growth, not unlike that experienced by Britain in the mid-nineteenth century, in which the great world depression represented no more than a temporary setback. Over the three or four decades prior to the Second World War, for example, Japan's gross national product grew at an average annual rate about twice that attained by the British economy. Much of the investment generated especially in the later stages of this period of growth went into the development of industry in Manchuria, and also into the further development of communications, the railway itself having taken by far the greatest share of investment in the earlier stages. The importance of the efforts made at the conclusion of the Russo-Japanese War, and the strain which those efforts had put on the national resources, were now seen in full perspective, and valued accordingly by the public in Japan.

Up to the end of the 1920s the initiative in Manchurian development had been taken, under the inspiration originally of Goto Shinpei, primarily by the SMR, which controlled most large enterprises in the railway zone, with the willing collaboration of the Kwantung Army. After 1931 the Kwantung Army came to dominate this partnership, to the extent even of assuming responsibility for the comprehensive reorganization of the SMR in 1933. Like the radical nationalists at home who had murdered Baron Dan in protest against the alleged lack of patriotic spirit in the Mitsui group, officers in the Kwantung Army regarded the established zaibatsu concerns with suspicion and contempt. They considered that the leaders of these great conglomerates had shown an inappropriate sympathy with Shidehara's policies of international co-operation, were at best half-hearted in their support of the army's imperial mission, and indulged deliberately in corrupt relationships with the political parties, which were themselves unprincipled and defeatist. The Kwantung Army encouraged and promoted the formation of new business groups, notably the Nippon Sangyo Kaisha (Nissan) and, after the outbreak of war with China, the Manchukuo Heavy Industry Development Company. The fact that the chief executive and moving spirit of Nissan was connected both with the Mitsubishi leadership and indirectly, through his original patron, Prince Inoue, with Mitsui, was overlooked by the army: this may serve as a reminder that in discussion of a closely knit but complex society the dangers of oversimplification are always present.

The army justified its attitude towards the old-established industrial groups partly by an insistence on the need for Japan to build what government, under increasingly persistent military influence and pressure, came to accept and describe as a quasi-wartime economy (*junsenji keizai*). This led to the gradual imposition of central control on a progressively wider range of industrial activity, reversing the earlier trend under which industries originally requiring government support had been transferred successively into private management. Resistance to this reversal of policy was understandably cautious on the part of the zaibatsu, given the prevailing climate of opinion and the trend of policy.

In keeping with this trend, legislation which had been introduced to rationalize industry, so that it might be able better to ride out the slump, was retained to facilitate the degree of central control now thought necessary: from rationalization to nationalization, the transition was justified on the simple grounds of national interest, with no special appeal on the part of government to ideology. In 1934 the Japan Iron and Steel Company was formed by the amalgamation of six large private concerns with the state-owned Yawata plant. Other examples of creeping central control were the obligation put on oil companies to hold substantial stocks, and the close supervision of their programme of operations to which both they and the powerful shipping companies were subjected. Japan had the world's third biggest merchant shipping fleet by the mid-1930s, largely composed of fast vessels recently constructed under the 'scrap and build' scheme by which the government had helped the shipbuilders to come through the recession. The shipbuilding capacity and that of the merchant fleet were both obviously of first-rate strategic importance.

The merchant fleet was well equipped to cope with the changes which were also taking place in the composition, balance and direction of Japan's foreign trade. The sale of a wide range of manufactured goods throughout the countries of Asia became increasingly important in the early 1930s, while the demand for manufactured imports from North America and Europe tended to decline, except for the most sophisticated products. Dependence on cotton from the United States and wool from Australia, on the other hand, grew. The importance of trade as a whole with the United States had fallen very sharply on account of the depression in the raw silk trade. Rising exports to Manchuria more than offset losses in the main China market, and consisted to a large extent of capital goods. Even before the development of the yen bloc, which followed the outbreak of war with China, trade with both Taiwan and Korea prospered, the colonies accounting for about a quarter of Japan's total exports and imports.

This latter characteristic of the period owed much to the demand for the establishment of a quasi-wartime economy. The autarkical and protectionist tendencies in world trade as a whole, after the slump, were as much of political as of economic significance. The Smoot-Hawley Tariff Act of 1930 and the Ottawa Conference of 1932 were taken by the Japanese authorities to be indicators of a climate increasingly hostile to the expansion of manufactured exports, which they were determined to promote. Japan's share of world exports in 1936 was still less than 4 per cent, but Japan was competing successfully in markets formerly dominated by one or another of the older Powers, while the latter were still suffering severely from the effects of the slump. The impact of Japanese exports, especially in narrow market sectors such as cotton piece-goods, was out of all proportion to their overall scale. By contrast, the full extent of Japan's commitment on the mainland of North-East Asia was not widely understood.

The economic changes which took place in these years hinged above all on the expansion of Japanese activity in North-East Asia. The principal reason why criticism of the Kwantung Army's initiatives was so meagre in Japan itself was that, on the left no less than on the right, many rapidly came to see it as providing the best hope of recovery, especially for the most distressed rural communities, but also for industrial workers. By the time of the Manchurian Incident, Japanese civilians in China, mostly active in commerce and industry, represented some 70 per cent of all foreigners resident there. Although the total sums of British and United States investment in China were each still greater than that of Japan, the latter represented some 80 per cent of total Japanese overseas investment, while the comparable figures for Britain and the USA were no more than 6 and 2 per cent respectively. Japan's share of China's foreign trade was three times the annual value of Britain's, and was worth half as much again as that of the United States. These were commitments which would carry weight proportionately with decision-makers in Tokyo, whoever might come to power.

Although the prospect of expansion was widely welcomed in Japan, there had been some demonstrations against the Manchurian adventure. But the popular vote for the non-communist proletarian parties which opposed it fell sharply in the general elections of 1932. The Japan Communist Party was naturally hostile to any move which might threaten or carry the risk of conflict with the Soviet Union. At this time it was in sympathy with the Communist Party of China which, from Kiangsi, had actually declared war on Japan early in 1932. The Comintern put out a Thesis on Japan at that time, which called first of all for the destruction of 'the Emperor system', and proceeded to attack Japanese landlords, the influence of religious thought in Japan, and the conditions imposed on Japanese workers and peasants by 'the ruling classes and the social democrats', with their 'antidemocratic, imperialistic and counter-revolutionary slogans'. The Japan Communist Party was, of course, consistently regarded by the authorities in Tokyo as dangerously subversive, and had always been suppressed harshly by the police. By the end of 1933 most of its leaders had been tried and imprisoned, or had gone into exile; a few had recanted. Most other organizations on the left were tempted, at least, to accept that there would be advantages in territorial expansion. Many recognized that castigating the excesses of those responsible for Japan's advance in North-East Asia was not the best way of appealing to the poor and disadvantaged, especially not to those in the agricultural regions of the country, who might well look towards the continent for new opportunities of earning their livelihood.

This was a situation of which conservative officials, including some who might themselves be sceptical of imperialist pretensions, knew how to take advantage. Whether or not willing to tolerate indiscipline on the part of the army itself, such officials were disposed to share military views of the need for social discipline and patriotism in civil life. The Minister for Home Affairs in Saito's cabinet demanded the dismissal of a professor of law at Kyoto Imperial University for alleged communist sympathies, in 1933. A number of senior members of the university resigned in sympathy with Professor Takigawa, but the renewed authoritarian trend in government was unmistakably established by this time.

As a consequence of this, the parties of the non-communist proletarian left had drawn closer together in the Diet, merging in 1932 to form the Socialist Masses Party (Shakai Taishuto), in which leaders of the Labour-Peasant Party, such as Kawakami Jotaro and Asanuma Inejiro, worked in partnership with Katayama Tetsu and Nishio Suehiro of the former Social-Democratic Party. As separate parties, earlier in the year, both had seen their support fall away badly in the general elections of 1932. The merger came under attack from the extreme left, but there were also some defections from socialism to Fascism. The newly merged party itself gradually came – by way of reluctant approval of increased expenditure for military purposes, in order to stimulate economic recovery – to the eventual support of a war policy.

In retaining Araki as War Minister and appointing General Muto as Commander-in-Chief of the Kwantung Army, to be concurrently both Governor-General of the Kwantung Territory and ambassador to Manchukuo, Saito may unintentionally have made the gradual adoption of a war policy more probable and, in attempting to appease the army, rendered the task of reasserting political control over its most headstrong elements more formidable. At the international level, the prospects for realization of a worthy system of collective security diminished progressively. Following Japan's withdrawal from the assembly, the League of Nations toyed elaborately with the idea of sanctions, but ended by restricting the outcome of its consideration of the whole affair to a call for the non-recognition of Manchukuo. Franklin D. Roosevelt, newly elected President of the United States, appointed Cordell Hull Secretary of State, and appealed to Heads of State for endorsement of the principle of non-aggression; but his need to concentrate on the New Deal at home precluded a vigorous follow-up. Isolationism and pacifism were both rather popular with the American public at this time. Hitler, having become Chancellor of Germany in January 1933, was already claiming the attention of the other European Powers and the possessions of his neighbours. His avowed sympathy with the more ambitious Japanese strategists balanced, and would soon outweigh, Germany's military collaboration with Chiang Kai-shek.

The Chinese Nationalists for their part, deeply disappointed in the League of Nations and defeated in the continuing fighting with the Kwantung Army around Jehol, were obliged in the spring of 1933 to negotiate a ceasefire, known as the Tangku Truce, with the Japanese commanders. This provided, rather imprecisely, for a demilitarized zone south of the Great Wall. It was to allow plenty of scope for officers in the Kwantung Army to persist in activities aimed at subverting or intimidating Chinese northern provincial officials and local commanders, and undermining their allegiance to Nanking. In September 1933 Saito appointed Hirota Koki, formerly ambassador in Moscow, as Foreign Minister. Hirota believed in the desirability of co-operation between Japan and China. Later, he also insisted on the need for the 'liberation' of China from 'the Red menace'. On assumption of office, he stated that Japan's foreign policy would be based on the recent Imperial Rescript, with its reference to Japan's intention of promoting wider international co-operation. He spoke of respecting the independence of Manchukuo. Addressing the Diet in January 1934, however, he said that 'Japan, serving as the only cornerstone for the edifice of the peace of East Asia, bears the entire burden of responsibility.' In April 1934, in the much-debated statement made by Amau of the Foreign Office in Tokyo, there was a more far-reaching and outspoken assertion of the exclusive and dominating position now claimed by Japan in China. Though Saito's government appeared to distance itself from this statement, even to disown it, it was taken to reflect a view commonly held within the leadership. A short time before this, the Japanese government brought in a Trade Protection Act, which would enable it to retaliate against high tariffs or other protectionist measures frustrating Japanese exports. The maintenance of an Open Door policy in the Kwantung Territory, as in the rest of the Empire, might depend upon reciprocity. In the rest of Manchuria, it might depend upon the recognition of Manchukuo as an independent state.

Official talks were resumed in London in 1934 on naval arms limitation. From the preparatory stage, the Japanese government insisted that only a common limit would be acceptable. Long before the conference itself took place, it became clear that the so-called fleet faction of the navy was not going to permit a repetition of the Washington and London agreements of 1921 and 1930. The other participating countries, having persevered in the full formal negotiation, were able to reach a new formula in 1935, but were eventually obliged to incorporate in their agreement an escalation clause applying to Japan. The seaworthiness of the new agreement was later tested to destruction by Hitler. It was Japan which had set the example of inability to sustain the Washington regime of restraint. Hirota offered to negotiate a bilateral arrangement with the United States, but the Roosevelt administration was not prepared to abandon the Washington system, although, after Japan's formal defection, the naval component of the system was bound to give way to an arms race. The Japanese government, in 1934 and 1935, struggling to retain control over the army, could not afford a repetition of the divisions with the navy, and within it, which had caused so much pain in 1930. At the same time, Germany having departed both from the League of Nations and from the main negotiations on disarmament at Geneva, and with British attention concentrated on attempts to preserve the Locarno Treaty as the basis for peace in Europe, those in Japan who were determined to consolidate gains already made on the continent were not persuaded of the need for moderation. Naval strategists foresaw that the army's existing commitments in North-East Asia would require a high level of support at sea. They were also beginning to argue that it would be necessary to ensure not only access to the raw material resources of South-East Asia but also the security of the sea lanes to the south, even if the main thrust of any expansion was in China and the main threat in the long term to the integrity of gains already made was from the Soviet Union. The Soviets, though they agreed in 1934 to sell the Chinese Eastern Railway to Japan, had also begun to strengthen their defences in the Far East.

Early in the preparatory stage of the naval talks, Admiral Saito's government was brought down by a financial scandal over dealings in the shares of the Teijin (Imperial Rayon) Company. (Later all the accused in this case, including a former railway minister, were acquitted of the charges brought against them.) In the selection of Saito's successor, the Jushin (committee of former prime ministers) played a prominent part. As the sole remaining Genro, Saionji was increasingly reluctant to act without the full backing of the Jushin or the Privy Council, or both. The choice fell on Admiral Okada Keisuke, who had been Navy Minister in Saito's cabinet. He was entrusted with the formation of another Government of National Unity, to be constituted with a strong bureaucratic element and modest representation from the political parties. In the Diet, it enjoyed the minority support of the Minseito. Hirota was retained as Foreign Minister, and General Hayashi Senjuro, who had succeeded Araki earlier in the year, on the latter's resignation on grounds of ill-health, as War Minister. Hayashi, who had been in command in Korea at the time of the outbreak of the Manchurian Incident and had committed his troops across the border on his own authority, had now become to the Toseiha, in terms of leadership, what Araki and his associate, General Mazaki Jinzaburo, were to the Kodoha.

The results of the general elections of January 1935 suggested that the people were reacting against the increasing dominance of the military in policy-making. The Minseito made modest gains. Nevertheless, international developments seemed to boost the case for strong Japanese policies. These developments were, notably, German rearmament, the Italian invasion of Abyssinia and the apparent implications of United States policy, both in the promise of independence for the Philippines and in the Roosevelt administration's interventions in China (sometimes, as in the Silver Purchase Act of 1934, against the interests of the Chinese Nationalists). Strong policies accordingly continued to be advocated by the majority of influential soldiers, by the fleet faction of the navy, by revisionist officials in the bureaucracy, by the patriotic and secret societies of the right, and by those Diet members who either sympathized with these activists or thought it politic not to oppose them. It was not clear at this time whether the prospects in China itself had been improved by the forced withdrawal of Communist forces on the Long March to Yenan, but the decision to mount a major campaign against them had weakened the capacity of the Nationalists to maintain their defences in the north. In June 1935, Major-General Umezu Yoshijiro secured the withdrawal of Kuomintang troops from Hopei and Chahar, in the interests of 'preserving peace'. To the people at home it looked as though the Kwantung Army was continuing to do well. To those who wished to reassert the supremacy of the civil power, however, it was plain that they were not in control of events on the frontiers of the Empire.

The philosophical, constitutional and legal aspects of the principle of the supremacy of the civil power had for many years been at the heart of the work of Professor Minobe Tatsukichi of Tokyo Imperial University. A violent attack on Minobe was launched early in 1935 by one of his colleagues in the House of Peers, with vociferous public support from the right, including that of Hayashi, the War Minister. Minobe's best-known thesis, that the Emperor was an organ of the state, and did not embody constitutional sovereignty in his own person, had been a matter of some controversy when first propounded; but it had been widely acceptable in Japan and respected by international scholars of constitutional law for two decades. It was now denounced as treasonable and heretical. Minobe's books were banned and he was forced to relinquish his honours and to resign from the House of Peers. He was subsequently assaulted by a would-be assassin, but survived the attack. The episode illustrated more vividly than any other single development how the political culture of Japan was hardening. Not content with ruining the life of a highly distinguished scholar and public servant, the supporters of the 'Showa Restoration' now demanded clarification of the national polity, the *kokutai*, in order to consolidate their advance.

The persecution of Minobe was an indication of the accumulating influence of forces intent on promoting and exploiting a spirit of patriotic zealotry based not on a political ideology, such as those which guided totalitarian regimes in Europe, but on the manipulation of traditional ideas about the supremacy of the warrior class, with added hints of privileged access to imperial counsels and intuitive knowledge of the interests of the imperial divinity (without scruple in regard to the actual wishes of the Emperor himself, who is known, to continue with the example of this particular case, to have valued Professor Minobe's learning). In the competition for power, the objectives of the extreme rightists included the indirect discrediting of Prince Saionji and others of the Emperor's advisers whose influence would always be liable to frustrate them.

These forces were not themselves unified, any more than their disparate opponents. In July 1935, intrigue on the part of the Toseiha, who took advantage of Hayashi's championship of their cause, led to the enforced resignation of General Mazaki, hero of the Kodoha, from the key post of Inspector-General of Military Training. The following month, Major-General Nagata Tetsuzan, whose responsibilities as Chief of the General Affairs Bureau at the War Ministry would have included the submission of the recommendation for the dismissal of Mazaki, was murdered at his desk by Lieutenant-Colonel Aizawa Saburo, who had travelled up to central Tokyo in uniform from his distant quarters to do this deed, which he performed with his sword. Aizawa's earlier protest against Mazaki's retirement had resulted only in his receiving an intimation of his own posting to Formosa. His reaction now inevitably sharpened the dispute between the main factions into which the army was already divided.

Despite the bitterness of this dispute, there was broad agreement between the army's factions as to the need for a strong policy in China. The urgency of this need seemed to have been underlined by the adoption at the seventh Comintern Congress in Moscow, in July 1935, of the thesis establishing a 'popular front' against Fascism. The Soviet government, recognized now by the Powers, and lately having assumed membership of the League of Nations, was evidently taking up a position of direct opposition to the extension of Japanese influence in China, regardless of the enmity between the Nationalist authorities in Nanking and the Chinese Communist Party. If the sympathy with the Nationalists already displayed by the Western democracies were to be supplemented internationally by the extreme left, the attainment by Japan of hegemony in East Asia could be gravely prejudiced.

This line of thinking in Tokyo was a part of the background against which the Japanese government received Sir Frederick Leith-Ross in September 1935. He came, on his way to China, for informal discussion of proposals, known to have considerable backing in Whitehall, for a fresh cooperative effort to put China's financial affairs on to a sound basis. Hirota was already engaged in the management of negotiations with the Chinese Nationalists, with a view to securing Nanking's recognition of the independence of Manchukuo; but these negotiations were being conducted on a strictly bilateral basis. To have explored Leith-Ross's proposals positively, including the advantages of enlisting the participation of the United States in the project, would have been taken to imply a willingness to consider meeting some of Nanking's principal requirements before having extracted any concessions from them over Manchukuo. In addition, it would have involved something very like a tacit agreement to the reactivation of the Washington system. Hirota preferred not to abandon the bilateral negotiations on which he had embarked. He knew also that co-operation with the British would not have been easily accepted in military or rightist circles, where the supplanting of British interests and the curtailment of British influence in China was by this time generally regarded as a highly desirable objective. Leith-Ross was therefore obliged to drop the idea of partnership with Japan. In the tense world of the mid-1930s, crowded with grandiose pretensions, a constructive idea of scope and quality was thus allowed to slip away, almost unnoticed by the public.

At about the same time, Takahashi, who had returned to the Finance Ministry a year before, after a brief absence in the first few months of Okada's premiership, began to tighten control of public expenditure. The earlier policy of reflation had served its purpose. Allocations for the armed services came under scrutiny. This naturally caused concern. There was more immediate disquiet about the consequences for the army of the murder of Nagata. Preparations were in hand for the trial of Aizawa. His crime had followed the detection in 1934 of yet another plot to attack cabinet ministers. The atmosphere remained tense. Some officers prominent in the Kodoha were liable to be dispersed, in postings designed as a precaution against further outbreaks of violence and terrorism. It was the intended dispatch of the army's First Division to Manchuria which precipitated the 26 February Rising of 1936. Led by young officers, themselves inspired by professional agitators from the ultra-nationalist societies, soldiers of this division seized the War Ministry, police headquarters and other buildings in central Tokyo, close to the Imperial Palace, while murder squads went out to attack public figures whom they held responsible, among other offences, for preventing the realization of a 'true relationship' between the Emperor and his people. They called for a Showa Restoration to promote the national spirit, and to bring about the abolition of political parties and democratic institutions.

Those murdered were the Lord Keeper of the Privy Seal and former Prime Minister, Admiral Viscount Saito Makoto; the Finance Minister and stalwart supporter of constitutional government, Viscount Takahashi Korekiyo; General Watanabe Jotaro, whose principal offence was to have succeeded Mazaki as Inspector-General of Military Training; and Colonel Matsuo, brother-in-law of the Prime Minister, who was mistaken for Okada. Those on the rebels' hit-list who escaped, in addition to the Prime Minister, were the last Genro, Saionji himself, who was alerted to the danger; and Count Makino, former diplomatist and Imperial Household Minister, who had very recently completed ten years' service as Lord Keeper of the Privy Seal, whose escape was owed in large part to his granddaughter, Kazuko, later Mrs Aso Takakichi – for her, the first of many achievements and distinctions in a life of public service, most notably in support of her father, Yoshida Shigeru, and of his aims.

For the best part of three days, the outcome of the uprising was in some doubt. The leaders of the attempted *coup d'état* refused an appeal from their hero, General Mazaki, to return to discipline. A crucial factor was the insistence of the Emperor, confronted with weakness and confusion among those who happened to be around him when news of the incident broke, that the rebels be treated as such. Loyal troops took up positions surrounding the centre of the city, and it was made clear that ships of the fleet, lying in Tokyo Bay, were prepared to shell the insurgents. Many of the rebel soldiers were at last persuaded to return to their barracks. One or two of their leaders committed suicide; the remainder were arrested on 29 February. The most senior officer directly implicated was of no higher than captain's rank. Most of the young officers involved were from comparatively well-to-do families; they were not the desperate sons of impoverished tenant farmers. Prosecutions were brought against 124 offenders. Trial proceedings were held in secret, 13 officers and 4 civilians being convicted. Those officers were executed in July, as was Aizawa. The civilians sentenced to death, including Kita Ikki and Nishida Mitsugu, whose ideas were said to have influenced the leaders of the rebellion, were executed in the autumn of the following year.

Admiral Okada, who had escaped from the Prime Minister's official residence only by passing himself off as a mourner among those following behind the bearers of a corpse which was still believed to be the remains of himself, resigned in early March, his own authority and that of his entire cabinet irreparably damaged. Although the Minseito had done well in general elections held a few days before the 26 February Rising (as had the

101

Shakai Taishuto, but still as a very minor party) the effect of the insurrection was to strengthen the army's Toseiha, rather than to restore confidence in the political parties. The integrity of the Constitution had been threatened by the army; but the army was also seen as its only possible saviour. General Terauchi Hisaichi, who was appointed War Minister in the new cabinet, was determined to restore discipline throughout the army, but he was not ready to see government entrusted to the political parties. Hirota had become Prime Minister of another Government of National Unity, with former bureaucrats as ministers in charge of most departments. He was not able to act independently, even in respect of appointments to his own cabinet. He would have liked to have Yoshida Shigeru as Foreign Minister, but the army preferred Arita.

Saionji had proposed Prince Konoye as Prime Minister, before turning to Hirota, and had been embarrassed by Konoye's refusal, based on a plea of ill-health. Saionji had also been reluctant to acquiesce in the promotion of Baron Hiranuma Kiichiro to be president of the Privy Council, even though Hiranuma agreed to the dissolution of the Kokuhonsha, a reactionary society of some influence, over which he had presided ever since founding it in 1924. There were some links between Saionji and senior officers in the Toseiha, but while the latter were in the ascendant after the 26 February incident, Saionji never fully recovered the power or the prestige of earlier days. He retained close connections in court circles, through Yuasa, who succeeded Saito as Lord Keeper of the Privy Seal, and through Matsudaira Tsuneo, former ambassador in London, Yuasa's successor as Minister of the Imperial Household. Power was already largely in the hands of those intent upon total national mobilization for the fulfilment of Japan's destiny in Asia; and activists in this cause increasingly tended to regard Saionji and his associates as weak liberals.

The shift of power in favour of adventure was greatly accelerated by the revival in May 1936 of the ordinance laying down that appointments as ministers of war and of the navy must be made from among senior officers still on the active lists. Early in the following year Hirota was obliged to resign, primarily as a consequence of a dispute between the Minister of War and a member of the Diet who had criticized Terauchi in the strongest terms. When it was proposed that retired General Ugaki should succeed Hirota, the army frustrated his appointment, despite its having been approved in due form by the Emperor himself, by refusing to nominate a new war minister.

Meanwhile, the policy of Hirota's government had owed its direction largely to the military planners. No progress had been achieved towards the goal of a bilateral settlement with the Nationalist Chinese, for which both Hirota and Arita had worked. The Cabinet approved a paper on the strategic outlook, which recommended preparations for confrontation with the Soviet Union, linked with the consolidation of Japan's position on the continent and a new emphasis on the possibility of moves to secure natural resources available in South-East Asia. The planners were making detailed assessments of the external requirements of the 'quasi-wartime economy'. The navy was thus associated more closely than before with the army's longer-term thinking, but differences persisted both between the two general staffs, and the two ministries, and within each of these four centres of strategic planning. Despite these differences, there was a broad range of measures acceptable to all concerned, including some of first-rate importance, such as the subsidizing of shipbuilding and the further development of mining and heavy industry in Manchuria.

In November 1936, owing especially to the work of Major-General Oshima Hiroshi, military attaché at the Japanese embassy in Berlin, who had initiated preliminary discussions before the Gaimusho assumed responsibility, in April, for the formal negotiations, the Anti-Comintern Pact was concluded with Germany. This came as something of a shock to public opinion, not only in Japan. It was presented as a defensive reaction to the popular front tactics of the Soviet Union, and was intended in Tokyo also as a warning to China. To some, including Oshima himself, it gave recognition to the growing similarity of outlook between Hitler's regime and the military planners in Japan. Its significance for Japan's future relations with China, and to a lesser extent with the Soviet Union, was more than counterbalanced by the effects of the Sian Incident, which took place in December. The capture of Chiang Kai-shek by Chang Hsueh-liang's men in Sian that month led to the adoption of the united front strategy against Japan by Nationalists and Communists, their mutual enmity apparently put aside. The full implications of the Sian Incident were not immediately obvious. It soon became clear, however, that the depth and strength of Chinese hostility towards Japan, and of Chinese nationalism as a motivating force, had been widely underrated.

It was not until April 1937 that the Kuomintang and the Chinese Communist Party agreed the terms of their united front alliance. In Japan, Hirota had been succeeded as Prime Minister by General Hayashi Senjuro, Ugaki having been kept out because he was not acceptable to the Toseiha. The latter's domination of every aspect of government being increasingly unpopular, and irksome to the political parties, the Minseito and Seiyukai began to find it possible to co-operate. They passed the biggest army budget yet in Japan's history, but otherwise made difficulties for Hayashi, who responded abruptly, at the end of March, by insisting on the dissolution of the House of Representatives. Hayashi himself was closely identified with the radical nationalism of the Toseiha, especially in support of the total mobilization of national resources. He favoured the introduction of military training and discipline in all schools, to the extent of supervising it personally, as his own Minister of Education. Redefinition of the national polity was also undertaken at this time, in the publication *Kokutai no Hongi*, which became the holy writ of ultra-nationalism. Saionji regarded it with disdain. At the same time, Hayashi was prepared to listen to views now expressed in general staff circles that the time had come to desist from encouraging separatist movements in north China, lest this lead to operations on a scale for which some staff officers considered that the army was not ready. Further, he had included in his cabinet Sato Naotake as Foreign Minister and Admiral Yonai Mitsumasa as Navy Minister, both notable supporters of policies of co-operation with Britain and the United States. Sato, who had been ambassador in Paris, believed in the economic interdependence of the non-communist Powers, and argued that Japan needed to work for open world markets. The doctrine of self-sufficiency was, however, not one which the most influential military planners were readily going to modify. Sato was not given time to overcome the prevalent orthodoxy.

However, Hayashi's Minister of Finance, Yuki Tokutaro, brought into government from his position at the head of the Industrial Bank, did take action to correct the serious deterioration in the country's economic position which had resulted from the reversal by his predecessor, Baba Eiichi, of the measures of retrenchment initiated by Takahashi before his assassination. With Ikeda Seihin, recently retired from Mitsui, being persuaded to become president of the Bank of Japan, the outlook for business and finance improved. It had become very gloomy indeed under Hirota. Despite these improvements, military planners such as Ishiwara Kanji continued to exercise a strong influence on economic policy. No less than half the national budget was by this time accounted for by the putative demands of defence, and, although the requirements of the army and the navy served to stimulate industrial production, military expenditure was not under proper control.

When Hayashi dissolved the lower House of the Diet, it was in the expectation that the electorate would support the extreme right, but the small ultra-nationalist party on which the fulfilment of this expectation depended actually lost seats. Gains were made by both Minseito and Seiyukai. A few weeks later, Hayashi resigned.

Prince Konoye now became Prime Minister, in his mid-forties. He seemed to embody the widespread desire for harmony in government, and for stability in society. He enjoyed strong support on all sides: in the armed services, among the 'new' bureaucrats, from politicians and industrialists. He was Saionji's protégé; and, for all his loss of effective power, Saionji retained unequalled personal prestige. Konoye was known to have held, ever since the Paris Peace Conference, the revisionist view that Japan, as a 'have-not' nation, was entitled to a share of the world's resources more appropriate to the country's status as a Power. He considered that Japan was entitled to exercise authority over Manchuria. His brand of revisionism applied to the domestic political system as much as to the international status quo. At the same time he shared a cosmopolitan outlook, in the liberal tradition, with those to whom, critical as they might be of Anglo-Saxon privilege, the direct, deliberate alienation of the Western democracies would have been unthinkable. Konoye seemed enigmatic, even to his peers and contemporaries, in a style which would have been regarded as anachronistic in anyone not descended from one of the great families of the nobility and the court. He listened sympathetically to each successive approach for his understanding or support, yet without disclosing his own views or intentions. He consulted widely, and was a pioneer in the use of what later came to be known as the think-tank, to devise and test options for policy.

Konoye brought back Hirota as Foreign Minister, retained both Admiral Yonai and General Sugiyama, and introduced Kaya Okinori as Minister of Finance. He had scarcely settled to his task, which he certainly saw as involving the reassertion of political control over the military, in the spirit of the Meiji Constitution, when fighting broke out in north China on 7 July. Japanese troops on night exercises at and around the Marco Polo bridge, near Peking, clashed with the local Chinese garrison. Responsibility for the initiation of hostilities on this occasion has never been apportioned conclusively between the parties. After an early ceasefire, attempts were made to settle the incident locally, but hostilities were resumed before the end of the month, spreading to Shanghai in mid-August, then becoming general. As early as 11 July the Cabinet in Tokyo decided on mobilization; and Konoye acceded to the army's demand for reinforcements. Three divisions were ordered on 26 July to move from Japan to China, in accordance with a contingency plan drawn up immediately after the original clash.

Washington appealed for a peaceful settlement on 16 July, but took no more concrete action and did not accept a proposal from London for joint mediation. The Powers other than Japan were greatly preoccupied with the Spanish Civil War, now a year old and increasingly attracting the intervention of Fascist and communist regimes.

Chiang Kai-shek committed the Nationalist government of China to armed resistance of any Japanese advance, while calling on the international community to condemn Japan, invoking in particular the protection of the League and of the Nine Power Treaty, and seeking supplies of equipment from both the Germans and the Russians. The response of the latter, more forthcoming than expected, was a warning to the more cautious Japanese not to place excessive reliance on the initial success of their operations in China.

This success was none the less encouraging to all those who believed that China could be brought to accept a settlement on terms, including further demilitarization in the north, the conceding of autonomy to Outer Mongolia, and even peaceful coexistence with an independent Manchukuo, which would be advantageous to Japan and at the same time would permit early reconstruction of the bilateral relationship between Japan and China, to their genuine mutual benefit.

Hirota had always favoured the bilateral approach to this key relationship. The Japanese government, though prepared to explore a German offer of mediation, accordingly responded to criticism made in the assembly of the League, and by other signatories of the Nine Power Treaty at the meeting they held at Brussels in November, by reiterating the claim, constantly asserted in offical statements in Tokyo, that their actions in China were justified in self-defence and were designed to restore stability in North-East Asia.

The speech by President Roosevelt, in October, in which he proposed the imposition of measures of 'quarantine' on the aggressor nations, was not followed by any suggestion of willingness on the part of the United States to support proposals for sanctions, at the Brussels meeting. International disapproval nevertheless caused some concern in Tokyo. There was a clear desire, shared by a good many senior army and navy officers, to bring the China incident to an end. Following an amphibious operation which rendered their positions around Shanghai untenable, the Chinese Nationalist forces were driven back beyond Nanking. That city's occupation was accompanied by the gratuitous slaughter of great numbers of Chinese soldiers, irregulars and civilians. The nature and scale of the atrocities committed by the Japanese Army in and around Nanking ensured the irreconcilable hostility of the mass of the Chinese people, and was bound to affect not only the reputation but also in the long term the morale of the army itself. The grave damage caused to Japan's international image was added to by the attack on the US Navy's gunboat *Panay*. For this incident, prompt reparations were made; but, whatever the intentions of the government in Tokyo might be, it became clear that some of the Japanese officers in the field were glad to take opportunities to harm foreign interests and harass foreign representatives in China. The earlier wounding of the British ambassador in China, from the air, was accidental, but the shelling of HMS *Ladybird* was a deliberate action taken on the orders of Colonel Hashimoto Kingoro, who was put on the retired list for the second time, in consequence, but was not silenced.

In the autumn of 1937 Italy joined the Anti-Comintern Pact, and in February 1938, Hitler, abandoning years of endeavour on the part of the extensive German military mission in China, made public his support for Japan's 'fight against Communism' and his intention of recognizing Manchukuo, duly put into effect in May. Hitler's primary objective in drawing closer to Japan was to reduce both the British and the Soviet Russian inclination and capacity to interfere with his plans in Europe. Those in Tokyo who favoured the development of ties with Berlin were mostly thinking, at this stage, of countering the threat from the Soviet Union.

Oshima and his associates were, however, intent upon a full military alliance with Germany, as a means of deterring the Anglo-Saxon Powers from interfering with Japan's plans in East Asia and the Pacific.

In January 1938 Konoye declared that his government would not deal with the Nationalists in China (*aite ni sezu*). By May, as military operations on the continent expanded inexorably, he lost confidence in the efficacy of pressure alone to produce an early conclusion to the China Incident. He brought General Ugaki into his cabinet as Foreign Minister, in place of Hirota. Ugaki attempted not only to revive negotiations with Chiang Kai-shek but also to improve relations with Britain and the United States. To this end, he engaged Sato Naotake as his special adviser. Their efforts were interrupted in July by the outbreak of fighting between Japanese and Soviet forces at Changkufeng, near the intersection of the borders of Korea, Manchuria and the Soviet Maritime Province. A truce was achieved in August, but by this time Ugaki felt his authority threatened by Konoye's agreement to the establishment of a China Board, which would take authority over policy in China away from the Gaimusho. He resigned at the end of September. The Munich agreement of that month was widely regarded in Japan as evidence that the Western democracies were on the defensive.

Although Konoye's foreign policy fluctuated, his first cabinet took measures to make the machinery of government more effective and better coordinated, which also brought Japan more closely into line with the fashionable practices of the totalitarian regimes. The Cabinet Planning Board was set up in October 1937, and the Imperial Headquarters in the following month. This improved co-ordination between ministries, including civil departments, between the armed services, and overall. The military planners were already sharing resources for economic research with the SMR. Now central controls were placed on trade and on capital movements, to ensure that military requirements had appropriate priority. The National Mobilization Law of April 1938 gave the government powers to regulate every aspect of economic activity: wages and prices, labour and manufacturing production, transport and the supply of materials, and the direction of industrial research and development. At the centre itself, the Liaison Conference was established, to supplement *ad hoc* ministerial committees, as the forum in which senior members of the Cabinet discussed the key issues of policy with the brass hats.

Within this machinery, the nature of the alliance with Germany became increasingly contentious. In late October 1938 Konoye brought Arita into the Cabinet, as Foreign Minister. Arita favoured the tie with Germany, but specifically as a deterrent to Soviet Russia: he did not see it as an appropriate instrument with which to challenge the European colonial Powers in Asia, or the United States in the Pacific. Konoye himself issued a statement in early November setting out his conception of a 'new order for ensuring permanent stability in East Asia'. Both China, having abandoned the current mistaken policies of the Nationalists, and Manchukuo were to co-operate in this, under Japan's leadership. This assertion of hegemony, coupled with the continuing expansion of military operations in China, gave rise to strong protest from Washington against the denial of American rights in China, and of the principle of the Open Door. Arita responded with a reiteration of Japan's claim, in effect, to an exclusive sphere of influence in East Asia, in terms which amounted to an explicit, even emphatic, renouncement of collaboration on the lines envisaged in the Washington Treaty system.

In late December, Wang Ching-wei, thitherto Chiang Kai-shek's jealous deputy, flew to Hanoi to work for the establishment of a pro-Japanese regime in China. The Japanese government declared its willingness to 'adjust its relations with a new China'. Chiang Kai-shek, however, from his capital in Chungking, where his government had been based since the fall of Hankow, was firm in his resistance; and in this he enjoyed continuing popular support. With the capture of Canton by the Japanese Army, the front in China now stretched for over 2,000 miles. The demands of the campaign on the national resources seemed endless, and out of proportion to its achievements. In the New Year of 1939 Konoye resigned, giving up for the time being his plans for further changes in the structure of government, including reform of the House of Peers and of the electoral system.

Hiranuma, who succeeded him, declared his intention of working with the political parties in the Diet, from which he might otherwise have expected obstruction. He retained Itagaki as Minister of War and Araki as Minister of Education, thus indicating a readiness for expansion on the continent as well as for nationalism at home. In keeping Arita at the Gaimusho, he had it in mind to limit the application of a strengthened alliance with Germany. A dispute with Britain over Tientsin, on which a compromise was reached eventually, brought him under pressure to accede to Oshima's project for a full military alliance with Berlin, which he barely resisted. Meanwhile, a renewal of local but quite large-scale hostilities with Soviet forces, this time arising out of clashes between the Kwantung Army and Outer Mongolian troops near Nomonhan in May, led to a series of defeats in August, and was not settled until after the outbreak of war in Europe. At the time of the Nomonhan Incident, the scale and nature of which was as far as possible concealed from the outside world, the Japanese government was deeply embarrassed by the announcement of the Nazi–Soviet Non-Aggression Pact. This followed the notification in July of the Roosevelt administration's decision to abrogate the bilateral Treaty of Commerce and Navigation, which had been in force since 1911, with effect from January 1940. This would enable the United States to take economic sanctions against Japan, and was clearly at least a potential turning-point.

It was, however, the immediate impact of Hitler's apparent accommodation with Stalin, and all that this implied for the Anti-Comintern Pact (of which it looked like a betrayal) and for the continuing negotiations in Berlin, which forced Hiranuma to resign before the end of August, by which time war in Europe seemed inevitable.

Saionji was unable to form a view as to who should succeed Hiranuma, so deeply was he resigned to the prospect of further military intrigue and general mismanagement. Yuasa, as Lord Keeper of the Privy Seal, having consulted Hirota, who declined to be a candidate, accepted the army's nomination of General Abe Nobuyuki. Moderate both in his views and in the forcefulness of his character, Abe was chosen, despite his links with Ugaki, at a juncture when opinions in the army were confused by the shock of events. General Hata Shunroku, who believed in the need to restore discipline, became Minister of War. Admiral Yonai's departure weakened the Cabinet, but Admiral Nomura Kichisaburo came in as Foreign Minister on the understanding that the Kwantung Army would be brought under control. He proceeded to initiate talks with United States Ambassador Grew, with a view to negotiating a new treaty of commerce and averting the threatened application of economic sanctions, which all could see as a potential disaster. Indeed, this was so clear that it stimulated military planning for a southward advance, to secure the natural resources of South-East Asia, especially of the Netherlands East Indies and of Malaya. Japan's obvious vulnerability to any embargo on the supply of certain materials, including above all oil and scrap iron, coupled with the need to stand by the European democracies, caused a stiffening of attitudes in the Roosevelt administration, most significantly on the part of Morgenthau at the Treasury, of Secretary of the Interior Ickes, and of senior officials such as Hornbeck at the State Department. Deterrence was the word in Washington. Japan was required to return to the status quo ante the China Incident. Such a concession was not acceptable to the Japanese Army. Unable to make progress, Abe resigned in January 1940.

His successor, Admiral Yonai Mitsumasa, and Arita, who once more became Foreign Minister, were anxious to avoid a breakdown in relations with the United States, but the abrogation by Washington of the commercial treaty came into effect very soon after the formation of Yonai's cabinet. The Cabinet made proposals for reduction in the scale of the military effort in China, but was prevailed upon by the army to increase it, with the usual argument that this would produce victory; and with the result of confirming Washington's scepticism of Tokyo's motives and intentions. In the Diet also, after so much acquiescence, there was some expression of disquiet. In particular, the veteran Minseito member Saito Takao attacked the army's case for the continued prosecution of war against China, and demanded a redefinition of Japan's objectives. The House voted for his expulsion, little

attempt having been made by any of his colleagues to resist this infringe-
ment of the member's rights. The government's attempt to render convinc-
ing the claim of Wang Ching-wei, installed by the Japanese themselves
in Nanking, to represent the true government of Nationalist China, was
unsuccessful.

In addition, there was continual trouble with Britain over such incidents
as the wounding of the chairman of the Shanghai Municipal Council, at a
ratepayers' meeting, by the leader of the Japanese Committee; and over the
removal from a Japanese ship, *Asama Maru*, of some German nationals, by
the Royal Navy, exercising belligerent's rights. Anti-British demonstrations,
as at the time of the Tientsin Incident, were not altogether spontaneous. The
atmosphere changed, however, with the ending of the phoney war in Europe, and with the fall of France. The Japanese press, which had retained a
certain respect for the Western democracies, now turned strongly against
the British in particular, and in favour of the Germans, who were seen, in
the popular view, to be winning victories by virtue of their superior national
spirit. Thus assisted, the army brought great pressure to bear on Yonai's
cabinet to concede the desirability of a full alliance with Berlin; and this,
coupled with the attraction of ideas for a 'new structure' in politics, which
Konoye was advocating, led to Yonai's resignation, in July. By this time the
British had been obliged to concede the closing of the Burma Road, though
only for three months; and the Vichy authorities had accepted a degree of
Japanese supervision of the supply routes through Indo-China. Japanese
planners were recommending the establishment of airfields in Indo-China
and Siam (Thailand) not primarily to extend operations against the Chinese
Nationalists, but to facilitate the seizure of British and Dutch possessions in
South-East Asia. Roosevelt's support for Britain seemed the greatest impedi-
ment to a strike in the south by Japan; but, although the bulk of the
American fleet was kept in Hawaiian waters in the summer of 1940,
contrary to normal practice and as a warning to Japan, it was evident that
the United States was by no means ready for war.

When Prince Konoye formed his second government, following Yonai's
resignation, he did so, once again, as the leader generally acceptable to all
the most influential groups in the country. The army recognized his attachment to the idea of Japanese leadership in Asia. His reforming zeal suited
the revisionist bureaucrats. His aristocratic credentials comforted conservatives. He was the best hope of those who wished to avoid an open clash with
the Western democracies, and above all to achieve an understanding with
the United States. Accordingly, he was favoured in court circles, and acceptable to industrial opinion. Many politicians, conscious of their subordination to the military in recent years, looked to him to restore its dignity to the
Imperial Diet. The Jushin and the Privy Council were grateful to find a

champion who seemed ready to take up the poisoned chalice as if it held nothing worse than a rather bitter summer drink.

Konoye appointed as Foreign Minister Matsuoka Yosuke, whose theme was that Japan could attain its rightful position in Asia without provoking a wider conflict; and as his Minister of War Tojo Hideki, formerly head of the Kempei in Manchuria, Chief of Staff of the Kwantung Army, and Deputy Minister of War. A leader of the dominant Control faction, he had the reputation of a brilliant staff officer, who believed that war with the United States was unavoidable. (Whether Konoye would have been allowed a free choice of his Minister of War must be doubted; but he may have been under no compulsion to select Matsuoka. He was surely not a consistently good judge of character, but rather susceptible to the blandishments of the glib and plausible.) Konoye easily persuaded the political parties that the concentration and unification of their influence and resources in the central organization of his 'new political structure', the Imperial Rule Assistance Association (IRAA, Taisei Yokusankai), would be in their own and the nation's best interests. There were a number of Diet members who looked askance at this parliamentary mainifestation of the totalitarian tendency, but they were too few to dismiss it. Some, like Ozaki Yukio, who stood out against it, were made to suffer for their idiosyncrasies. Outside the Diet, organized labour was willing to play its part in what had become the national war effort. Society at large, though with much scepticism among the sophisticated, accepted the enhanced sense of unity produced by the new neighbourhood associations (*tonarigumi*), and tolerated the enhanced supervision which was an increasingly notable feature of the system. People had grown accustomed to a repressive climate. There was a keen sense of dutiful patriotism, despite the frustrations of the war in China. Many were ready to help push the old empires out of the way of the full realization of Konoye's new order in Asia.

As with society as a whole, so with industry: private companies learned not to oppose the army directly, and to look for profit in projects approved by the military. Those among the leaders of business, such as Ikeda Seihin, their doyen, who maintained consistently that conflict with the United States would be fatal to the Japanese economy, relied on the probability that the manifest logic of their argument would prevail before any irrevocable moves were made in the contrary direction. Some outstanding elements of this argument were well known: Japan's production of steel in 1941 was running at one-tenth that of the United States, in volume; stocks of essential materials were good for no more than two years, less in some instances, if wider war were to come; undisputed access to all the resources of South-East Asia would not make up for the closure of other sources of supply; the loss of world markets would distort the economy badly. Effects of the war in Europe had shown up the deficiencies of policies of import substitution and of maximizing trade in the Empire and with other Asian countries. For defence production alone, there were still requirements which could be obtained only in or through the capitalist countries of the West.

Yet, even before the formal inauguration of the IRAA, Konoye had assented, in September 1940, to conversion of the pact with Germany and Italy into a full alliance. At this critical juncture in world affairs, the advocates of this move were insistent that it would deter the United States both from entering the war in Europe and from interfering with the development of Japan's plans for the new order in Greater East Asia. The new order was recognized in the text of the Tripartite Pact itself, and a certain significance attached to German and Italian endorsement of Japan's leading role in Asia. It seemed to validate the nationalist ideal of Hakko Ichiu, promising to bring the eight corners of the Asian world under Japan's protective domination. At the same time, the further victory of the European Axis seemed certain to many in Tokyo (though not to Saionji, even in the last weeks before his death in November 1940). For many of those middle-ranking staff officers and civil servants, whose influence tended to predominate, the pact was prelude to the seizure of the Netherlands East Indies and of all British and French possessions in South-East Asia and the south-west Pacific. They went to work in Indo-China, stimulating the Thais to make territorial claims against the French, then acting as arbitrators, and gradually asserting effective control over the representatives of Vichy France.

Matsuoka calculated that the new order in Greater East Asia, which in the New Year of 1941 began to be referred to as the Greater East Asia Co-Prosperity Sphere, might well come about through the simple collapse of the old order, that the European colonial Powers would be obliged to withdraw as a result of their humiliation in Europe, and that the United States would not go to war to prevent this, nor to assist the Nationalist Chinese, though Roosevelt, re-elected for his third term in November 1940, had authorized the provision of a major loan to sustain Chungking. Matsuoka combined a shrewd caution with an entirely contrary, impulsive tendency to believe his own propaganda, both characteristics being expressed in a voluble rhetorical style. Soon after returning to office he had intervened to secure the release of a number of British residents in Japan arrested by the Kempeitai (with the exception of the Reuters representative, Melville Cox, who died while in their custody). In February 1941, in response to a warning sent by British Foreign Secretary Eden, through Shigemitsu Mamoru, the Japanese ambassador in London, he asserted that Japan stood for 'no conquest, no oppression, no exploitation'; and he went so far as to offer Japan's mediation in the war in Europe. This caused some difficulty with Berlin, which Matsuoka arranged to visit officially in March 1941.

Before going to Europe, Matsuoka initiated another unsuccessful attempt to bring the China Incident to a conclusion, by seeking to draw Chiang Kai-shek into a three-sided negotiation with the Japanese government and its instrument, Wang Ching-wei. Confident of growing sympathy in Washington, Chiang was not tempted. Matsuoka set off in March, first to explore in Moscow the prospect for an arrangement which would relieve Tokyo, at least temporarily, of the Soviet threat. Proceeding to Berlin, he found the Germans surprisingly unchanged in their hostility towards their partners in the Ribbentrop–Molotov Pact. He was unable to give the Nazis the commitment they wanted from Tokyo to an attack on Singapore at an early date. While he was on his tour, Matsuoka was sent some questions by Mr Churchill, throwing doubt on the wisdom of counting on German and Italian victory in the war, and recommending the most careful consideration of where Japan's interests lay. He told the press, on his second halt in Moscow in April, that England would be beaten by the end of the year, before help from the United States could be decisive. He then concluded a five-year Pact of Neutrality with the Soviet leaders. This was designed to ensure peaceful bilateral relations and respect for the integrity of Manchukuo and of the Mongolian People's Republic. The Soviet leaders were already aware from the reports of their agent, Sorge, in Tokyo, both that they should not place their trust in the agreement with Ribbentrop and that the Japanese were developing plans for operations in South-East Asia which might prove more attractive to them than any possible move in the north. Stalin, however, did not draw the conclusion that it would be safe greatly to reduce Soviet forces in the Far East in order to strengthen his defences in the West.

On his return to Tokyo, Matsuoka found that Konoye had authorized the start of talks in Washington, through the Japanese ambassador, Admiral Nomura Kichisaburo, to seek the establishment of a *modus vivendi* with the United States. Matsuoka, who had insisted on the dismissal of a number of officials in the Gaimusho and at posts abroad on the grounds of their excessive attachment to the idea that Japan's best interests were likely to lie in collaboration with the Anglo-Saxon Powers, was suspicious of arguments about the need for compromise in pursuit of hegemony in East Asia, or in prosecuting what had come to be called Japan's holy war in China. When the Germans attacked the Soviet Union, Matsuoka's reputation suffered. He had been in Berlin only a few weeks before the date by which Hitler had required that the plans for Operation Barbarossa should be completed, yet he had been vouchsafed no confidences by his Nazi allies. He took part in a Liaison Conference in Tokyo on 25 June, followed by an Imperial Conference in early July, at which it was resolved that Japan should move into south Indo-China, should be ready for war with both the United States and Britain, and should not intervene in the Russo-German conflict unless the

Soviet Union was clearly on the verge of defeat. Matsuoka himself was against the further move into Indo-China, and in favour of attacking the Russians forthwith, the terms of the pact which he had just concluded in Moscow notwithstanding.

Japan's new advance in Indo-China was countered by the freezing of Japanese assets by the United States and Britain, previous prohibitions and limits on the export to Japan of various items of strategic significance no longer seeming to have sufficiently high deterrent value. Washington, which had put forward proposals for a *modus vivendi* with Japan immediately prior to the German assault on the Soviet Union, was now evidently deeply concerned to restrain the Japanese, and to sustain Chiang Kai-shek; but remained by no means ready for war. Consultation between the United States, Britain and the Netherlands had become close. All were increasingly supportive of Nationalist China. In Japan, the talk was all of encirclement by the ABCD Powers. The British and the Dutch, however, while accepting responsibility for the defence of their own colonial territories, and in Britain's case for co-ordination with the Dominions, had agreed that the United States should represent the interests of the Western democracies as a group, in their negotiations with Japan. It was plain to Konoye that the only alternative to war was to reach an understanding with Washington. Considering this more likely to be achieved without Matsuoka's direct participation, he submitted the resignation of his whole cabinet, and formed a new one, with Admiral Toyoda Teijiro as Foreign Minister.

Proposals already put forward by the United States made any relaxation of economic sanctions conditional upon a Japanese undertaking to withdraw from China. The probability that the position reached in Manchuria might now be acceptable to the Anglo-Saxon Powers, as a *fait accompli*, hardly seemed to affect the outcome of further discussion. The war in China had become such a combination of mission, commitment, challenge and frustration, and was above all so closely connected with the army's hold on power in Japan itself, that even a good measure of international recognition of Manchukuo now seemed an inadequate return for a decade of effort; and even those senior officers who were fully aware of the risks inevitably involved in any confrontation with the United States were reluctant to abandon hope of outright victory in China. The number of Japanese troops actively involved in hostilities there was by now about 850,000. Unable to bring any really substantial enemy forces to battle, they were exposed to persistent attack by guerrilla units and were obliged to protect their greatly extended lines of communication by constructing and manning blockhouses every few miles along each railway line, and dispersing their own strength in static garrisons. The effect on morale and on standards of conduct was as negative as it was pervasive. In response to the Hundred Regiments Offensive launched by the Chinese, the Japanese Army mounted a 'three-alls' campaign: kill all, burn all, loot all. It was the worst possible prelude to a wider war, yet a wider war had begun to seem to offer the best prospect of bringing it to a successful conclusion.

A thrust southwards, though its main practical purpose would be to gain control of natural resources, and its presentational aim would be the attainment of a grand Asian hegemony at the expense of older empires, also held out the prospect of cutting off Chungking's principal remaining routes of supply from the outside world. Though there were sharp differences of view about the strategy to be adopted, both between the army and the navy and within the central staff of each service, there was also a range of attractive benefits to be expected from success, and planning went ahead accordingly. Pressure built up for early action. It was desirable to take advantage of Axis successes in Europe, to move before the United States was ready to intervene effectively in the first stages of the Japanese advance, and to strike during the winter in order to reduce the risk of a dangerous Soviet counterstroke in the north. The complete denial of oil supplies from the United States, which was imposed in August 1941 following that of scrap-iron at the turn of the year, was a very much more serious sanction than the licensing regime operated by Washington from the previous summer. It gave the Imperial Navy no alternative but to argue that, if there was to be a war, it must be started without delay. As discussion proceeded, Admiral Yamamoto Isoroku, Commander-in-Chief of the combined fleet, made no secret of his doubt as to the navy's, and thus the nation's, capacity to sustain a prolonged war, even with the early acquisition of the oilfields in the Dutch East Indies.

Economic blueprints for the Greater East Asia Co-Prosperity Sphere were tinged with wishful thinking from the outset. The idea that this regional organization could if necessary (depending on political and strategic developments elsewhere) achieve complete self-sufficiency was more often assumed than argued with any rigour. The arguments for peace – including the consideration that the economy had shown an average annual growth rate of about 3.7 per cent from the earliest years of the century until 1937, and that this exceptionally good performance had faltered only, or primarily, because of distortions resulting from the war with China – were not allowed to deflect attention from the vision of empire, or alternatively from the threat of encirclement. The warnings of experienced and successful industrialists such as Ikeda Seihin went for nothing in an assertive climate of opinion, itself created largely by the army.

The requirements of the military leaders may have distorted the economy, but it was also evident that they had done much to create the new, heavy industrial base which enabled Japan to consider new options. By 1940 heavy industry accounted for nearly 60 per cent of total manufacturing output. The production of iron and steel, and of armaments, continued to expand. In shipbuilding, Japan's share of the world's gross tonnage

115

launched in 1939 was second only to that of Britain. By 1940, exports of heavy manufactures exceeded imports. Exports as a whole maintained the surge built up after the slump, and went predominantly to Asian markets. Half Japan's imports came from Asian countries. But this was still a long way from regional self-sufficiency.

The importance of the role of government in the development of industrial strength was also continuing to grow. Like shipbuilding, the motor industry received official support which was crucial to its success. Under the Automobile Manufacturing Law of 1936, Toyota and Nissan received benefits so substantial as to enable them to drive American competition out of the Empire. Those sectors of manufacturing industry which were of secondary importance to the 'quasi-wartime economy' were required to form cartels, for which their own representatives shared responsibility with the appropriate ministry. This arrangement tended to strengthen the influence of zaibatsu affiliates, and thus of their parent groups, so that any dissatisfaction felt by smaller private interests was outweighed by the accretion of power in the hands of the conglomerates. The incomes of industrial workers were still rising, and the level of savings was high. In the most advanced sectors of industry there was a sense of common endeavour by management, labour, the bureaucracy and the armed services. But the quality and availability of consumer goods generally, and of food in particular, began to deteriorate in the late 1930s. In the agricultural sector there was little improvement and much discontent: landlords were often disposed to obstruct reform.

Japanese agricultural policy was perhaps more successful in the colonies than at home, during this period. Korea and Taiwan were sources of inexpensive rice, imported in bulk with advantages in keeping down the cost of living and the pressure for higher wages in the urban and industrial centres of Japan, but with the effect of prolonging the depression in rural areas. Something like 20 per cent of productive agricultural land in both Taiwan and Korea was in Japanese ownership. Neither of those colonial territories was as important as Kwantung as a supplier of industrial raw materials. Kwantung and Manchukuo were also the recipients of the bulk of Japanese industrial investment overseas in the 1930s, though a good deal of this had not become fully productive by the end of the decade.

All the overseas territories of the Empire benefited from government investment in infrastructure and services, including communications, medical services and education. Formal education was, however, developed primarily for the Japanese expatriate community, which numbered about a million persons, in civilian occupations, in the Empire as a whole, by the late 1930s. Colonial governments gave priority to Japanese industrial and commercial organizations, as opposed to indigenous enterprises, in promoting industrial development. This enabled the zaibatsu concerns to profit from collaboration with established policy, without having to fight for advantage, except sometimes between themselves, when there was no implicit agreement on market shares. In mining and heavy industry, semi-governmental corporations were also prominent. Tokyo subsidized the colonial governments of Korea and Kwantung, while that in Taiwan was self-supporting. In all the territories, the systems of taxation favoured the corporate sectors, each of which was dominated by Japanese interests. Thus, while the export surpluses generated in the colonies were put back into their own economies, the beneficiaries were for the most part Japanese. During the 1930s colonial development was progressively more closely connected with the requirements of Japan's 'quasi-wartime economy'. Governors-general were usually senior military figures with political experience. The Kwantung Army effectively ran Manchukuo throughout its period of nominal independence. But the colonial administrations also consistently took the army's interests fully into account.

This was yet another area in which the army's influence had been unchallenged. It was in large part for reasons of political doctrine, but it was also with a view to subsuming this military influence within a larger national organization and a more varied climate of opinion, that Prince Konoye had brought the IRAA into being. Once it was established, however, its control eluded him, and senior appointments there, too, went to military men, many of the remaining forceful and independent personalities in the Diet having kept aloof from it. The military view that there was neither need nor room for concessions, and that it would be a national humiliation to abandon the objectives of the war in China after four years of sacrifice, was widely accepted. Those who persisted in the belief that war with the United States and Britain was unthinkable were no longer capable of decisive influence. The press was mostly jingoistic. Publicists out of sympathy with the trend towards ultra-nationalism, or simply critical of some specific aspect of government policy, had to be careful how they sought to express their views. Earlier repressive legislation had been reinforced to the extent that, ever since the beginning of the war in China, information about new developments either in the national economy or in foreign affairs could be published only with the permission of the authorities. The Atlantic Charter of August sounded faint and distant to the public in Japan, and could be presented as a sign, not of the determination of Washington to put down Fascism, but of the United States' preoccupation with the war in Europe.

In reality, the principles enunciated in the Atlantic Charter came to stand in the way of Konoye's proposal for a personal meeting with President Roosevelt. Konoye's advisers would not have permitted him to endorse any such principles in advance of a meeting, while Roosevelt's advisers could see no likely benefit from a meeting without his having done so. In September 1941 a decision was made, and confirmed at the highest level, that Japan

117

should be prepared to go to war with the United States, Britain and other countries associated with them, including if necessary the Soviet Union, if no acceptable alternative course of action could be arrived at through the Washington negotiations, by late October.

Prince Konoye had had doubts not only about the Axis Pact itself, but also about the agreement made with Vichy France over Indo-China. He regarded the proposal for a meeting with President Roosevelt as having offered the only way by which he might have reached towards a compromise acceptable to his own colleagues. When the response to this proposal was seen to amount in effect to a repetition of the position taken by Secretary of State Cordell Hull throughout the previous discussions, Konoye felt obliged to resign. He would have been aware by mid-October that his reputation and authority were bound to suffer from the discovery that the Soviet agent Sorge had penetrated his private office, through his close adviser, Ozaki Hotsumi. But the more compelling reason for resignation was that it enabled the September decision, with its imminent deadline, to be reconsidered.

The appointment of Konoye's War Minister, General Tojo Hideki, to succeed him as Prime Minister was recommended by the Lord Keeper, Kido Koichi, with the approval of the Jushin. Tojo enjoyed the army's confidence, and was known to have adopted, in Konoye's cabinet, a hard line towards the negotiations in Washington, refusing to contemplate any commitment to withdraw from China. His appointment of Togo Shigenori as Foreign Minister, however, was among indications that he intended to make a last attempt to avoid war. Those in favour of compromise regarded him as possibly the only man capable of imposing his will on the army. Time was very short. According to the military planners, if a strike were not made in December it would have to be put off until the spring. A postponement of that length would risk reducing the navy's oil stocks well below the level considered essential for success in the operations to be undertaken. The Cabinet agreed a modification of the deadline, and modified instructions for the negotiating team in Washington, now led by Kurusu Saburo, working in an uneasy partnership with Nomura.

There was a fleeting chance that a *modus vivendi* might be developed, based in part on the beginning of a process of withdrawal by the Japanese, from Indo-China. But the price was judged in Washington to be likely seriously to impair Nationalist China's will to sustain resistance, and thus also to threaten the continued co-ordination of all the interests represented on their side of the talks; and so, far beyond the purview of the talks themselves, to have consequences detrimental to the cause of the democracies. When the Japanese government received Secretary Hull's note of 26 November, in which he reiterated once again the basic principles underlying the United States' position, they chose to interpret this as an ultimatum.

They proceeded accordingly, on lines agreed at liaison and imperial conferences earlier in the month, and now confirmed, to supervise the implementation of the plans for attack. They knew it was a gamble. They thought it preferable to the acceptance of a subordinate position in a new Washington system.

6

War, Occupation and Renewal, 1941–52

The seizure and securing of all the territory required to complete the Greater East Asia Co-Prosperity Sphere, which would involve conflict with British, Dutch and Australian forces, and with all the Commonwealth and eventually with all the Allies, was to be combined with and facilitated by the immediate crippling of the United States' naval power in the Pacific. The element of tactical surprise was essential to the success of the initial attack on the US Pacific Fleet at Pearl Harbor on 7 December 1941. Delay in presenting to Secretary Hull in Washington the exculpatory note in which the Japanese government conveyed its decision to break off diplomatic relations, whether or not due to difficulties in the transmission and deciphering of an unusually long text, added a seemingly deliberate element of treachery, and served to stimulate a determined reaction. The attack on Malaya, advertised in advance by suspect movements of troop ships and transports in the Gulf of Siam, about which the British ambassador had made representations in Tokyo, preceded that on Pearl Harbor briefly, in real time. But the approach to Oahu by the striking force under Vice-Admiral Nagumo, which had assembled in great secrecy and sailed from Tankan Bay in the Kurile Island of Etorofu as early as 26 November, escaped detection. At little cost, carrier-based Japanese aircraft sank half the battleships in the US Pacific Fleet, and severely damaged most of the others, causing heavy casualties. Many American aircraft were also destroyed on the ground. However, none of the Pacific Fleet's three aircraft-carriers was in Hawaiian waters, so that what the attack on Pearl Harbor failed to achieve also proved to be of very great significance.

The Japanese drive southwards was even more overwhelmingly successful, most objectives being secured in less time than the planners had allowed. Hong Kong, Malaya, Singapore, Borneo and the Netherlands East Indies were all taken over by the end of March 1942. With the sinking of HMS *Prince of Wales* and *Repulse*, and the elimination of United States air and naval power in the Philippines, at the outset of the campaign, and with the defeat of allied naval forces under the Dutch Admiral Doorman in the Battle of the Java Sea in late February, the Japanese had achieved command of the sea within the extended perimeter of the Empire. The Japanese XV Army, having taken Rangoon, was moving further north into Burma, to cut the only overland route by which supplies from the West could reach Nationalist China. Although Corregidor did not fall until May, General MacArthur himself had withdrawn from the Philippines to Australia in mid-March. The islands of Wake and Guam had been captured. In addition to the heavy blows sustained by their naval forces, and the vast concessions of territory, Allied losses of manpower, especially in the surrender of Singapore, were extremely serious.

Japan's access to essential raw materials, to tin and rubber in Malaya, and especially to oil in the Netherlands East Indies and Borneo, was seemingly assured. A perimeter was established for the Greater East Asia Co-Prosperity Sphere, and thus effectively for the Empire of Japan, which stretched from the Kuriles in the north, by way of Wake Island and the Marshalls and Gilberts down to the Bismarck archipelago and the northern coast of New Guinea, taking in Timor, Java, Sumatra and Malaya, to reach in northern Burma a tentative link with the older war against Nationalist China.

Vast as was the area now occupied, there were temptations to go further. Japanese warships debouched into the Indian Ocean. There were some whose ambitions extended to bringing both India and Australasia into Greater East Asia. The dangers of overstretch were clear, and it was only a few months after the drive south that the Army General Staff argued for some thinning out of garrisons in the newly occupied southern region, in order to secure advances in China. It was the Imperial Navy, originally more cautious than the army about the prospects for the wider war, which now advocated a sustained strategy of aggression in the south. Their objective was to provoke a fleet action in the Pacific before the United States Navy could replace the losses suffered at Pearl Harbor. Victory in such an action would have implications similar to those which the Battle of Tsushima had had for the war with Russia in 1905.

No political or military strategy had been devised explicitly to cover circumstances which might become less than wholly favourable. In the autumn of 1941, however, when the decision to go to war was still conditional upon the outcome of the negotiations in Washington, the president of the Privy Council, Baron Hara Yoshimichi, had made clear in discussion with his colleagues in the leadership his view that the wider war, if it had to come, must be kept short. The conflicting view – that the extended perimeter, as established in the opening phase of operations, could be held indefinitely against Allies preoccupied and even perhaps fatally weakened by the war in the West – was strengthened by the dramatic success of those operations. It was shown to be untenable within a year of the attack on Pearl Harbor, but this was not so readily apparent as to govern the conduct of the war. In any case, the impossibility of reconciling any substantial withdrawal from China with the maintenance of the army's dominant position in government was to remain a bar to any compromise or negotiated settlement of the broad issues. It was the army's realization that the retention of their position in Tokyo no less than in the field was likely to depend upon the complete defeat or destruction of American naval power in the Pacific that gave Admiral Yamamoto his authority in the counsels of a government otherwise more intent on satisfying the army's requirements. Even so, agreement between the service chiefs was always difficult to achieve, at Imperial Headquarters; and inter-service co-operation was seldom smooth, despite its obvious and continuing importance, in the Pacific theatre above all.

The urgency of working for conclusive victory in the Pacific meant that the political, as opposed to the military and strategic, consolidation of the extended Empire took a lower priority for the Japanese government. The advance was presented as having been inspired by a vision of Pan-Asian solidarity. The region now dominated by Japan was generally referred to as the Co-Prosperity Sphere rather than the Empire. Plans for political evolution were drawn up by the Gaimusho; but serious advocates of the development of truly autonomous, let alone wholly independent, regimes in the occupied territories had no part in their administration at this stage, when it was naturally regarded by the local army commanders as a matter of military necessity. The exigences of war, and their own traditions, saw to it that local commanders were seldom able to relinquish close control over civil affairs. There was a tendency among Japanese army officers to treat civilian populations with scant consideration, even with contempt. This made the task of administration harder, in the short term. Eventually, it meant that the attainment of independence was not, in most cases, attributed with gratitude to the Japanese war effort. The long, bitter struggle in China, against Nationalists and Communists alike, had been allowed to exert a pervasive, brutalizing influence on the Japanese Army.

In addition, the ill-treatment of Allied prisoners of war and civilians was in part a deliberate policy of humiliation of the rival, established, non-Asian colonial Powers. In part, it too reflected experience in China, in part the ethos which led Japanese troops themselves to fight to the end, against any odds, in the conviction that capture was a disgraceful fate, to which a glorious death in the Emperor's service was always to be preferred. Reminders of obligations which had long been accepted internationally were received, and disregarded. Some voices were raised in Tokyo in protest about reports of indiscipline and cruelty, but in vain. Measures such as those which had been taken to register at least a mild formal disapproval of the earlier excesses at Nanking were apparently not repeated. It is doubtful whether either the scale or the systematic character of the atrocious offences committed by their troops overseas in the field, and in prison camps, was understood by the people of Japan until long after their own sufferings in the closing stages of the war had inured them to all such considerations. By that time, many local commanders had paid the highest penalty for cruelties for which they were held responsible.

In the early months of 1942, while the Japanese conquests were being completed, the United States Navy concentrated on establishing a secure southern Pacific route to Australia. Some Japanese island garrisons were lightly harassed, bombarded but not assaulted. Japanese seaborne communications were not exposed to serious disruption by submarine attack, partly because of the unreliability, at this stage, of American torpedoes. But the air raid on Tokyo led by Colonel Doolittle on 18 April was significant both in psychological terms, for the doubt which it cast on popular assumptions in Japan of security and invincibility, and militarily, for the impetus which it provided for Admiral Yamamoto's plan to bring about a major fleet engagement with the enemy.

The Americans, who had been able to read one series of encrypted Japanese diplomatic communications since before the war (the product known in intelligence circles as Magic) now acquired the capability to intercept Japanese naval signals. This facilitated the US Navy's success, as the result of the battle of the Coral Sea, in early May, in turning back an intended Japanese amphibious attack on Port Moresby. This was a costly success, against formidably efficient Japanese aircraft and crews. But it began a process of attrition of experienced Japanese pilots which was to have a profound influence on the course of the war in the Pacific.

A much more serious setback for Japan, long to remain concealed from the public, was incurred in the battle of Midway a month later. Admiral Yamamoto combined an attack on the Aleutians, designed to draw the US Pacific Fleet away to the north, with a preliminary bombardment of Midway Island from Admiral Nagumo's carriers, which was to be followed by the occupation of the airfield there for use as a base to support the Japanese Combined Fleet, at full strength, in the main battle against Admiral Nimitz in which the operation would culminate. Misjudgements as to the likely whereabouts of the American carriers under Admirals Spruance and Fletcher, and consequent inadequacies in his air search, led Nagumo to expose his own carriers to attack. All four were lost, and, although the United States losses, especially of aircraft and crews, had been heavy, and the carrier *Yorktown* had been crippled (and was to be sunk by submarine attack as she limped away after the battle) this obliged Yamamoto to order a general retirement.

The decisive character of the battle of Midway was easily overlooked at the time, even by those allowed to know the facts. The main body of Yamamoto's Combined Fleet had not even been engaged. Carriers could be replaced, even if trained crews, and especially the crews of hundreds of aircraft, were admitted to be a grievous loss. The enemy had suffered too. The perimeter of Japanese conquest, so far from being penetrated, had actually been enlarged, if marginally, in the Aleutians. The war in the West was still developing favourably for the Axis Powers. The German armies might have been halted in Russia, but could be expected to resume the offensive. Hitler, who had declared war on the United States in solidarity with the Japanese immediately after the attack on Pearl Harbor, although neither consulted nor warned of it by Tokyo in advance, was causing terrible losses to Allied shipping in the Atlantic. Soon after Midway, there was also some compensatory encouragement for Imperial Headquarters in Tokyo, in the news that Rommel had taken Tobruk and was threatening the British position in Egypt, and thus throughout the Middle East.

In the latter half of 1942, however, the prospect for the Axis Powers as a whole began gradually to darken, and the brilliance of Japan's initial successes continued to fade, if at first almost imperceptibly to all but the most closely informed. By the end of July the Japanese had been turned back by the Australians on the Kokoda track through the Owen Stanley Mountains. The fighting in the fearful conditions of this terrain was on a comparatively small scale, but it signalled the end of what had come to seem a prescriptive right to victory for the Japanese Army. The retreat from Milne Bay the following month meant that the Japanese could only with difficulty hold on to a contracting beachhead in the Papuan peninsula, though they were not finally driven out of Buna until January 1943, and their positions on the northern coast of New Guinea, further west, remained formidably strong.

The achievement of the US marines in fighting their way ashore on the island of Guadalcanal, in the Solomons, on 7 August 1942 was most significant for the whole future course of the war in the Pacific. Their unexpected landing and their success in consolidating the initial gains made in this first of the long series of amphibious assaults, and the establishment of close air support on what became famous as Henderson Field, was followed by months of uncertain conflict. Both combatants were heavily reinforced, the Americans building up eventually to a strength of 50,000 men on the island, the Japanese bringing in fresh reserves at night by naval convoy, the 'Tokyo Express'. In a series of naval engagements in the surrounding waters, losses were heavy on both sides. The Japanese had the better of the battle of Savo Island, at the outset of this first Allied offensive campaign. But their losses in the subsequent clashes at sea, and especially in the three-day battle of Guadalcanal itself, in November, amounted to a very serious drain on their resources of trained men, and of ships and aircraft; above all, of experienced pilots. In the struggle on the island, the belated all-out attempt by General Hyakutake's XVII Army, based on Rabaul in New

Britain, to recapture Henderson Field was decisively defeated, but Japanese resistance on Guadalcanal was not finally overcome until February 1943.

By this time, having completed the conquest of Burma, the Japanese had taken a decision to go over to an essentially defensive strategy on that front, at the furthest extension of their advance. They were unable to prevent supplies to the Nationalist Chinese from being flown in, over 'the Hump' from India. In China itself they were keeping up the pressure, but with neither military nor political solutions in early prospect. Their Axis partners were no longer prospering in the West. Rommel had been defeated at Alamein in early November 1942, and Anglo-American forces had landed in French North Africa. Hitler was making the strategic error of reinforcing failure in that theatre. In January 1943 the Russians destroyed the German Sixth Army at Stalingrad. The investment of Leningrad was broken. Meeting at Casablanca that same January, Roosevelt and Churchill agreed to the former's proposal that they adopt a policy of demanding unconditional surrender by their enemies. American strength was growing massively. The production of war material in the United States was by now probably five times as great as that achieved by the maximum effort in Japan. The bulk of US production, however, was still being sent to sustain the war in the West, to which the Allies had declared repeatedly that they were giving priority; and losses of Allied shipping to German U-boat attack reached their highest, devastating level in the spring of 1943. They began at last to turn down in the early summer.

In well-informed and liberal circles in Japan, there was persistent scepticism about the war policy. The dramatic initial successes of Pearl Harbor and the sweep southwards, however, induced a degree of euphoria in the collective consciousness of the general public, which the media were officially encouraged to stimulate. The atmosphere of patriotic and nationalistic conformity, which had already been fostered for a decade, reached a stifling intensity. 'Spiritual mobilization' had been the watchword in education for three years before the outbreak of war in the Pacific, and the elementary schools were instructed in the spring of 1941 to put a strong emphasis on the national heritage, history and culture of Japan. They were now known as national schools (*Kokumin Gakko*). At about the same time, the Home Ministry completed the organization of neighbourhood associations (*tonarigumi*) throughout the country. Since every adult's entitlement to rationed food depended on his or her membership of the appropriate *tonarigumi*, the system was genuinely comprehensive. It gave officials of the Ministry a firm structure by means of which to maintain social discipline and administrative control. Its institution was designed, in part, to forestall the development of the IRAA.

The IRAA may well itself have been intended by Prince Konoye to enable the civil leaders in government to outflank and ultimately to dominate the military, by the sheer weight of a regimented people capable of being manipulated directly by the Prime Minister. However that may be, the IRAA was seen by officials of the Home Ministry as a weapon threatening bureaucratic authority, whether it was to be wielded by the Prince, as a politician, or by the generals, as his effective masters. This perception led the bureaucrats to devise a competing instrument and bring it into operation in time to win them substantial advantage in terms of the domestic balance of power and influence. By doing so, they may, perhaps even intentionally, have spared their fellow citizens subjection to extreme totalitarian tyranny, though such political distinctions were to seem of little account during the later wartime privations.

In any case, repression was harsh enough. Measures were introduced in 1941 to strengthen the Peace Preservation Law, with a view especially to outlawing both the Communist Party and communist propaganda; and the National Defence Security Law brought in the death penalty for the disclosure of strategically sensitive information. Many arrests had been made before the war of people suspected of subversive activity, and more were taken into preventive detention in 1941, and thereafter. The Special Emergency Act of December 1942 prohibited unauthorized assembly, and imposed penalties for spreading damaging rumours. The Special Higher Police (Tokko) and the Military Police (Kempei) thus had very extensive powers, which they used effectively. Suspects under interrogation were often tortured. Life in civil prisons was grim, and in the later wartime years malnutrition was almost as severe as in the prisoner-of-war camps. But the rate of executions of criminals seems not to have varied greatly from pre-war years. There were no mass killings of civilians believed to oppose wartime governments, in Japan itself. Nor, on the home front, was there any openly avowed policy of racial persecution, in particular not against Jews. Of those arrested for offences connected with religion, in wartime Japan, only about one in nine was Christian. Among civilians belonging to the Empire, those who suffered most grievously at the hands of government in Tokyo were the tens of thousands of Koreans and Taiwanese who were taken south as labourers to fortify the perimeter defences, and kept there to the end.

Just as in education, and in civilian life generally, central control had been built up progressively in the pre-war years, so had the participation of government in certain key sectors of industry. This process involved direct participation, as in iron and steel, and shipbuilding; and also compulsory cartelization through control associations (*toseikai*). It had tended in peacetime to increase the reach and influence of the zaibatsu groups, but the onset of hostilities inevitably meant managerial subordination to the military in decision-making, at least on all major issues. The military distrusted the zaibatsu, regarding them as half-hearted supporters; and their professions of willingness to collaborate had long been referred to as 'camouflage policy'.

Nevertheless, the military were to some extent in the hands of those with industrial experience, particularly when it came to methods of production, and the optimum siting and scale of manufacturing facilities. The great corporations were indispensable, and they flourished accordingly, enlarging their interests in heavy industry especially, even if they had little say in the formation of policy at national level. Their trading interests, however, largely gave way from the end of 1941 to the business of procurement, transport and distribution of raw materials and other supplies for the wartime economy. They had to work closely with bureaucrats and military planners.

Tojo had included some senior bureaucrats in his cabinet, notably Togo Shigenori at the Foreign Ministry, Kaya Okinori as Minister of Finance, and Kishi Nobusuke, fresh from his highly successful supervision of the industrial development of Manchuria, as Commerce and Industry Minister. Tojo himself remained as War Minister, concurrently with his assumption of the premiership, and took charge briefly also of the Home Ministry. He felt the need to consolidate and formalize his government's political support. The dissolution of the Diet was in any case overdue. There seemed likely to be advantage in holding general elections in the spring of 1942, preferably before reports of victory on all the fighting fronts might be interrupted, or might have to be qualified. It was decided in January that polling day should be 30 April 1942.

Tojo arranged through the IRAA to have a list of 'patriotic candidates' drawn up, so that voters could readily identify those whom the government recommended for election. There were 466 names on this list, and each of these candidates received a subvention secretly authorized by Tojo to be disbursed from the army's 'special fund'. (Tojo was restrained by some of his ministerial colleagues from making full use of the IRAA Young Men's Corps to the same end.) There were also 613 independent candidates, ranging from former Diet members of liberal views, most of whom belonged to an informal group, the Like-Minded Association (Dokokai), to a small party on the extreme right wing, which expressed disappointment that the IRAA was not shaping up on sufficiently thoroughgoing totalitarian lines. Independent candidates, though their patriotism might be suspect in some quarters, were often well supported, including Saito Takao, expelled from the Diet in 1940 for criticizing the military, who was to top the poll in his electoral district. His was one of a number of election campaigns hampered or frustrated by the police. Both Ozaki Yukio and Ashida Hitoshi, among the 37 Dokokai candidates, were arrested during the campaign, and Ozaki was later prosecuted: nine of the Dokokai were successful in the elections. At the height of the electoral campaign, the Doolittle air raids of 18 April caused the government some embarrassment, reflected in the executions of airmen on this mission who were captured. There was an exceptionally high turnout at the polls on 30 April, of over 80 per cent of the electorate. The officially recommended candidates received 66 per cent of the votes, and won 80 per cent of the seats. When the new Diet met, in May, all but a few unredeemed independent members of the lower House joined IRAPA, the reconstructed parliamentary arm of IRAA, to show their solidarity with the war effort.

Before these elections, Tojo's cabinet had included no members of the lower House. Kishi and Ino Hiroya, the Minister of Agriculture and Forestry, were returned as members at the polls on 30 April, and Tojo instituted a system of consultative committees, through which Diet members were kept in touch with the work of the ministries. Later, to acknowledge the continuing significance of allegiances to the pre-war parties, he introduced one representative each of Minseito and Seiyukai opinion into his government. So long as the constitutional proprieties were observed, Tojo needed to retain a working relationship with the Diet, above all to ensure the approval of budgetary measures.

Unlike his Axis partners, Tojo never had dictatorial powers. He had to cultivate, or at least to take into account, the views of all the groups on whose acquiescence in government policy domestic harmony and stability, and hence Japan's success in the war, depended. This included the views of his senior ministerial colleagues, of the senior officials in all their departments, of the Court, the Diet, industry, the press, and even of the people themselves; and above all of the senior officers in the armed services. Tojo's decision to create a Great East Asia Ministry in the autumn of 1942, to look after the 'sister countries' in South-East Asia now under Japanese occupation, lost him the support of Togo Shigenori, whose resignation signified the resentment of the Foreign Ministry over this loss of departmental clout. The army regarded Foreign Ministry officials as dangerously liberal (though this was hardly true of the faction of reformist officials, the Kakushinha, who had caused so much trouble within the Gaimusho). And in his own service Tojo was junior, for example, to General Count Terauchi Hisaichi, who was in command of all armies in the southern region of operations; to General Hata Shunroku, commander of the Expeditionary Army in China; and to General Sugiyama Hajime, the army Chief of Staff. All three were soon to be promoted Field Marshal, a rank never attained by Tojo. His Navy Minister, Admiral Shimada Shigetaro, was unpopular with his own service contemporaries, because he seemed willing to subordinate the navy's interests and requirements to those of the army, and to treat Tojo with excessive respect.

Tojo was vulnerable to criticism at a certain level. There was no praetorian guard devoted to him personally, no figure with the equivalent of Himmler's mastery of domestic terror. The suppression of isolated or uninfluential individuals or groups could not eliminate the expression of dissatisfaction among sophisticated and securely privileged officials and politicians, still less in court circles. In 1943 such criticism was becoming widespread, at that level. The close censorship of news about the progress of the war itself merely enabled critics to enlist rumour on their side.

1943 was the year in which the fortunes of the Axis partners gradually declined beyond recovery. After Stalingrad, the Germans faced a sustained Soviet Russian counter-offensive. Expelled from North Africa, and then from Sicily, they were forced on to the defensive in the West, also. In July, Mussolini fell, and Badoglio asked for an armistice for Italy early in September. The bombing offensive against Germany was stepped up, while Allied losses at sea fell away, as the menace of the U-boats was gradually mastered.

In the Pacific, Japanese losses to submarine attack rose sharply in 1943, greatly reducing below expectations the value of access to the raw materials of South-East Asia. In the south and south-west Pacific, the United States and Australian forces made headway against Japanese resistance, invariably of the most determined quality, both in the Solomons and in New Guinea. On 18 April Admiral Yamamoto was killed while on a tour of inspection, his aircraft being shot down over Bougainville following the interception by radio and cryptography of a message giving details of his programme and route. His prestige was such that the news of his death, when later released, was felt as a heavy blow. In May the Japanese garrison on Attu, in the Aleutians, was destroyed, and became famous as the exemplar of heroic defence, to be followed over and over again. By the late autumn, United States forces had assaulted New Georgia and Bougainville in the Solomons, and Tarawa in the Gilberts. The same amphibious techniques which had been developed in operations against the smaller islands by the combined Australian, New Zealand and United States forces, of all three services, were used in the advance along the northern coast of New Guinea to isolate the base at Wewak of General Adachi's XVIII Army.

In the summer and autumn of 1943 a degree of independence was conferred on regimes established in the Philippines and Burma, but subject to restrictions, indeed to Japanese authority, for the duration of the war at least. In November the Great East Asia Conference was held in Tokyo, with ceremony. Leaders from throughout the Co-Prosperity Sphere subscribed to a declaration in support of Japan's war aims; but they could already see, more clearly than their hosts, that all was not well.

By early 1944 Japanese Imperial Headquarters had decided that a contracted perimeter should be defended, running from Timor by way of western New Guinea to Truk and the Marianas. This was unrealistic, as their hold on New Guinea was already looking untenable; and by February 1944 their heavy losses, especially at Kwajalein in the Marshalls, indicated that the increasing weight of American and Allied assault capability was irresistible when thrown against any single island fortress. A decisive fleet action was the only possible means of holding back the tide of Allied recovery.

In 1943 the Japanese planned major offensives to take place in 1944, both in China and from Burma into Assam. A British and Indian offensive in the Arakan in 1943 had been turned back, at and around Donbaik, by Lieutenant-General Koga's 55th Division. But the first deep raid into Burma by Major-General Wingate's Long Range Penetration Group (the Chindits) influenced the Japanese to attempt to resume the offensive themselves in 1944. This led to the repulse of General Mutaguchi Renya's XV Army from Imphal, with the loss of half its strength; and to the further disasters in Burma, where the Japanese Army received its largest single defeat, General Kurabe's command incurring casualties of over 100,000 men in all, in the final campaign of 1944–45.

The Japanese Ichigo (No. 1) offensive in China in 1944 was successful in its primary objective of gaining control of a number of airfields of great significance to the United States' ability to support Chiang Kai-shek. But Hata's armies, with a total strength still of well over 600,000 men, could not contrive to bring either the Nationalists or the Chinese Communists to a decisive battle. From late 1944, developments in the Pacific rendered Hata's further plans of marginal significance, though his campaigns had greatly weakened the future prospects of Chiang and of the Kuomintang. In order to bring about this limited success, and to improve the general co-ordination of the war effort, Tojo had created a Ministry of Munitions in late 1943, which he at first supervised himself, with Kishi as Vice-Minister. He also sought to streamline the structure of command by taking over as Chief of Army Staff himself, and having Admiral Shimada similarly combine the post of Navy Minister with that of Chief of Naval Staff. This led Sugiyama, ousted by his junior in the service, to denounce Tojo to the Emperor, as a would-be dictator. Tojo was also under attack by Admiral Okada, and members of Konoye's circle, including Yoshida Shigeru and Shigemitsu Mamoru (the last two pre-war ambassadors in London), were known to be hostile to his continuing in office.

In July 1944 the so-called Zone of Absolute National Defence was penetrated in the Marianas, with the fall of Saipan after a desperate resistance. For Tokyo, increasingly remote from the wider conflict, this was a more ominous setback than the fall of Rome or the Allied invasion of Normandy, which had both taken place in the previous month. The seriousness of the loss of Saipan could be neither ignored nor concealed. The breach of the defensive perimeter and its implications for the future vulnerability of Japan to attack from the air amounted to a disaster, recognizable as such by all those closely involved in the direction of the war effort. It led straight to Tojo's resignation, his attempts to regain confidence by making changes in his team having been frustrated as a result of the Lord Keeper's determination that he should go, combined with the recalcitrance of some of his colleagues, including Kishi.

Tojo retained the dignity of his political rank, and was consulted, along with the other former prime ministers (Jushin) until the end of the war. He was replaced as War Minister by Sugiyama, and as Prime Minister by General Koiso Kuniaki, who had been Governor-General of Korea since May 1942 and who was assisted in forming his cabinet by Admiral Yonai. From rather different points of view (Koiso had been a member of the nationalistic Kokuhonsha, while Yonai had been for co-operation with the Anglo-Saxon Powers) both understood why much influential opinion in Tokyo was now in favour of seeking a compromise on the basis of which the war could be ended. The military, however, remained adamant that any such move must await the achievement of one decisive victory.

MacArthur was pressing forward steadily in the south and Nimitz in the central Pacific. Even if the disasters impending in Burma could be kept from view, it was apparent that successive island garrisons much nearer home were being destroyed or cut off, ineluctably. Losses of shipping by submarine attack were nullifying the advantages of high productivity in the manufacturing industries, and especially in the production of munitions and armaments, and were threatening the fuel and food supplies on which civil and military efforts alike depended. In August 1944 Admiral Nagumo perished, and Guam fell. In October the Imperial Navy, once again seeking decisive victory in a fleet action, suffered devastating defeat in the battle of Leyte Gulf, losing not only 10 cruisers, 4 carriers and 3 battleships, including the majestic 64,000-ton *Musashi*, but also no fewer than 346 planes, ten times the American losses in the air battle. General Yamashita's Fourteenth Area armies now fought a defensive campaign in the Philippines. Manila fell in March 1945, as did the island fortress of Iwojima. The United States Air Force's bomber aircraft were now based no further away than the Bonins, the group of islands nearest, in the south, to Tokyo itself. The raid of the B29s of 9 March 1945, on Tokyo, in which 300 of these superfortresses dropped some seven tons of incendiary bombs each, into a wind strong enough to create a firestorm of great areas of the city, was by far the most destructive bombardment in history. In the same season, 66 of Japan's cities were very heavily attacked from the air. On 1 April the Americans assaulted Okinawa, the US Navy suffering severely here from the deliberately suicidal attacks of the kamikaze pilots (to which the steel reinforcement of their decks made the carriers of the Royal Navy much less vulnerable).

The situation was now manifestly desperate for Japan. But Koiso could find no escape from it. He was succeeded early in April by old Admiral Suzuki Kantaro, who was personally close to the Emperor. It was generally presumed that he was intent upon bringing the war to a conclusion, but he seems to have persisted in the belief that an honourable conclusion would be

131

attained only if the Japanese succeeded, as the result of a last, great defensive battle, now inevitably on land, in procuring some modification in the terms of unconditional surrender demanded by the Allies, such as would at least ensure the continuance of the imperial dynasty. Certainly, that was still the belief of most of those who spoke for the armed services, and it remained so to the end. There was now, in some quarters in Tokyo, a growing dread of revolution; and Konoye was arguing that this was more greatly to be feared than defeat itself. Some of his political circle, including Yoshida Shigeru, were arrested for a time on account of their association with such views. Togo, who was once more Foreign Minister, in charge of the occupied territories as well as of Japan's international relations as a whole, thought it necessary to work towards a negotiated peace. Suzuki, contrary to the advice of Sato Naotake from the embassy in Moscow, insisted on exploring Soviet Russia's willingness to mediate, unaware that Stalin had already undertaken at Yalta to come into the war against Japan.

Finally, Suzuki's failing judgement led him to announce that the Japanese government would ignore the Allied declaration made at Potsdam on 26 July, which stated that for Japan the alternative to surrender was 'prompt and utter destruction'. Atomic bombs were dropped on Hiroshima on 6 August and on Nagasaki three days later. On 8 August, the Russians declared war, and much of what was left of the Kwantung Army scrambled back, leaving many thousand civilians to face captivity. On 14 August the Emperor led the government to accept surrender, and, after a night during which mutiny was narrowly defeated, in and around the grounds of the palace itself, his announcement of that decision was broadcast to the nation. Emissaries closely connected with the Emperor were sent out to all fronts, to ensure compliance in the field. On 17 August Prince Higashikuni was appointed Prime Minister, with a mandate to oversee the surrender proceedings, and, after detailed negotiation of the modalities, the instrument of surrender was signed on board USS *Missouri* in Tokyo Bay, on 2 September.

Pretty well the entire able-bodied, adult civilian population of Japan had been enrolled in the People's Volunteer Fighting Corps (*Kokumin Giyutai*) during the closing months of the war. This facilitated the maintenance of law and order during the tense period surrounding the surrender. The Japanese Army still had 5.5 million men under arms, and the Imperial Navy more than 1.5 million. Though provisions of every kind were in critically short supply, there could have been the most formidable resistance, in a last defensive struggle, as the Allies were well aware. Once the Emperor's message had been absorbed, however, acceptance of its authority was evidently assured. Some Japanese troops were actively employed for a time on internal security duties in both French Indo-China and the Netherlands East Indies. In China, some units even operated briefly in support of the Nationalist forces against the communist People's Liberation Army. But all were soon disarmed and demobilized. In the months immediately following the surrender, shipping had to be found for the repatriation from all occupied territories, and from the former colonies, of all Japanese nationals stationed or domiciled overseas, some 6 million in all, of whom about half were civilians.

They were brought back to a desolated country, in which food and shelter were already hopelessly inadequate, especially for its huge urban communities. Almost all the people in the cities, and many of those evacuated to rural provinces, were suffering from malnutrition. Many were dazed and disoriented. The end of the war seemed like the aftermath of a series of natural disasters of unprecedented ferocity. It was as though earthquakes, tidal waves, typhoons, fire and flood had swept across the entire country, and much of the known world. On top of this sensation, some knowledge of the effects of the atomic bombardment of Hiroshima and Nagasaki was gradually disseminated, together with much rumour and anxious speculation.

General MacArthur's instructions, as Supreme Commander for the Allied Powers (SCAP), were to ensure that Japan would never again pose a threat to international security; and that responsible and peaceful government was introduced at every level in Japanese society. Allied policy was in principle co-ordinated in the Far Eastern Commission in Washington; while in Tokyo the advice of the Allied Council for Japan was available to SCAP. In practice, the presence of Soviet Russian representatives handicapped both these bodies from the start, so that consultation between the Allies was largely conducted informally in Washington. MacArthur, though he never enjoyed the full confidence of President Truman at the personal level, was clearly seen to have wide scope for independent judgement and decision, in pursuit of the twin objectives of demilitarization and democratization, especially during the first eighteen months or so of the Occupation. During that period, though Allied difficulties with the Soviet Union steadily increased, furtherance of the ideals set out in the Charter of the United Nations was not yet wholly frustrated by the exigences of the cold war.

It was assumed in Washington's post-war policy-making that Japan's economy would in due course reassert its own viability, but the active promotion of economic recovery within Japan was given a low priority. Among pressures for the modification of policy, which soon built up from various causes, was the early realization that merely to keep the Japanese people from starvation, in the country's condition of complete destitution, would cost the United States $400 million a year, a huge subsidy at values then current. While plans for the destruction of weapons and of plants exclusively for their production went ahead immediately, the original intention of destroying heavy industrial capacity in general was seen to require further consideration. It would be a rash undertaking so long as the preservation of law and order among the mass of the population was itself liable to prove difficult to achieve. By the time that the Pawley Report came to be written, in 1946, the idea of removing heavy industrial plant from Japan in order to meet the requirement for reparations in countries previously occupied by the Japanese forces was beginning to look unrealistic. Circumstances were changing very rapidly for the wartime Allies, both within Japan and throughout East and South-East Asia.

First, the assumption that Chiang Kai-shek's Nationalist China would be the bulwark of peace and stability in Asia was open to question almost as soon as the Pacific war itself was over, though massive assistance from the United States served to conceal for some time, from the view of those who authorized it, the extent to which incompetence and corruption were undermining the Nationalist cause. Secondly, the Soviet Union's actions and attitudes in East Asia gave rise to concern in Washington long before the cold war as a whole was generally perceived to be dominating international affairs. As early as December 1945, the United States found it necessary to have the question of Korea placed on the agenda of the Council of Foreign Ministers, for their meeting in Moscow, following the inability of the Soviet commander in the field to respond to General Hodge's proposals for the unification of the Korean economy and administration.

Thirdly, there was the rapid development of domestic social and political affairs in Japan itself, and the interaction between this development and the worldwide influence and infiltration of communist ideology and Soviet subversion. The discrediting of Japan's pre-war and wartime leadership, taken together with trends apparent in the outside world, gave a strong boost to the left in Japan; and the granting of freedom for the formation of new political parties was naturally one of the earliest measures taken by SCAP, in the interests of Japan's democracy. There was as it were a competition for public attention at this time between the explosive demolition of an edifice of unwanted controls and the patient reconstruction of liberal foundations. All political prisoners were set free in September 1946. At the same time, a degree of press freedom was established which was almost absolute in respect of Japanese government authority (as opposed to that of SCAP itself). Legislation was in preparation, and came into force in the Trade Union Law of December 1945, which gave workers the right to join trade unions and to bargain collectively through them with employers about pay and conditions. Above all, the Constitution itself was known to be under review, together with the entire systems of education, the ownership of land, and the concentration of business interests.

Finally, there was a disturbing uncertainty about questions of responsibility and retribution for pre-war and wartime errors and crimes. Prince Higashikuni's cabinet, though its purpose was to accommodate Allied policy, included some members, even such as Ogata Taketora and Prince Konoye himself, whose records or associations were bound to be regarded as equivocal, or suspect, by SCAP. In addition, there were early difficulties over the release of political prisoners and the repeal of the Peace Preservation Law; and Higashikuni was obliged to resign in October 1945, by which time it was clear that some of his ministerial colleagues would be proceeded against by SCAP or 'another of the United Nations'. One or two of them survived in office, to serve under Shidehara in the next administration, notably Yoshida Shigeru, who had succeeded Shigemitsu as Foreign Minister in September. He had played a major role from the very initiation of SCAP's authority, by virtue of his own character and record and of his grasp of the work of the Central Liaison Office, the organ through which senior Japanese civil servants conducted the business of government, in consultation with or in pursuance of directives received from SCAP. It was Yoshida, more than any other person or interest, who was to give this key organization its philosophy, and thus to influence the outcome of the original Allied decision that SCAP should have the necessary reforms carried out through the existing Japanese machinery of government. In the circumstances, this meant primarily through the bureaucracy. Yoshida combined a mastery of bureaucratic technique with a certain aristocratic detachment. He was experienced, and very tough, but also deeply cultivated; conservative, but also pragmatic and constructive. He brought to the handling of the wholly new problems of post-war Japan the same spirit as that which had animated the outstanding leaders of the Meiji period, such as Ito Hirobumi. Above all, he believed in his countrymen's capacity for recovery.

In particular, it was Yoshida's view that national recovery would be promoted most effectively if Japan's leading, established industrial and commercial enterprises were given a free hand. He rejected the widespread view that the zaibatsu groups had given zealous support to the pre-war ambitions of the militarists and expansionists. There was discussion in SCAP of a programme of antitrust legislation which would lead to the permanent dismantling of these groups. In an attempt to forestall the threat of damaging interference, the Yasuda plan was put forward from the Japanese side as early as October 1945, based on the presumption that the importance of free market operations would be accepted by an occupation regime whose instructions came from the country in which, for all the achievements of the New Deal, the virtues of a capitalist system were best understood. The issue remained unresolved. Measures adopted in April 1946, with a view to liquidating the holding companies at the centre of each of the zaibatsu groups, did not destroy their cohesion.

In the New Year of 1946, the formal exclusion from public office of all who were deemed to have given their support to, or been associated *ex officio* with, policies of war was enacted in the first and most drastic of SCAP's 'purges'. The politicians were most severely affected (the military themselves having been disbanded separately); only about one in ten members of the lower House remained free to pursue their public activities. The ban, which affected some 200,000 persons, was extended to cover local government and economic and cultural circles in November 1946.

Meanwhile, many of those directly accused of war crimes had been brought before courts martial, both in Yokohama and overseas in formerly occupied territories. Hundreds had been found guilty on capital charges, and executed; thousands were sentenced to varying terms of imprisonment. In late 1945 preparations were made for the hearing of charges of major war crimes by the International Military Tribunal for the Far East, a court composed of judicial representatives of those Allied countries which had subscribed to the terms of Japan's surrender. Its proceedings were to last from May 1946 until November 1948, 28 individuals being arraigned as Class A war criminals. At the outset, public reaction in Japan to these proceedings was resigned or muted. Prince Konoye, on learning, in December 1945, that he was to be arrested and indicted as a major war criminal, took his own life.

In these circumstances, renewed political activity was at first more lively than effective. It was known that the House of Peers, like the peerage itself, would not survive the promulgation of the projected new Constitution. The lower House had been almost purged away. But early elections were to be expected, if only because Shidehara's government lacked democratic validity. New parties proliferated on the left; and the return of Nosaka Sanzo, who enjoyed a considerable personal following, after years of work with the Comintern in Moscow and with the Chinese Communists in Yenan, gave a particular fillip to the revival of the Japan Communist Party (JCP). The Japan Socialist Party, founded in November 1945, was led by pre-war social democrats such as Nishio Suehiro and Katayama Tetsu. The principal conservative parties, having their roots in the Seiyukai and the Minseito respectively, were the Liberals (Jiyuto), led by Hatoyama Ichiro, and the Progressives (Shimpoto). There was also a centre-right Cooperative Party (Kyodoto).

In January 1946, the Emperor formally renounced his divinity. The Japanese committee charged by SCAP with formulating proposals for a revised Constitution, however, favoured the retention of untrammelled imperial sovereignty. In the text eventually adopted – which was presented to both Houses of the Diet in accordance with the provisions of its predecessor, the Meiji Constitution, and promulgated by the Emperor in November 1946, to take effect on 3 May 1947 – the Emperor himself became 'the symbol of the State and of the unity of the people, deriving his position from the will of the people with whom resides sovereign power'. The second principle of the Constitution was pacifism: the people's desire for peace having been set out in the preamble, the people renounced war as a sovereign right of the nation, and the threat or use of force to settle international

disputes, in Article 9. This was soon interpreted as permitting the maintenance of sufficient forces to sustain the right of self-defence, although such
an interpretation was not acceptable to the parties of the left.

Human rights including equality under the law, and the freedoms of
thought and conscience, religion, assembly and speech, were established;
universal adult suffrage meant votes for women, the voting age being
reduced also, to twenty; and provision was made for the separation of
powers as between the legislative, executive and judicial branches of government. The Diet was made the highest organ of the state, and the Cabinet
became responsible to it. Both Houses were to be elected by popular vote.

Many of the provisions of the new Constitution, adopted under the aegis
of SCAP's Government Section, posed difficulties for the Japanese government, including those covering the Emperor's position. In conservative
circles, there was much opposition to certain changes, and to their 'foreign'
character. Yoshida himself always maintained that the Meiji Constitution
had been fundamentally democratic. The State Minister responsible for the
handling of the constitutional issue was hard put to it to argue that the
concept of the *kokutai* stood unaltered; but he did so. On the political left,
though there were strong demands for more revolutionary change, there
was also a tendency to look upon the new text as a gift for whose preservation the supporters of democratic ideals might well have to fight in the
future.

Elections were held in April 1946, still under the Meiji Constitution, but
under a revised Election Law providing votes for women, and the lower
voting age, in large, multi-member constituencies; and it appeared that
Hatoyama had emerged victorious, to lead a conservative, coalition government, supported by Liberals and Progressives. Before he could form his
cabinet, however, Hatoyama was purged by SCAP, and obliged to hand
over the party leadership and the premiership to Yoshida.

It was a tumultuous and dangerous time, when the administration was
both exposed to threats against public order and required to carry out an
exceptionally heavy legislative programme. Within the newly flourishing
labour movement, there was a vociferous demand for 'workers' control of
production'. Managers of major concerns were locked into their offices, in
attempts to force concessions from them. There were threats of a general
strike, and MacArthur had to lay it down that no strikes would be tolerated
which were injurious to the objects of SCAP. In May, while Yoshida was
still in the process of forming his first cabinet; in August 1946; and again in
the following February, there was some doubt whether it would prove
possible for the civil power to maintain law and order unaided. Yoshida
himself was inclined to the view that revolution was but narrowly averted.
He stood firm, and remained cool, but he was conscious that his resources
were slender. The modest police force was at full stretch, but it was recog-

nized that any widespread deployment of the army of occupation in support of the police might have served only to provoke a further deterioration of social discipline.

Although there was great scope for revolutionaries, and able revolutionaries such as Nosaka and Tokuda of the JCP were at work, there was also among the mass of industrial workers a recognition that productive employment would give them the best prospect of security and their country the best hope of recovery. Managers might be locked into their offices, but what they had to say was not ignored. It was gradually conceded that adequate wages could come only from adequate levels of production, and rising wages only from rising productivity. Some of the deals struck between management and labour during the early years of the Occupation proved to be of permanent value. The two main nationwide labour organizations at this stage, between them comprehending about 40 per cent of the entire industrial labour force by the end of 1946, were Sodomei, a federation of moderate unions, and Sanbetsu Kaigi, which was dominated by the communists. At corporate level, there was evidence early in the post-war period that the company union in Japan is often not the tame 'house union' of folklore. It often embodies a tradition of robust and challenging partnership with management, born in the years of greatest hardship. These years also saw the beginnings of production by some of the most technologically innovative corporations of post-war Japan, such as Sony and Honda. They saw the revival of pre-war relationships between major established Japanese companies and their Western, especially their United States, counterparts. Occupation policy was watched closely by guardians of the interests of private enterprise. In such matters, when it came to resisting what might be regarded as excessively interventionist occupation policies, Yoshida had friends across the Pacific.

Agriculture was a less controversial sector than manufacturing industry. Moreover, major changes in the structure of the rural economy had been under discussion since before the war, and had been initiated during the war. Rents had then been subject to control. More significantly, a dual price system had benefited the owner-farmer, as opposed to the landlord, and had given the latter an incentive to sell to his tenants, with the result that the proportion of arable land held by tenant-farmers had already fallen sharply from pre-war levels, before the Occupation reforms were devised. These reforms were, however, instrumental in accelerating and consolidating the trend already in operation. The Land Reform Law, passed in October 1946, was rightly regarded as one of the most far-reaching and valuable of the measures taken during the Occupation. Land was purchased compulsorily by the government both from absentee landlords and from all landlords and tenants who held more than a few acres, and sold to existing smaller tenants, at the same price. This bore hardly on landlords, whose terms of compensation were punitive. They were given low prices for their land, at a time when food prices were high and the rate of inflation was rising rapidly. The achievement of the reform, however, was to put 90 per cent of all cultivated land, as opposed to forest land, into the hands of owner-farmers. It also reduced the sense of social dependence in the countryside, and the tensions which had given rise to so much unrest in the past.

Yoshida's surprising choice as Minister of Agriculture and Forestry of the left-wing socialist, and former bureaucrat, Wada Hiroo, did not last beyond January 1947; but it was arguably more successful than that of Ishibashi Tanzan as Finance Minister. It was the high rate of inflation which probably contributed more than any other factor to the success of the Japan Socialist Party. It gained 143 seats in the lower House, compared with the Liberals' 133, in the general elections of April 1947. But there was also widespread indignation against the Liberals and Democrats (as the former Progressives were now known) on account of their having forced through the House a further revised Election Law, which brought back the constituency system favoured by the conservative parties in the pre-war period.

The Democrats, however, led by Ashida Hitoshi, did succeed in winning 126 seats in these 1947 elections. Ashida agreed to join the Cabinet as Foreign Minister, under the premiership of Katayama Tetsu, the Christian leader of the Japan Socialist Party, whose coalition government also embraced the Co-operative Party (Kyodoto). Katayama's cabinet brought in legislation enabling the new Constitution to come into effect, with all its far-reaching consequences, including not only the transfer of power and the grant of guaranteed rights to the people, but also the extension of democratic electoral procedures throughout local government, and the establishment of a high degree of autonomy at prefectural level.

Under some pressure from SCAP, the flow of social legislation was constantly maintained. The Labour Standards Law, enacted in the spring and effective from the autumn of 1947, gave some assurance to the labour movement that reasonable aspirations were recognized. Large enterprises were generally prepared to implement its provisions conscientiously, but its application could never be supervised effectively in the many areas in which cottage industry remained significant.

In 1947 also, the treasured Imperial Rescript on Education of 1890 was superseded by a new Basic Law on Education, which reflected the liberal principles of the new Constitution and governed the adoption of a unitary school system closely based on that followed in the United States. It was a truly radical reform, involving not only the extension of compulsory education from six to nine years, but also the wholesale reorganization of educational administration and of the school curriculum. The Basic Law, popularly known as the 'education constitution', has an idealistic preamble in which an international outlook is assumed, while reference is also made to the dignity of the individual. The aims of education are stated to include the contribution to human welfare, the full development of the personality, the love of truth and justice, and the building of a peaceful state and society. There is a commitment to academic freedom, equal opportunity and coeducation. The parallel School Education Law, also of 1947, guarantees free primary (six years) and middle-school (three years) education to all Japanese citizens. Three-year high schools and four-year universities are then available, with additional options, including courses at technical colleges. More universities were to be established, and the operation of the system would be controlled largely by locally elected boards of education. The omission of the teaching of ethics (an instrument widely considered to have been misused in the pre-war system) was criticized by Yoshida and by most of those on his political right, and there was later to be movement towards closer central control of education. But, at the time, grumbles about Americanization were as far as most critics were prepared to go. Education was too important to be allowed to suffer from avoidable controversy or obstruction.

Towards the end of 1947 Katayama's government also introduced the Economic Deconcentration Law, the long-awaited outcome of intensive discussions within SCAP, and consultations with Japanese officials. Intended originally as the decisive antitrust instrument, which would finally ensure the break-up of the zaibatsu groups, by the time this measure was enacted its character and purpose had become highly controversial in terms of occupation policy. There were increasing doubts among conservative legislators and industrialists in the United States about the desirability and wisdom of intervention on such a scale in the structure and conduct of private enterprise in Japan. Industrial production in Japan was running at no more than one-third of the level attained in the early 1930s. To risk depressing it still further was likely to be of advantage neither to the United States and the Allies nor to those countries of Asia which were counting upon substantial reparations from Japan. The law was never rigorously enforced, and its main provisions were allowed to fall quietly into abeyance.

Changes in the climate of opinion in which SCAP operated were now accelerating. As early as March 1947 General MacArthur himself had announced the intention of working towards the conclusion of a full treaty of peace with Japan. In the summer, Dean Acheson, as Secretary of State, began to canvass international support for the convening of a peace conference, meeting objections in China and from the Soviet Union, but finding encouragement and co-operation in Britain and the Commonwealth. Disillusionment with the prospects for effective government in China, despite General Marshall's prolonged efforts to bring about improvement, was leading Washington to look ever more purposefully towards Japan as the necessary base from which to promote and pursue reconstruction in

Asia, and resistance to communist subversion and to the spread of Soviet influence.

The evolution of cold war politics, publicly acknowledged as such from the time of Churchill's Iron Curtain speech at Fulton, in March 1946, gave an impetus to the views of the Intelligence Section (G2) of SCAP, whose concern with the threat of communism now balanced that of the Government Section in respect of the democratic framework of Japanese domestic affairs. Various elements, both political and economic, influenced the adoption of what came to be known as the 'reverse course' in occupation policy, a process of adjustment easily made to look capricious but which represented essentially a pragmatic reaction to the tactics of the Kremlin and the Cominform. The Strike and Johnston Reports of 1948 both powerfully advocated promotion of the economic recovery of Japan. They had influence not only in Washington but also, in the latter case, with Chiang Kai-shek. In the autumn of 1948, the British Foreign Secretary, Ernest Bevin, spoke at the British Labour Party Conference in favour of an early Japanese peace conference.

The changes in the international environment facilitated the achievement by the Katayama cabinet of the first post-war trade agreements, with the Netherlands, Britain and some other Commonwealth governments. But the left wing of the JSP, led by Suzuki Mosaburo, refused to co-operate with various moderate economic and budgetary proposals put forward on behalf of the government whose formation they had supported, in particular resisting any idea of control over wage levels. With violence threatening from the equally radical left wing of the organized labour movement, and amid strong public criticism of widespread black market operations, and of spectacular but questionable dealings in the disposal of supplies originating from wartime stockpiles (for which it was not suggested that he had any share of direct responsibility), Katayama resigned in February 1948. The House of Councillors wanted Yoshida to take his place as Prime Minister, but precedence was correctly accorded to the view of the House of Representatives that Ashida Hitoshi should do so, as the alternative leader of the existing coalition of parties of the centre and left.

Ashida himself was a robust opponent of communism. But his willingness to associate closely with the socialists strained the loyalty of his more conservative supporters. At the same time, it was never likely that the Socialist Party would perform harmoniously under his baton. As it was, Ashida found himself required by directives from SCAP to remove from the public and government services' trade unions not only the right to strike but also even the right to collective bargaining over wages and conditions of employment. By this time, some 50 per cent of all industrial workers throughout Japan were members of trade unions, and their unions were almost all affiliated to one or other of the two principal federations. Considerable discord and disturbance was aroused by the spectacle of a government which enjoyed support from parties of the left nevertheless being prepared to impose constraints on the union movement. It was, however, not this but a scandal over 'recovery funds' allegedly granted corruptly by government ministers to the Showa Denko Company which brought about the fall of Ashida's government, in October 1948. Nishio Suehiro, the right-wing Socialist who had been Ashida's deputy, was among the first to be arrested, and Ashida himself was arrested briefly, after his resignation. Both men were eventually acquitted on all the charges brought against them. Nishio recovered his position of leadership of moderate socialism, but the Showa Denko scandal damaged the JSP. Ashida's party, on the other hand, was always destined to be absorbed into the mainstream of Japanese conservatism.

This was already strengthening, and, although he now had to resume office in unfavourable circumstances, Yoshida seized the opportunity to consolidate its course. In December he was in receipt of a memorandum from SCAP which called for measures of retrenchment in the economy, likely to prove unpopular, but intended to facilitate recovery not only of the economy itself but of economic independence.

This memorandum set out the main points of what came to be known as the Dodge Plan, after the appointment of the American banker Joseph Dodge as special adviser on Japanese economic policy, from early 1949. These were points, aiming at a strictly disinflationary programme, and balanced budgets, which SCAP had been urging on the Japanese Economic Stabilization Board since the summer of 1948. The application of this programme was bound to cause greatly increased unemployment and hardship. The necessity for action on these lines was difficult to dispute, but the prospect, in the distressed conditions of post-war Japan, was gloomy and oppressive.

The International Military Tribunal for the Far East, after proceedings which had lasted more than two and a half years, announced its verdicts in November 1948, and the sentences of death passed on seven of the defendants were carried out in the following month. The reactions in Japanese society were not uniform in character, but they were uniformly subdued. Many people were still deeply preoccupied with the problems of their own survival, and that of their families.

In the confused and depressing winter of 1948, Yoshida's caretaker government could not expect to enjoy the confidence of a majority in the lower House. But in the campaign leading up to the elections of January 1949, Yoshida and his closest associates spoke up with conviction for the ending of socialist controls and of state ownership. They called, for example, for the privatization of the coal-mining industry. Their victory, essentially a triumph for the conservative right, was balanced by a sharp increase in support for the extreme left, the moderate left suffering proportionately from this apparent polarization of opinion. Yoshida's newly combined Democratic Liberal Party won a clear majority of 264 out of the 466 seats contested for membership in the House of Representatives, the Socialists falling from 143 to 48, while the JCP won 35 seats where they had held only 4 in the previous session. The Democratic Party went down from 121 seats to 69.

Yoshida saw to it that his successful supporters included experienced bureaucrats, such as, most notably, Sato Eisaku and Ikeda Hayato, and was enabled to strengthen his third cabinet in consequence. Ikeda, who had been the senior official in the Ministry of Finance, was sent straight back there as Minister, and took charge of the crucial programme of economic stabilization.

The severity of the Dodge line, now followed in the Japanese government's economic policy, may be judged by its having entailed, among its consequences, the dismissal of one in every four of those employed in the government service itself. The general effect on employment was to weaken the position of the national federations of trade unions and, at corporate level, to strengthen that of management. The policy of retrenchment also led to the intensification of constructive co-operation between government (at the political level and at official level, through the bureaucracy) and industry, the latter acting increasingly through the Federation of Economic Organizations (Keidanren), both partners being anxious to promote the earliest possible recovery. The formation in 1949 of the Ministry of International Trade and Industry (MITI) gave effective expression to the determination of the government, and especially of Yoshida himself, to play a full part in the development of a positive relationship with industry, and to build up Japan's export performance. This was the period in which the technique of extending administrative guidance to industry was adopted by the government departments concerned, as a way of avoiding conflict between the efficient deployment of resources and the provisions of antitrust legislation.

Although the bargaining power of Japanese labour had been weakened, moderate unionists were making efforts to reduce the influence of political troublemakers within their own organizations. Violence and subversion from the extreme left were also giving continuous, serious concern to the Japanese government and to SCAP. A number of incidents in 1949 deepened this concern. The 'Red Purge' which began in 1949 and gathered momentum in 1950 was partly a spontaneous Japanese reaction to a perceived threat to national security, and partly imposed by SCAP.

By 1949, the need to contain and counter the spread of communist ideology and of Soviet power and influence was preoccupying Western governments. The establishment of NATO was evidence of their growing will to mobilize resources for the construction of a new system of collective security. The coming to power in Peking of the government of the People's Republic of China (PRC) under Mao Tse-tung (Mao Zedong), though viewed by many experts as a development with potentially hopeful aspects, added further significance to the responsibilities of the United States and the Allies in and towards Japan, and to strategic decisions affecting East Asia more generally.

The United States' military aid programme for the Republic of Korea was in the early stages of implementation, and American forces, apart from a Military Advisory Group of 500 officers and men, had been withdrawn from Korea (as, apparently had Soviet forces, though the United Nations Commission on Korea was never permitted to verify this) when the North Koreans launched their unexpected attack in June 1950. The political and strategic importance to Japan of the Korean War was as plain as was Japan's incapacity to bring direct influence to bear on the conduct or course of operations. In terms of supply, logistics and communications, however, Japan was a key factor in determining the strategy of the United States and their allies in the UN Command (UNC), and the facilities available in Japan were indispensable to its success. In return for the use of these facilities, the war brought to Japanese industry procurement orders on a large scale, which were crucial to the much-needed acceleration of recovery throughout the country's economy.

The outbreak of the Korean War led Washington to stimulate serious negotiations, in consultations with the Allies conducted primarily by John Foster Dulles, for a peace treaty with Japan. There were intensive negotiations for about a year, from the beginning of the UN General Assembly in the summer of 1950. The Soviet government was among those consulted. Meanwhile, the communist Chinese intervened in Korea, General MacArthur was dismissed by President Truman, to the astonishment of the Japanese public, and bitter fighting continued long after the opening of armistice talks in the summer of 1951. By this time, the United States had circulated a draft treaty of peace with Japan, in early 1951, to which the United Kingdom responded with a paper based on the results of meetings held by the Commonwealth countries concerned. A third text, combining these two drafts, was produced in July 1951, following which the US and British governments jointly sponsored invitations to a conference to be held at the San Francisco Memorial Opera House in September, to conclude a peace treaty. It was attended by the representatives of fifty-one nations, most of which signed the finished document; but not by those which preferred to make separate arrangements, or were dissatisfied with reparations and, most significantly, not by the Soviet Union, Czechoslovakia or Poland.

By this treaty, which was brought into effect on 28 April 1952, having received the necessary ratifications, the full independence of Japan, consisting of the four main islands, was recovered. Japan accepted that the US might exercise trusteeship over the Bonin and Ryukyu Islands, including Okinawa; recognized the independence of Korea; and renounced all claims to the other territories formerly annexed within the Empire or administered under mandate. Japan formally accepted all obligations set out in the UN Charter, and the Allied Powers confirmed that they would abide by the charter in their relations with Japan. Japan's right of self-defence was recognized, and it was envisaged that Japan might wish to enter voluntarily into international arrangements for collective security. Japan's obligation to pay reparations for suffering and damage caused by it during the Second World War was recorded in the treaty, which, taking account of economic reality, incorporated the suggestion that countries with claims on Japan might arrange to receive consumer goods and industrial equipment from Japan, in return for their own raw materials.

Outside the treaty, arrangements were made by the United States to provide assurances relating to the future security of the Philippines, in a bilateral agreement; and of Australia and New Zealand, in the Anzus Pact. Of more immediate importance, a separate US–Japan Security Treaty was concluded in tandem with the Peace Treaty, which provided for the retention by the United States of the use of base facilities in Japan, and for the continued stationing of American forces there. Later, additional agreements were necessary to cover the status of American forces in Japan, after the resumption of full independence; and of other forces, primarily British and Commonwealth, which remained there in support of the operations of UN Command in Korea. It was relevant to the wider issues of security that Yoshida had already agreed, with some reluctance, at the outbreak of war in Korea, to the formation in Japan of a new National Police Reserve, 75,000 strong, and to an increase in the strength of the Maritime Safety Board.

Major questions left unsettled by the conclusion of the Peace Treaty included all those involving Japan's relations with the communist world. The Soviet Union was outmanoeuvred at San Francisco, over the Peace Treaty, as it had been over the setting up of the UN Command in Korea. Post-war Soviet policy towards Japan had varied from cool to cold. At first unwilling even to admit that, together with nearly 100,000 prisoners of war, they had detained and were holding some hundreds of thousands of Japanese civilians rounded up in Manchuria in 1945, the Russians had repatriated some of these people in 1949, then fallen silent again about the rest. There were problems impending over fishing rights in northern waters. And the legitimacy of the Soviet occupation of the northern islands of Habomai and Shikotan, arguably not properly to be regarded as separate territory from Hokkaido, and Etorofu and Kunashiri, was strongly contested by Japan.

Japan's future relations with China constituted the most complex and difficult of all the sets of problems which had necessarily to be discussed before the conclusion of the Peace Treaty. There was a presumption that Japan would wish to do business with the People's Republic, whose *de facto* authority as the government of China could no longer be doubted. It was tempting to assert that the British example in recognizing Peking should be followed by an independent Japan. On the other hand, some post-war ties had been developed with the Nationalists, and there were prospects of substantial trade with Formosa. The decisive consideration was simply that the United States would make it a condition of the completion of preparations for the San Francisco Peace Treaty Conference that the Japanese Prime Minister should give an undertaking to enter into negotiations for the conclusion of a separate peace treaty with the Nationalist government of Chiang Kai-shek in Formosa. Yoshida signed his famous letter accordingly.

The clarity of Yoshida's perception of Japan's national interests, especially throughout the harsh and joyless period of the Occupation, and of the limits placed on his tenacious pursuit of those interests, later won for him a place of great honour in his country's history. His achievement in working for and securing the resumption of independence in 1952 was uniquely the product of his character and personality. He saw and persuaded others of the possibility of a great national recovery, and of the need to work with the former enemy, up to the limit of the tolerable and the practicable. Co-operation was never more finely tempered with obstruction, nor determination better seasoned with humour and humanity. He was capable of dealing equally shrewdly with General MacArthur as with Tokuda Kyuichi, the Communist leader; and he chose his own advisers with great care. In the final, complex negotiations before the San Francisco Conference, for example, he relied greatly on a few, intimate confidants, notably Ikeda Hayato and Shirasu Jiro. He was also responsible for the selection and promotion of a school of tough administrators who shared his outlook and would keep its pragmatism alive. Several future prime ministers of Japan were indebted to him for early promotion. Among the youngest of the strong team he led to San Francisco was Miyazawa Kiichi, who was to attain the premiership forty years later. Yoshida was not widely popular in his own time, being considered autocratic, but he inspired a certain affectionate regard even among his critics. All those who worked closely with him knew the quality of his leadership.

7

Fevered Politics, Robust Industry, 1952–72

Although the resumption of independence and full national sovereignty in the spring of 1952 was a high point for Japan, it was not one from which people could easily discern a bright or prosperous future. There had been much hasty and patchy reconstruction in devastated city centres, but stretches of utter desolation remained. Many people were still homeless, sleeping rough, under railway viaducts or in the shells of buildings awaiting repair or demolition. Groups of disabled ex-servicemen were still to be seen on the streets, wearing the white kimono of convalescent uniform, holding out battered khaki caps for alms. On May Day 1952, seemingly endless columns of unemployed, long-demobilized, hungry men, near desperation, converged on the plaza in front of the Imperial Palace, in the centre of Tokyo. They were incited by communists and other troublemakers to take violent and revolutionary action. They contented themselves with setting light to a few American vehicles carelessly but conveniently parked beside the moat surrounding the palace, before disbanding sullenly rather than engage in serious hostilities with a strong but nervous police force.

Prime Minister Yoshida had done well to obtain the National Diet's assent to the ratification of his work at San Francisco within two months of his return from the conference, but the mood of the country was grim. He himself, though referring casually in public to 'the excesses of the Occupation' (a turn of phrase typical of his caustic, partly humorous style, and deliberately not specific), was widely regarded as 'pro-American', as having acquiesced too easily in Washington's plans, both for Japan and for security in Asia and militant opposition to communism. The Japanese public was scarcely beginning to understand the nature of the war in Korea, though fought so near to their own country, in the peninsula historically looked upon as the strategic key to the whole region of North-East Asia. The benefits that would accrue from procurement were not yet visible. In domestic affairs, many resented what they considered to be the high-handed arrogance of 'One-Man' Yoshida.

He was the obvious target for attack from the left. But he was also bitterly criticized not only by extreme reactionaries of the right, but also by those conservatives who believed that he should have returned the leadership of his party to Hatoyama Ichiro. The latter had been specially released in the summer of 1951 from the restrictions of the purge (now no longer operative, with the resumption of independence) in the expectation of his resuming a leading position in public life. But, quite apart from the consideration that Yoshida had by now achieved unique personal authority, there were differences of policy between them. In particular, despite his having kept his distance from the excesses of pre-war and wartime leaders, Hatoyama was becoming a principal advocate of the early revision of Article 9 of the 'Peace' Constitution, and was in favour of further modifying various reforms carried out under the Occupation, all of which were moves considered by Yoshida and his supporters to be inappropriate, unwise and impractical. The latter were prepared to go a certain way down the 'reverse course', but they were tacking rather than turning about. The former Democrats, known from early 1952 as the Reform Party (Kaishinto) and led by Shigemitsu Mamoru, represented another focus for conservative factionalism.

The significance of divisions among conservatives was, for the time being at least, much less than that of the rift in the Japan Socialist Party caused towards the end of 1951 by disagreement in reaction to the Security Treaty with the United States. The left wing of the JSP, led by Suzuki Mosaburo and supported by Sohyo, the federation of trade unions formed in the summer of 1950 and now dominant in the labour movement, was opposed to the Peace Treaty itself, as well as to the Security Treaty, and advocated neutrality for Japan. The right wing, under the leadership of Asanuma Inejiro, though rejecting the terms of the Security Treaty with the United States, accepted the Peace Treaty, and believed that Japan should remain aligned with the West. The balance of support within the JSP lay at first with the right wing, but the post-war appeal of pacifism, strengthened by hostility to the development of atomic weapons by the Western Powers and revulsion from the price seemingly demanded for resistance to communism, judging this by the evidence of the Korean War, gradually shifted this balance towards the left.

Despite disaffection among his own crew, on the part of depurged politicians jealous of his achievements and hungry for office, and strong currents of radical hostility on the left, Yoshida held to his course. He negotiated and set up administrative arrangements necessary for the implementation of the Security Treaty with the United States; and agreed, early in 1952, that the National Police Reserve should be converted into a National Security Force, and enlarged to a strength of 110,000. He concluded a peace treaty with Chiang Kai-shek's Nationalists on Formosa, in fulfilment of the undertaking given to Dulles. In order to deal with the threat posed by open adoption of violent tactics by militant communism, he secured the reinforcement of government powers, through the Subversive Activities Law. He was concerned that the revised codes of law and the judiciary's independent place under the Constitution should be firmly established, as they came to be in the hands of the outstanding Chief Justice, Tanaka Kotaro.

Perhaps most significantly of all, a spirit of revival was nurtured in Yoshida's time, inspired and dominated by the new national aim of 'catching up with the West'. The principles of economic stabilization having been established and put into effect under the Dodge Plan, Yoshida concentrated on the promotion of further practical co-operation between the bureaucracy and industry. Key sectors were identified for special attention, both in manufacturing production and in the infrastructure. In the latter, the restoration and improvement of communications, and the development of additional resources of hydro-electric power took precedence. In manufacturing, though the older, established performers such as textiles, with a new stress on synthetic fibres, were not neglected, the strongest emphasis was on iron and steel, engineering and machinery, and chemicals, continuing the prewar trend but with particular concentration on the necessity of producing goods of the highest possible quality. Great impetus was given to recovery by procurement orders for the forces and agencies of the USA and the UN in Korea, which both stimulated production directly, as in their demand for trucks and lorries, and clothing, and also promoted and accelerated the revival of activity in the wider economy as a whole.

Once the economy began to pick up, it became possible to attract investment from the United States. Japanese funds were also used to buy selected technological know-how, again primarily from the United States. These funds had been mobilized through low-interest postal savings and through the commercial banks, with the support of the Industrial Bank of Japan, the Japan Development Bank and other quasi-governmental agencies, and with the understanding of the Bank of Japan, and of the Keidanren. At this stage (and for some time to come) Japanese industry concentrated on the development of advanced products for the market, rather than on basic research for exploitation in the longer term. Outstanding success was achieved by the shipbuilding industry, where techniques of production engineering were introduced which were ahead of any in use elsewhere. The practice was pioneered of designing standard types of functional vessels for sale in series, rather than building to individual specification. One of the leading exponents of this departure from traditional ways was to say that the radical methods of 'flow-assembly' employed in the new shipyards were based on those used in wartime for the mass production of fighter aircraft. The

149

methods used to attain accurate and economical control of quality and stock, however, which became such vital elements in the unprecedented growth of productivity throughout Japanese manufacturing industry, widely admired and later widely emulated, were based on the recommendations of American experts, at this period less highly regarded in their own country. These methods, together with the high gearing of corporate finances, based on the availability of funds at low rates of interest from banks which attached importance to growth prospects rather than to short-term returns, were instrumental in bringing about the 'economic miracle' of post-war Japanese industrial success. If there was an even more indispensable factor in operation, it was the spirit informing the whole endeavour. For the fostering of this spirit, credit must be given to Yoshida and his closest political associates, as well as to the managers, engineers and entrepreneurs, and to the teams of workers who recognized and responded to it.

Yoshida's decision that there should be general elections for the lower House of the Diet in October 1952 was unexpected, but the opposition parties were not caught unprepared. The Liberals' strength fell from 264 to 240 seats, and, although the Reformists made some gains at their expense, the principal beneficiaries were the two wings of the Socialist Party, which together won 111 seats, compared with the 48 won by the then united JSP in January 1949. The JCP, however, collapsed, as perhaps Yoshida had foreseen, owing to the unpopularity of their official adoption of the tactics of violence: they lost all 35 seats held at the dissolution, and made no single compensating gain. A process of polarization had begun, which largely excluded both extremes of the political spectrum, faithfully reflecting the general approach of the Japanese electorate to post-war democratic politics.

After these elections, Yoshida's position in the Diet deteriorated, on account of the sharpening of factional divisions among conservatives rather than of the additions to the opposition properly so designated. At the end of November a motion of no confidence was passed against Ikeda Hayato individually, in his ministerial capacity. Earlier in the autumn, Ikeda, as Minister of Finance, had taken part on Yoshida's behalf in negotiations with senior representatives of the United States administration, on issues of security policy, and he had been frank in public about the unresolved difficulties involved. Yoshida, who continued justifiably to rate his ability highly, had brought Ikeda into his new cabinet as Minister of International Trade and Industry, and Director of the Economic Council Agency. His dismissal detracted from the strength of the Cabinet, and was a blow to Yoshida personally. Although the wider environment was improving, with a clear prospect of an end to the fighting in Korea, Yoshida was forced into a further dissolution of the House of Representatives in the spring of 1953, following a great show of parliamentary indignation over his having aimed a mild but contemptuous swear-word at a member whose interpellation had caused him some irritation. The seats held by Liberals loyal to Yoshida, in the subsequent elections, fell to 199, while dissident former Liberals openly defecting to Hatoyama's now distinct cause took 35. Those won by the Socialists' two wings combined rose to 138.

Yoshida persevered. It might for once be fairer to say, of this highly idiosyncratic statesman, not that he clung to power, but that he stayed where he was because of the strength of his conviction of the country's need for consistency in the further pursuit of what he saw as a policy of plain common sense. The priority attached to economic recovery must not be endangered by adventures which might also prejudice the gradual reassertion of true independence. The national interest, as he and what came to be known as his 'school' interpreted it, required that the maximum of friendly co-operation with the United States be combined with great caution over wide, strategic commitment and over the expansion of Japan's defence capabilities, for political as well as for economic reasons. The maintenance of a firm position against threats of subversion at home must be distinguished clearly from any temptation to prepare for an active role in the strategic containment of communism worldwide. The war in Korea would soon be over, but President Syngman Rhee would never accept that there could be a military role for Japan, even to keep the peace, in the peninsula. Nor was Japan's potential defence capability in the least relevant to the current communist menace in Malaya, Indonesia or Indo-China. It would be more appropriate for Japan to attend to the outstanding questions of reparations, and to build up relations of confidence with governments which wished to be assured that the era of colonialism was truly ended. Equally realistically, there was no place in present circumstances for strategic considerations in the delicate and difficult relationship with Formosa, let alone in planning to deal with mainland China. In the long run, of course, Japan and China would be the principal Powers in East Asia. For the present, to build up Japan's economic strength remained the basic priority for policy, in the foreign just as in the domestic context. For these purposes there was no need to consider revising the Constitution, and it was preferable not to invite the scale of confrontation with the left which any attempt to do that would inevitably provoke.

Eisenhower's election promise to see to it that wars for Asian freedom would in future be fought by Asians had made a deep impression in Japan, and helped to persuade some of the more thoughtful conservatives that it was right to sustain their support for Yoshida. Some ground was, nevertheless, conceded to Washington's persistent urging of a greater Japanese contribution at least towards the security of the Japanese Islands themselves. In 1954, the Self-Defence Force (SDF) assumed a lasting shape, with the establishment of the Defence Agency, under a minister of state, to co-ordinate its activities and control its development. Legislation was passed, largely on the initiative of Shigemitsu and Ashida and their associates, to set up a National Defence Council and a Joint Staff Council, with the principle of civilian control firmly maintained at Yoshida's insistence. A Mutual Security Assistance (MSA) Agreement was signed with the United States Ambassador Allison by Foreign Minister Okazaki Katsuo, who had built on the work done by Ikeda in the previous year. This brought some economic advantages, and useful extensions in the field of procurement, but imposed no substantial new obligations on Japan.

The Economic Plan for 1953–58, for which, also, Ikeda had been chiefly responsible, was helping to sustain confidence in the prospects for recovery, but it was not yet clear in 1954 that the annual rate of growth of 5 per cent which it predicted would prove to have been doubled for each of the first two years. In short, Yoshida derived little direct benefit, in terms of his own, immediate political standing, from the effort put by the government into economic recovery during his premiership. Indirectly, his authority was reduced by the scandal over subsidies for the shipbuilding industry, in which some of his political associates were allegedly implicated, which dragged on through much of 1954.

In the spring, too, much discontent and indignation was caused by the subjection of the crew of a Japanese fishing vessel, *Fukuryu Maru* (the Lucky Dragon) to radioactive fall-out from the testing of United States weapons on Bikini Atoll, as the result of which one seaman died. The contamination of the ship's entire catch provoked additional anxiety about the future of one of the country's most valuable industries. The incident stimulated a new wave of anti-American sentiment in Japan, from which Yoshida's cabinet inevitably suffered; and led to the inauguration of Gensuikyo, the anti-nuclear movement, as a prominent focus of popular protest, almost exclusively anti-Western in its direction.

The opposition parties were largely united in furious objection to the proposed revision of the Police Law, and above all to the government's insistence on forcing this measure through the necessary Diet procedures by early June, after several impromptu extensions of the parliamentary session. The proposals, for which it was claimed by the Cabinet that they struck a fair balance between too great a degree of autonomy for local police forces on the one hand and excessive centralization on the other, were seen by the opposition as dangerously reactionary in intention. A similar issue was made of the Local Tax Law, but objection was not pressed to the same limits of acceptability, or legitimacy. Physical obstruction was used in attempts to frustrate the amendment of the Police Law, and police officers had to be called in to restore order in the chamber of the Diet.

Yoshida would have been prepared to go on facing down the Socialist opposition until the end of time. But he was constantly made aware of the growing bitterness of Hatoyama's supporters, and he was willing to listen to those of his own associates, notably Ogata Taketora, who felt that the achievement of greater solidarity in the conservative movement as a whole was essential to its continued predominance, and that this would be facilitated by a change of leadership. In the knowledge that industrial opinion, likewise, was putting increasing emphasis on the need for reconciliation within the conservative camp, Yoshida resigned in December 1954 in favour of Hatoyama, who assumed the premiership as leader of the Japan Democratic Party, together with the former Reformists, and dissolved the Diet in preparation for general elections in February 1955.

At the age of seventy-six, Yoshida easily assumed the role of elder statesman. In the nature of events, it was not generally perceived at the time what a solid foundation he had caused to be laid for Japan's entire post-war development. Men of his school were to be prominent in Japanese politics, and in industry, finance and commerce, throughout the succeeding generation, indeed for longer than the normal span of a further single generation's activity. But it was he who saw which way the country should go, and who saw this clearly, at a time of difficulty and uncertainty for which it would be hard to find a parallel.

By the time of Yoshida's retirement, the crucial importance to both partners of the new relationship between the world of business and finance, the *zaikai*, and conservative politics was well understood. The third component in the effective machinery of government, the bureaucracy, was the essential complement to the other two, but, while it could exercise a major influence in favour of wealth creation and over the disbursement of budgetary allocations for example, the bureaucracy could never be directly responsible for the generation of funds in the private sector, on which so much depended. The leaders of the *zaikai* at this time were a remarkable band, perhaps the most distinguished team of this kind in the whole of modern Japanese history. The greatest figures among them included Ishizaka Taizo of Toshiba and the Keidanren, himself indisputably *primus inter pares*, Fujiyama Aiichiro of the Japan Chamber of Commerce and Industry, Yusukawa Daigoro and Matsunaga Yasuzaemon, pre-eminent in the electric power industry. An unprecedented degree of co-ordination was achieved between industrial leaders more widely: in iron and steel, shipping and shipbuilding, in banking and in textile manufacture, in the heart of the Kansai and throughout western Japan as well as in the Kanto and in the north, with the great trading companies (*sogo shosha*) and with the pioneers of new technology in electrical and electronic engineering, in chemicals and pharmaceuticals, with newspaper proprietors and publishers.

Corporations from the pre-war zaibatsu groups were coming together in new, looser combinations (*keiretsu*), without holding companies, and without family control, but each with a bank at its centre. It was, however, the wider organization of industrial opinion on the national scale, and especially through the Keidanren, which affected the actual conduct of political and government business. The leaders of the *zaikai*, then, their success in the realization of solid economic recovery now proven, set out to ensure that the politicians, who depended upon their support, could be depended upon in return to produce a stable political environment in which business enterprise could continue to prosper, for the national benefit. The industrialists' influence was reinforced by the consideration that they stood higher in public esteem than the politicians.

Nevertheless, Hatoyama enjoyed an unusually high degree of popular support when he first came into power. He appointed a strong cabinet, whose three most outstanding personalities were retained throughout his premiership: Shigemitsu Mamoru as Foreign Minister, Ichimada Hisato, former Governor of the Bank of Japan, as Minister of Finance, and the distinguished economist and editor, Ishibashi Tanzan, at the MITI. These appointments were satisfactory to the industrialists, who also approved Hatoyama's negotiation of Japan's entry into the General Agreement on Tariffs and Trade (GATT) in 1955, despite the denial of full reciprocity by some important signatories; and into the United Nations, in 1956. But there was disappointment over the margin of Hatoyama's victory in the lower House elections of February 1955. True, his Democratic Party made substantial gains, to win 185 seats. But the Liberals retained 112, which denied him full conservative endorsement, while the Socialists of both wings made further advances, with the result that their combined strength reached 156.

This outcome persuaded the factional leaders and local 'bosses' of both conservative parties, conscious also of a growing impatience in industrial circles, energetically to explore the possibility of unification. There was a sense, stimulated by the persistent electoral success of the Socialists, that the opportunity to establish stable conservative government, in other words a substantial and lasting majority of seats in the Diet, might elude them if they perpetuated their essentially artificial division. Negotiations were in the hands primarily of Ono Bamboku for the Liberals, and Miki Bukichi for the Democrats. In the event, the two wings of the Socialist Party, in which there were parallel developments, were reunited in October 1955. The conservative merger followed in November, the combined forces calling themselves the Liberal Democratic Party (LDP).

The process of this conservative merger, though it produced formal and sustained unity at the level of the contest in national democratic politics, in the essentially two-party contest known as 'the 1955 set-up', also had the effect of sharpening and hardening divisions between the factions of which the Liberal Democratic Party was composed. At its inception, the LDP comprised eight distinct factions, in each of which personal loyalties were very strong. Hatoyama became the party's first president, following Ogata's sudden death, in April 1956. But he never commanded the allegiance of all the factions. Given the multi-member constituency as the basis of the electoral system for the lower House, factional allegiance was inevitably a crucial consideration in local politics, where parliamentary candidates had always to compete with others from the same party. Hatoyama attempted to get support for legislation to reinstitute the single-member constituency, but the attempt was a much-publicized failure. His long-standing determination to revise the Constitution also proved divisive in conservative political circles, as well as being more widely unpopular. He secured the passage of a bill providing for a cabinet commission to investigate constitutional revision, but it went no further.

Towards the end of his premiership, Hatoyama was himself closely engaged in negotiating the restoration of normal relations with the Soviet Union. This was a substantial achievement, bringing with it advantages in the agreement of arrangements for trade, and for fisheries. But its timing did not altogether please the *zaikai*, and it was no surprise when Hatoyama resigned in December 1956, in favour of Ishibashi Tanzan.

Although economic recovery was proceeding satisfactorily in the latter half of the 1950s, Japan's scope for activity in international affairs remained tightly constricted. Even in economic matters, relations with the United States, which accounted for about one-third of Japan's total foreign trade, were always the dominant consideration. Cautious progress was made towards further settlements with countries of South-East Asia of their claims for reparations, and in the development of trade. But in connection with the Geneva Conference, the conclusion of a ceasefire (for the time being) in Indo-China, the establishment of the South-East Asia Treaty Organization (SEATO), or the preliminaries and proceedings of the first Afro-Asian Conference, the Japanese government was conscious of being able to exert very little, if any, direct influence. In this respect, things remained much as they had been at the outset of the Korean War.

For the public in Japan, even the sensational events in Egypt and Hungary in the autumn of 1956, observed from what had become a very great distance indeed, seemed significant as providing confirmation of existing prejudices, rather than as enlarging their understanding of the outside world. For the leading politicians of both left and right, however, a suspicion that the country's new licence to participate in world affairs was proving largely ineffectual bred increasing frustration. The driving motivations for the Socialists were their desires to break away from the policies of the United States, to adopt a neutral position in the struggle between East and West, and to concentrate in domestic affairs on the protection of the Constitution and the realization of the ideals of the French Revolution, as interpreted in the light of Marxist-Leninist economic theory. A broad programme served to conceal wide differences among them. Politicians of the right were also concerned to reassert more truly independent lines of policy in international affairs. The differences among them were no less marked than those dividing the Socialists, but they were based on individual predilections and on personal loyalties rather than on considerations of theory, let alone of ideology, and they were more easily and more often exposed.

For example, the general approaches to the problems with which they were faced, of Hatoyama and of his two successors as president of the LDP and Prime Minister, could hardly have been more disparate. The industrialists might know that they could call the tune, but the apparent unification of the conservative factions had not greatly simplified for them the difficult choice of which piper to pay. In politics, as in finance, reinsurance was usually advisable. Besides, the industrialists also naturally differed among themselves over priorities and personalities. Nevertheless, they contributed to the ship of state, when necessary, a ballast of massive common sense.

The choice of Ishibashi Tanzan as Hatoyama's successor was reached only after a second ballot among LDP members of the Diet, Kishi Nobusuke having led on the first ballot, but without obtaining the support of a sufficient majority. Ishibashi appointed Kishi Foreign Minister in his cabinet. Given his own consistent opposition over many years to the whole idea of Japanese expansion at China's expense, and Kishi's background in the administration and development of Japanese interests in and around Manchuria, their partnership promised to be lively. Ishibashi was deeply concerned to promote good relations with the People's Republic of China, with which the only ties since 1952 had been through unofficial trade agreements; and he was to continue to advocate this until his death in 1973. But ill-health forced him to resign as Prime Minister after only two months in office. He was succeeded by Kishi, whose election as president of the party in March 1957 was not seriously contested.

Kishi's qualities as an administrator, and his ability to get things done, were widely admired. His links with heavy industry and in the financial world were strong, partly if not largely on account of the Manchurian connection. It was not forgotten that he had been on the list of those suspected of implication in major war crimes, and imprisoned, though not subsequently charged; nor, by contrast, that he had proved a recalcitrant member of Tojo's wartime cabinet, from which indeed he had resigned. He was a Choshu man, and was seen as representing a traditional heritage of stalwart patriotism. In his desire to effect revision of the Constitution, he seemed to be going no further than Ashida would have gone, or than Hatoyama had intended to go.

Kishi's premiership is remembered above all for the struggle brought on by his decision to renegotiate the terms of the Security Treaty with the United States. The result of this decision was to secure palpable improvements in the new treaty, especially in respect of proper recognition of

Japan's sovereign independence, which went far to dispose of arguments that the original instrument had been nothing other than a modern equivalent of the 'unequal treaties' so bitterly resented in Meiji times. The passionate opposition which developed to this enterprise was based not so much on the substance of the revision itself as on a combination of much broader issues. First, the renewal of the treaty in any form, after ten years' operation in the face of their consistent hostility, was a challenge to which the parties of the left could not fail to respond wholeheartedly and with all the resources at their disposal. For them, the treaty symbolized Japan's subordination to the interests of 'Wall Street capitalism' as well as its implication in the intrigues of 'Western Imperialism', including the 'criminal' reliance on nuclear weapons.

Secondly, the steady progress they had made in lower House elections, and to a lesser extent in the House of Councillors, led the Socialists to believe that power would be attainable through the democratic process: they must seize on this great issue, with its direct popular appeal, in order to enlarge their support decisively in all sections of the electorate. Thirdly, in mustering their forces for this struggle, some JSP leaders were confident that they could consolidate the fragile unity formally proclaimed in 1955. In making this last calculation, those on the farther left misjudged the character of their more moderate fellow-socialists, in particular the persuasive powers of Nishio Suehiro as well as the firmness of his convictions.

Almost as important as the great issue of the Security Treaty itself in building up the tension were the clear, prior and separate indications given by Kishi that he was intent on the pursuit of a broad line of policy which was thoroughly uncompromising towards the left, if not calculated to provoke, then certainly not designed to assuage their anxieties. His belief in the need to revise the Constitution was well known, but action here was for the time being held in check by the widespread persistence of doubts within his own party. Meanwhile, he lost no time in introducing legislation to make permanent certain restrictions on the rights to strike of miners and workers in the electric power industry, which had been brought in as temporary measures during the last year of Yoshida's premiership. He curtailed the rights of some classes of civil servants to maintain union membership, and prohibited the automatic deduction of union fees from wages and salaries.

By continuing the expansive thrust of economic policy initiated by Ishibashi, Kishi permitted a threat to develop to the maintenance of adequate reserves of foreign exchange, and had in consequence hurriedly to adopt stringent measures, which damaged his standing in industrial circles. Furthermore, his plan for bringing Japanese technology together with American capital for the economic development of South-East Asia was not sufficiently popular with either prospective partner to bring any advantage to himself, as author, or to the region. Making a new departure in parliamentary practice, he obtained the agreement of the opposition leader to the dissolution of the Diet; and general elections were called for 22 May 1958. In raising the number of seats won in the lower House to 166, the Socialists did less well than they had expected; but for the first time they could claim the support of one-third of all voters.

After these elections, Kishi's party exploited the slightly reduced, but still absolute, and at last nominally unified conservative majority in the lower House by arrogating to themselves the chairmanship of all its committees, having previously shared these key posts with the opposition. They also pushed for the institution, throughout the country, of a system for rating the efficiency of teachers, proposals for which had already been declared anathema by the Japan Teachers' Union (JTU). Members of the Cabinet, including Kishi himself, made no secret of their keenness to reduce the influence of the JTU, and with it that of Sohyo. The unions and the opposition parties set out to mobilize a 'national joint struggle' against what they claimed was a determination on Kishi's part to reverse the trend of post-war educational reform altogether, and to recentralize control. A bill dealing with the appointment of local school boards had caused serious trouble in the House of Councillors in 1956. Now the government risked igniting an already inflammatory situation by instructing schools, through the Ministry of Education, to reintroduce the teaching of ethics (*shushin*), which was closely associated in the public mind with indoctrination by supporters of militarism in the 1930s and during the Pacific War.

Matters were made worse, and Kishi's confrontation with the political left more bitter, by the government's introduction into the Diet, in October 1958, of a bill to amend the Police Duties Law. The amendments put forward did not involve drastic change, but they envisaged some extension of police powers, both of detention and of entry into private property. Given the trouble which had already arisen over legislative action in this field, the recent occurrence of one or two cases in which police officers had incurred charges of the excessive use of existing powers, and current criticism of the official handling of a major strike by workers at the Oji Paper Company's mills, these new proposals aroused the strongest protests and objections, the press campaign against them, in particular, inviting comparison with that mounted against the Katsura government in 1913. Controversy continued into December, by which time even those few newspapers which had been willing to concede at first that there might be some need to contemplate further curbs on subversive activity came out in criticism of the government's obduracy in proceeding with such a plainly unacceptable project. The eventual unanimity of the press in opposition to it was a most exceptional circumstance, and played a notable part in inducing the Cabinet finally to abandon the project; but not before it had damaged the government's standing badly, not merely with those permanently in opposition, but also with a number of moderate organizations not normally inclined to allow themselves to take sides on political issues, including some religious bodies. In industry, there was sympathy with the government's objectives, tempered with acknowledgement that it had not found the right way of pursuing them. The unanimous hostility of the press may, and should, have been taken as a warning to Kishi and his colleagues that doubts about their performance were not confined to circles in which opposition could be taken for granted.

This was the domestic background against which the movement of opposition to revision of the Security Treaty came to dominate political life in Japan at the end of the decade, up to the mid-summer of 1960. The Kishi government had concluded a peace treaty and an agreement on reparations with Indonesia in 1958, and were given some credit for this, in economic as much as in political circles, to offset their difficulties. These difficulties were partly self-inflicted, it seems clear, but they were also partly a reflection of wider events and movements of opinion. The spirit of Bandung, dressed in the attractive robes of neutralism, was present everywhere, like some pervasive subliminal advertisement. It affected Japanese opinion because of its Asian provenance, as well as by virtue of its pacifism. The advent to power in the Soviet Union of Khrushchev brought new dangers and opportunities. The government of the People's Republic of China was accused of spoiling the prospects of peaceful coexistence of the two superpowers, already at serious risk in the Middle East, by its threats of action against the Nationalists, in the offshore islands and in Formosa. Percipient observers in Japan could see the possibility of a Sino-Soviet split.

The struggle against the Security Treaty and its revision was conducted on a broad political front: by the Socialists, by Sohyo, working at first uneasily with the JCP, and by Zengakuren, the so-called students' union, the latter stealing the JCP's thunder by calling for an immediate revolution of the proletariat; also by numerous 'progressive' organizations normally devoted to single issues not directly related to defence and foreign policy, or even essentially apolitical in character. The People's Council for the Prevention of Revision of the Security Treaty, launched formally at the end of March 1959, sponsored the formation of local councils throughout the country, the most prominent being the Tokyo Joint Struggle Council, whose leaders effectively directed the national campaign. Drives were held frequently, to recruit further support and to sustain zeal for the cause, on the lines of the now traditional annual labour offensives, but harsher in tone and far more shrill and insistent in propaganda. The central theme of opposition to the Security Treaty (Ampo Joyaku) itself was linked with that of hostility to collective security systems in general (at any rate those devised in the West) and with impassioned advocacy of neutralism. The campaign got off to a brisk start on the strength of a ruling by the Tokyo District Court (later overturned by the Supreme Court) in connection with charges of trespass brought against opponents of the enlargement of a US Army base at Sunagawa, to the effect that the stationing of US forces in Japan was itself unconstitutional.

The extreme opponents of the Security Treaty, though they succeeded in mounting a campaign of unprecedented scale and vigour, destroyed the unity of the JSP. At the Party Congress in September 1959, Nishio Suehiro, now a principal faction-leader, but also a former Secretary-General, and deputy premier under Ashida, came under heavy attack on account of his more pragmatic approach to revision of the treaty and to the broad international situation, and a motion was carried referring his case to a disciplinary committee. He and his supporters thereupon resigned their positions in the party, and withdrew from the congress. He announced the formation of the new Democratic Socialist Party (DSP) the next month, following a formal vote of censure against him by the JSP committee, and secured the support of 37 lower House and 16 upper House members of the Diet. This was a development with long-term consequences for the structural pattern of Japanese politics, but it scarcely affected the current national discord.

Despite their unprecedented campaign, the opponents of the treaty were powerless to interfere with its renegotiation, which proceeded satisfactorily to both governments. The revised instrument dispensed with certain features of the original agreement, which were obviously no longer appropriate, notably provisions permitting American intervention to put down civil disturbances in Japan, if requested by the Japanese government, and requiring the latter to obtain Washington's consent before granting military rights to any third party. It recognized the obligation of both parties to settle disputes in accordance with the United Nations Charter, an improvement which, in calmer circumstances, might have gone some way to mollify the Japanese opposition.

Attempts to prevent Kishi's leaving Japan to sign the revised treaty having been thwarted, signature took place at the White House in Washington on 19 January 1960, and was attended by President Eisenhower. It was announced the following day that the President would make an official visit to Japan, arriving there about 20 June, and that there would also be a visit to the United States by Crown Prince Akihito in the course of the year. The conclusion of the revised treaty was at first taken fairly quietly by the opposition in Japan, anxious not to advertise their failure to avert it, though even the new DSP declared it unconstitutional. A prolonged debate followed in the Diet, where tactics of obstruction were employed from time to time by the Socialists, and in the media. The People's Council, exploring the possibility of frustrating or postponing ratification of the treaty, once more intensified its nationwide activities. Moderate and neutral opinion seemed to be moving against the government, of which the newspapers again became increasingly united in their criticism. They lectured Kishi on his duty to satisfy popular misgivings. An editorial in the *Asahi*, admittedly often left of centre in its views but still the leading daily newspaper, accused the government of lacking sincerity (an ominous charge in such circumstances) and insisted that there were outstanding issues which it should clarify. Then, on 1 May, came the shooting down of the American U2 'spy plane' over the Soviet Union. This instantly raised the temperature of the argument in Japan to a feverish level.

Kishi, however, made it plain on 19 May, when he arranged for the LDP formally to request an extension of the Diet session, that he intended to force the procedure of ratification through the lower House, so that the necessary complete approval could be obtained before President Eisenhower's proposed arrival a month later. He was able, in accordance with the Constitution, to calculate that the sanction of the House of Councillors would be 'automatic' thirty days after action was taken in the House of Representatives, no matter what view the Councillors might wish to take of the treaty. His decision to go for effective ratification that very day of 19 May, or in the early hours of the next morning as it turned out, took the opposition by surprise. When they understood his intentions, the Socialists resorted to methods of solid physical obstruction within the Diet, and the People's Council set out to muster protesting crowds outside. It was reckoned that some 15,000 demonstrators had assembled by evening. The Diet building was protected by 5,000 police officers. Later, for only the second time in the history of the Diet, police entered the chamber. The Speaker had authorized 500 police officers to come into the building, and they were eventually required to carry many Socialist members and their robust male secretaries bodily away, in order that the parliamentary business of the newly extended session might proceed. The treaty was given formal approval shortly after midnight.

There was a sense of shock, extending beyond the ranks of those previously mobilized in opposition to the treaty. The headline of the *Asahi*'s editorial for 20 May, 'The LDP and Government's Undemocratic Act', encapsulated a common view. To take the opposition by surprise, or to use your majority ruthlessly and without regard to the strength of your opponents' feelings on any particular issue, had come to be considered incompatible with good parliamentary practice in the democratic system as it was evolving in Japan. Kishi had offended on both counts. Even the *Nihon Keizai Shimbun* was sharply critical of the LDP for acting 'unilaterally'. Kishi made clear in public his own doubts about the newspapers' claim to exclusive rights in the interpretation of public opinion. The demonstrations against the government which now proliferated were for a time given encouragement by much of the press, with prudent and pious reservations

161

about the use of violence. When President Eisenhower's press secretary, Hagerty, had to be rescued by helicopter from the mob, near Haneda airport, the press deplored the damage done to Japan's international prestige and rounded on the demonstrators in condemnation of their reckless excesses. Further disturbances culminated in a grim battle outside the Diet, in which a student lost her life. The Japanese government concluded that the President's safety could not be guaranteed, and Eisenhower's visit was postponed indefinitely. Kishi resigned, in acknowledgement that the price paid for revision of the treaty, in terms of domestic disharmony and even of the cohesion of his own party, had been so high as to require this sacrifice. He wished to absolve others of responsibility.

Although the struggle over revision of the Security Treaty was the direct cause of Kishi's downfall, the ferocity with which his government was opposed was also affected by the coincidence of this struggle with another, itself among the most bitter in the post-war history of labour relations in Japan. This had first arisen in the previous summer, of 1959, and had still not reached its climax. It was caused by the decision of the Mitsui Mining Company to insist on redundancies at the Miike mine in Kyushu, the largest and most modern colliery in the whole country. The mining industry as a whole was facing great difficulties. Oil was already established as the principal source of energy for future industrial development. Overseas sources of supply of coal for the electric power and iron and steel industries, especially from Australia, were becoming increasingly attractive. Quite apart from the economics of supply, the quality of most of the coal still available in quantity in Japan did not meet the requirements of modern manufacturing or generating plant.

Redundancies, other than those which could be met by acceptable arrangements for voluntary retirement, were bitterly opposed by Sohyo, the biggest national federation of trades unions, supported by the dominant left wing of the JSP, and by Tanro, the national federation of miners' unions. They feared a breach of the unwritten obligation upon large-scale business concerns to provide continuing, lifetime employment. They maintained a determined opposition over many months, even though the management's case for redundancies was based partly on the need for technological improvements, in the interests of higher productivity, for which Japanese unions have usually tended to show understanding. The local branch of the federation of Mitsui Mining Company unions was in favour of compromise, but was repudiated by a majority of the workers at the Miike mine. The strength of feeling engendered by this case added to the willingness even of those best disposed towards Kishi, in his party and in industrial circles, to accept the necessity of his resignation.

The succession was contested at an extraordinary convention of the LDP held on 14 July. Ikeda Hayato – who had been MITI Minister in Kishi's last cabinet but whose main strength lay in support from the Yoshida school and from the mainstream of industrial opinion – failed to obtain an absolute majority on the first ballot. Fujiyama Aiichiro, Kishi's Foreign Minister, who had come third among the candidates, then stood down; and Ikeda prospered accordingly in the second ballot, while the challenger, Ishii Mitsujiro, was unable to improve on his earlier share of the vote. Ikeda brought leaders of certain of the other contending factions into his cabinet, though some were excluded, the principle later followed, of proportional representation from all factions, not yet being in operation.

Ikeda's priorities included the restoration of orderly co-operation as the characteristic of Japan's relations with the United States, and for this, as well as more generally, his choice of Kosaka Zentaro as Foreign Minister was well made. Ikeda was also concerned if possible to build up exchanges and closer understanding with Peking, despite the uncertainties added to the prospects there by the Great Leap Forward. In domestic as well as international political affairs, he let it be known that tolerance and patience were his watchwords. The use of the expression 'low posture' (*tei shisei*) to characterize Japan's foreign policy became current at this time, perhaps at Ikeda's instigation. Above all, however, he concentrated, more demonstratively, on high growth, on the consolidation and extension of Japan's industrial and economic strength, and on the further improvement of standards of living. His inspiration of the racy 'income-doubling' plan boosted public morale for years beyond his own premiership. His responsibility both for its conception and for its realization was more than a mere formality of office. That a programme designed to double the national income inside a decade should command public credibility, and be perceived as a success from its early stages, was in itself remarkable. In the first half of the 1960s Japan enjoyed a steady annual rate of growth in the gross national product of as much as 10 per cent, with the value of exports rising by an annual average of over 15 per cent. Progress in reconstruction was achieved at a visibly accelerating pace. The new prosperity was still based primarily on the reorganization and re-equipment of heavy industry, at this stage. Pay packets, however, seemed to grow in every sector and to do so consistently faster than the cost of living. The social cost of rising prosperity itself, especially in terms of environmental pollution, was not yet apparent, though it was soon to emerge.

Many factors contributed to this grand economic advance, which was indeed more like a thoroughly well organized expedition than like a miracle; more like the performance of a well trained team in an athletic contest than like that of a conjurer. Ikeda himself clearly understood the process of interaction of these factors. He had taken part for many years in the outline planning exercises which enabled government and industry to communicate in depth, to adapt to each other's reasoned requirements, to adopt mutually acceptable priorities and targets for development, and to reach a measure of preliminary agreement on the broad allocation of responsibilities, and to some extent of resources; but to do all this without detracting from the basic independence of groups and corporations in the private sector, or sheltering them from competition, except where cartelization was permitted to offset certain specific adversities. The recommendations arising from close collaboration of MITI and the Economic Planning Agency (EPA) with industrial groups and associations were likely to be supported also by the Ministry of Finance (MOF), with whose post-war methods of administration Ikeda was at least equally familiar.

In the period of most rapid industrial growth, which stretched for twenty years from the closing stages of the Korean War to the first oil crisis in 1973, major Japanese corporations typically operated on a ratio of debt to equity of about 80:20, almost the reverse of the ratios commonest among their counterparts in the United States or Britain, for example. They were able to aim at increasing their market shares over the long term, without having to consider the interests of exigent or impatient shareholders. Moreover, finance was always available to them at lower rates of interest, often far lower, than those current elsewhere in the industrialized world. The system was consolidated by the reconstitution of the old zaibatsu conglomerates into the new keiretsu groups, each with its bank at the centre of its affairs, and with private as well as corporate investors more intent upon the security of their investments than on their rates of return. The ratio of personal savings to disposable incomes was sustained at an exceptionally high level throughout the period of high growth. Within this much longer period, the early 1960s were especially well favoured.

As early as 1956, Japan had assumed the lead among the world's shipbuilding nations. Productivity at the new shipyards in Kyushu and on the main island of Honshu could be matched in the 1960s, if at all, only at the Arendal yard in Sweden. The benefits were passed on to the iron and steel industry, whose use of specialized bulk carriers to bring ore and coal alongside their modernized plants added to their competitive advantages. These were shared by the engineering and chemical industries. Machine tools, electronics, motor vehicles and aircraft were beginning to emulate the success already achieved by cameras and binoculars, in a growing range of export markets. Matching advances were made by the traditional sectors, including textiles, ceramics, woodworking and food and drink.

Emphasis was placed at this time on economies of scale, notably in vehicle production and in the great so-called 'kombinahts' built at intervals along the Pacific and Inland Sea coasts of Honshu to store, refine and further process the cargoes of oil brought in by the supertankers. By 1960, oil was of equal importance with coal as Japan's source of energy. As soon as he had taken office in succession to Kishi, Ikeda had moved to avert bloodshed in the miners' dispute, and had brought all concerned to accept a truce at Miike, but the future scope of the coal-mining industry was evidently limited, as was that for the construction of new hydro-electric power stations. Atomic energy was coming in, but not to the extent of taking the lead in supply. For the foreseeable future, the country's dependence on oil could only increase. Since some 80 per cent of oil supplies came from the Middle East, and very little was available from dependable sources nearer to Japan than Indonesia, this was the most vulnerable of all the factors making for continued prosperity. The implications for foreign policy, especially for relations with the United States, and in the longer term for defence policy, if that was to become a consideration separable from the Security Treaty, were inescapable.

This was another reason, in addition to the drive for sustained competitive vigour in both domestic and world markets, why innovation became a preoccupation of Japanese industry. Much technical know-how was bought in from abroad, at prices which at this time were influenced by the inaccessibility of the domestic market to direct exports by foreign manufacturers. In the Japanese manufacturing sector itself, as well as new methods of production engineering, there was a constant drive for greater technical sophistication, for incorporation in new products of fresh design. A high innovative capability characterized the Japanese electronics industry from the beginning, and the potential for advances such as that into colour television was quickly recognized. By the early 1960s, such was the rate of growth in industrial activity generally that the possibility of future labour shortages stimulated interest in automation as a principal means of ensuring gains in productivity. Management practice involved consultation with opinion on the shop floor, and teamwork at that level promoted innovation, as well as quality control.

In agriculture, output rose steadily, while manpower declined. Mechanization was linked with advances in the vehicle industry, and in engineering more generally, and increased yields followed from the growth in the chemical and pharmaceutical sectors. The development of automatic rice-planting machinery which could be drawn through the flooded paddyfields by small but powerful tractors revolutionized the lives of the farming communities throughout Japan. Rice remained the chief crop, but the support price paid to subsidize its production doubled during the 1960s. Measures designed to divert production from rice to those crops for which demand was increasing were not successful. Like agriculture, the fishery industry gained benefits from advances made in engineering. It also sustained its major contribution to exports.

By the late 1950s Japan's manufactured exports were depending progressively less on textiles and clothing, and more on the products of the heavy, capital-intensive engineering industries. Orders for the latter were coming proportionately less from the developing world, and more from the other industrialized countries, in whose markets Japan could compete successfully both in price and in quality. From as early as the mid-1950s, the rise in exports of machinery and transport equipment was the most striking single feature in the composition of Japan's foreign trade; and it was to retain a conspicuous place in the statistics, and on the agenda of international trade negotiations, for decades. By the end of the 1950s earlier assumptions that growth in international trade would depend substantially on the expansion of exchanges of raw materials from the less developed countries with the manufactured products of the leading industrialized countries were discredited. The fastest growth was in trade between the advanced industrial countries. But although the best markets for products of high technology were in Europe and North America, Japan also needed to invest in the development of the raw material resources of South-East Asia, in particular, and of oil supplies from the Gulf. In South-East Asia there was also great scope for investment in the labour-intensive textile and pottery industries, to take advantage of wage levels below those now prevailing in Japan itself. The subsidiaries and joint ventures of Japanese parent companies in these and other light manufacturing sectors made a profitable contribution to the development of other economies in the region, including those of Taiwan and the Republic of Korea. In all this, the large Japanese trading companies, eight or ten in number, which continued to handle more than half of Japan's total foreign trade, played major roles.

By 1960 the share of Japan's exports taken by Europe and North America had risen sharply, while that taken by Asian countries had fallen back. Switches in the structure and direction of trade had been partly responsible for balance of payments difficulties, which had added to Kishi's political and security problems. But the strong growth of exports in the early 1960s relieved economic policy-makers, for a time, of these anxieties. A boom in consumer spending in the domestic market both expressed and reinforced the recovery of confidence.

Ikeda himself was associated above all with the Ten-year Plan for doubling the national income, which was launched in 1960, and which, as already noted, succeeded at once in appealing to the public imagination. It actually underestimated the rate of growth to be achieved in the decade, partly because planners did not foresee the strength of private investment in industry. It confirmed the expectations of industrialists and the optimism of the public. The high point in confidence was reached in 1964, the year in which Japan took up membership both of the IMF and of the OECD; and in which the Olympic Games were staged in and around Tokyo, with conspicuous success. The two sports stadia designed for the Games by Japan's leading architect Tange Kenzo; the new Western-style hotels; the smooth operation of the *shinkansen* (the bullet train) and of the capital's new raised expressways (*shuto*), were among features which highlighted a sense of restored national pride in the prosperity and success which the people had earned. The leader chosen to represent the host country, in the preparation and oversight of the Olympic Games, and to preside, with Mr Avery Brundage, over their conduct, was Yasukawa Daigoro. The decisive function of the industrial organizations in the management of national recovery, and Yasukawa's pre-eminence in this larger enterprise, were thus appropriately recognized, just as that of Ishizaka Taizo was later to be acknowledged in his appointment to preside over the international exhibition, Expo '70.

In negotiations over the regulation of international trade, the way was still hard. The British government at the time of the San Francisco Peace Conference had abandoned only with some reluctance their desire to see limits put on Japan's future development in industrial competition, and their successors had withheld recognition of Japan's full rights under the GATT, upon the country's accession to that key instrument in 1955. A Treaty of Commerce was concluded with Britain in 1962. By this time, there was strong international pressure on Japan to liberalize quantitative restrictions on imports, to abandon export subsidies, and to relax the regime of exchange controls. In trading relations with the United States, from which Japan had received so much support, first in aid and later in procurement, serious problems began to emerge, at least from the mid-1950s. From 1956, for example, Japanese exports of cotton textiles to the USA were made subject to 'voluntary' quota controls, the Japanese government thus agreeing to the use of a technique whose extension was later frequently in demand by other trading partners. Complaints now brought against Japan related to various methods by which Japanese officials contrived to protect their manufacturers from foreign competition at home, and to strengthen their capacity to export. The primary objective of a visit to the United States by Ikeda, as Prime Minister, in 1961, was to resolve trade problems. A Joint Committee on Japan–US Trade and Economic Relations was established.

Before his visit to Washington in early 1961, Ikeda had already led the LDP through a general election campaign in the previous autumn, during which Asanuma, chairman of the JSP, had been assassinated, dying of stab-wounds received, in full view of television cameras, at a public meeting. The outcome of the elections of November 1960 was a gain of 9 seats in the lower House for the LDP, giving them 296 seats, while the JSP's total dropped to 145, the 17 seats won by Nishio's DSP largely accounting for their decline. In his new cabinet, Ikeda gave the MITI to Sato Eisaku, and brought in Miyazawa Kiichi as Director of the Economic Planning Agency. These and other appointments, including that of Tanaka Kakuei as Finance Minister, sustained the emphasis on economic policy, though

Tanaka's promotion was otherwise something of a departure from the established pattern.

Tanaka's career had followed a course which might have been regarded as conventional for a 'boss' in local politics, but which was unusual at national level. He was a man of boundless energy and self-confidence, who had amassed a huge fortune as owner and chief executive of a construction company in Niigata Prefecture, on the Japan Sea coast. He had used his wealth to striking effect in the party's interest, on the national scale, but primarily in favour of Sato's faction. He had enjoyed none of the educational or social advantages common to most ministers, nor the background of service in the bureaucracy which counted in favour of so many leading figures in the LDP. He exerted a new style of influence in the higher counsels of the party, where he had been consolidating an ever more powerful position since the early post-war years.

At this time, factional divisions within the LDP were both sharp and complex. A number of party elders were competing jealously, either for the leadership itself or for a dominant influence over succession to the leadership. Current factional loyalties did not always correspond with older loyalties, to Yoshida or Hatoyama, or to pre-war parties, or regional nobility, or business interest. Differences over domestic or foreign policy were liable to supervene. Ikeda's attempts to sustain party unity, increasingly by means of the proportionate allocation of cabinet posts to representatives of the factions, were only partially successful. Sato's refusal to continue in the Cabinet, in 1962, if Kono Ichiro was included, was an expression of rivalry as well as being the outcome of disagreement over foreign policy. At the time of the Cuban missile crisis, when Western unity was already under strain for other reasons, including the impact of de Gaulle's policies, Sato made no secret of his view that Kono's pursuit of improved relations with both China and the Soviet Union, and his advocacy of an altogether more independent policy for Japan – which of course meant a policy less closely attuned to Washington's – was untimely, even unseemly.

Ikeda himself kept to a moderate course. He made clear his concern that relations with the United States should return to the calm understanding which had mostly prevailed prior to the drama of 1960. At the same time, he worked for some expansion of exchanges with China, seeing this as being in the interests of the non-communist world, much as Lord Home would argue on his visit to Japan in April 1963. The so-called Liao-Takasaki Memorandum on Trade, which was concluded in November 1962, following negotiations coincidental both with the Cuban missile crisis and with the outbreak of fighting on the Sino-Indian border, provided a pragmatic and strictly non-governmental basis for an expansion of bilateral trade, and for some cultural exchanges. Ikeda's approach to the relationship was paralleled by that of Chou En-lai; indeed, there seems to have been something of a rapport between them. Chou accepted that Japan's opposition to China's membership of the UN, persisted in out of loyalty to the Nationalists as well as to Washington, need not preclude some development on an unofficial basis of what must inevitably become the most important relationship in the whole region of East Asia.

This development was subsequently inhibited once again by the deterioration of domestic conditions within China, where anti-rightist campaigns had followed the Great Leap Forward. The Sino-Soviet dispute, openly acknowledged in 1962, also came to preoccupy the Chinese leadership. The Japanese government watched this dispute, and the gradual evolution of its consequences – in Vietnam, in East–West relations, and throughout the Afro-Asian countries – with attention and anxiety. Their concern to avoid unnecessary and dangerous political entanglements served to re-emphasize their concentration on economic affairs.

The continuing success of the economy was the background to Ikeda's re-election as president of the LDP in 1962. In general elections in the following November, the party lost a handful of seats, but it was the DSP and minor parties which made gains, not the JSP. The Socialists had begun to split once again, the right now under the leadership of Eda Saburo, whose moderate vision involved the reform of the capitalist system from within; the left calling for Marxist revolution. The Japan Communist Party had reacted to the Sino-Soviet split by adopting a frankly nationalistic programme, but it was not itself united. The opposition thus posed no serious threat to the LDP. Nevertheless, Ikeda faced a challenge for the presidency from Sato, in the summer of 1964.

Factional differences within the LDP had grown even more pronounced. There was much uncertainty and equivocation, both over allegiances and over policies. The weaker groups feared the growing influence of Kono Ichiro, who was not a man for compromise and consensus. Internal dissension was reflected, and partly distorted, in disagreement over basic questions of foreign policy. On the one hand, it was argued that a substantial, if temporary, growth in trade with China, which had been marked in 1963 by the mounting of reciprocal trade fairs, involved a concentration of effort prejudicial to Japan's position in non-communist Asia, and especially in Taiwan, and, most seriously of all by far, to the maintenance of Washington's confidence in the direction of Japanese policy. On the other hand, clear signs of impending American commitment to massive intervention in Vietnam were disturbing to those in the LDP who, while wishing to preserve the advantages enjoyed under the Security Treaty, feared too close an identification with Washington's current, wider aims in Asia. With Yoshida's support in preserving the balance of his foreign policy, Ikeda survived Sato's challenge for the presidency of the LDP. Soon after the resounding success of the Tokyo Olympics, however, Ikeda was forced by ill-health to retire. His nomination of Sato as his successor was confirmed at a party convention.

Shortly before Sato came to power, the opposition parties and various activists of the left, including those working for communist front organizations, as well as pacifists and neutralists and the anti-nuclear groups, had formed a strong peace movement to protest against the United States' actions in Vietnam. The Chinese had held their first test of a nuclear explosive device. The situation seemed to call for the maintenance of the low posture in Tokyo's foreign policy. Sato was regarded with some suspicion in Peking, if only because he was Kishi's brother (adoption accounting for their different family-names). In fact, though by no means hostile towards China, he was disposed to ensure that Japan kept on the best possible terms with the United States, and to build on the economic success and prosperity already achieved.

In the conduct of relations with the United States, Sato worked from the beginning of his eight-year term as Prime Minister for the smooth continuation of the Security Treaty, which he duly secured when its extension became due, in 1970. He was also bent on recovering Okinawa for Japan, and was able to negotiate an agreement in 1969, which provided for this, for full implementation in 1972. He also welcomed the assistance of the United States in assuring a successful outcome to negotiations with the Republic of Korea, with which Japan re-established relations in 1965. In the following year there was a useful agreement with the Soviet Union, on trade. There was even talk of the joint development of Siberian resources, and even of the possible participation of United States capital; but this was abandoned after the Soviet invasion of Czechoslovakia in 1968. The Soviet negotiators, in any case, never offered terms which greatly attracted the leading Japanese industrialists of the Keidanren. From 1966, the outbreak of the Cultural Revolution in China had ruled out the possibility of progress in relations with Peking, regardless of the United States' position, for the time being. Part of the reason for Sato's eventual retirement was that he did not seem to be sensitive to the likelihood of a return to more pragmatic policies in China, perhaps out of a sense of obligation to Taiwan. The lack of warning of the fundamental change which took place in Washington's policy towards China is a separate consideration, one of the 'Nixon shocks' contributing more directly to the ending of Sato's premiership in 1972.

Meanwhile, the high rate of growth in the economy which had been achieved in Ikeda's time was sustained under Sato. In the latter half of the 1960s, Japan's GNP surpassed those of the four leading Western European countries successively, to attain the third place in world ranking. Japan's exports to the other industrialized countries were still made up predominantly of steel, ships, motor vehicles, machinery and instruments. Electronic products were beginning to excel, while transistor radios captured large consumer markets, textiles and pottery still accounted for substantial earnings abroad, and chemicals and pharmaceuticals were gaining in competitive strength. Improvements in productivity more than compensated for increased wages. At the same time, the value of Japan's direct foreign investments began to rise sharply.

The speed of Japan's advance in foreign trade, and the rapid changes in the composition of exports, together with the accompanying bilateral imbalances, aroused criticism in the United States and Europe; as well as demands for the faster liberalization of Japan's import controls and the opening of Japan's markets. It was the growing imbalance of trade which most seriously disturbed Japan's industrialized partners, who drew attention to the potentially destabilizing consequences for international financial arrangements. The result was the second of the 'Nixon shocks' of 1971, when the dollar was devalued against the yen in mid-August, and its links with gold broken, and surcharges were introduced on imports into the United States of certain Japanese goods. This caused confusion in financial markets and in trade, and a bout of severe inflation in Japan.

The effect of these developments on Sato's position were the more serious on account of its having been badly shaken by the first of the 'Nixon shocks', when the President's forthcoming visit to China had been announced, in July 1971, without effective warning to the Japanese government.

Sato had also encountered new problems at home. During the 1960s, the environmental cost of the hitherto almost uncontrolled expansion of industrial activity in Japan had attracted widespread attention, and increasingly strident criticism in the press. There was great, and growing, damage from pollution. In the most notorious local cases, industrial effluent had caused disease and death. The full story of suffering at Minamata, for example, was not disclosed until later; but public concern was now demanding action. The simplest manifestation of the scale of the threat was the deterioration in the atmosphere of Tokyo itself, where police officers on duty controlling the traffic were obliged to wear oxygen masks. Legislation was introduced which soon proved remarkably effective in combating atmospheric pollution. Other forms were not so easily overcome.

The danger of pollution from nuclear sources is a permanent concern of the Japanese public. The development of civil nuclear power has been possible only on the basis of prolonged and detailed negotiation with local interests, including those of inshore fishermen operating close to areas where it is proposed to discharge effluent. Although Japanese engineers designed and constructed a nuclear-powered ship, its use was rendered impossible by popular hostility. In the context of defence, Sato gained credit by his enunciation of three non-nuclear principles: that Japan would neither manufacture nor possess nuclear weapons, nor permit their introduction by others into Japan. This, coupled with his interest in international action on non-proliferation, went some way to assuage anxiety, but there were persistent doubts about the compliance of United States warships, in particular, with the Japanese government's requirements.

Sensitivity on matters of defence in general was especially pronounced during the Vietnam War, when criticism of the United States' strategy in Asia grew loud in Japan. Sato was cautious in his approach to the further expansion of the self-defence forces, and introduced the idea of limiting the defence budget to below 1 per cent of GNP, though this formulation was not officially endorsed until after his time. In appointing Nakasone Yasuhiro as Director of the Defence Agency for a time, in his third cabinet, however, Sato allowed himself to be associated with the least inhibited of all senior Japanese politicians at that time, in regard to the needs and role of the forces. Despite his forthright attitude, Nakasone, too, recognized that Japan's international standing would not in the future depend on military strength. In a speech in Washington in 1970, he said: 'In the history of mankind, countries which have become economically powerful have always been fated eventually to become military great powers as well. The new Japan challenges this commonly accepted rule of history.'

Such reflections made little impression on the peace movement, which had in any case condemned Sato merely for his association with policies of co-operation with Washington, carrying, however indirectly, the taint of Vietnam. The 'struggle' of the peace movement, given new life by the war in Vietnam, became linked in 1968–70 with a great upsurge of discontent in the universities of Japan. This may have had its origins in discontent with the conditions imposed on medical students in Tokyo University, but it came to embrace every cause opposed to 'the establishment', to conservatism, to authority itself in any form. It led to violent disputes between competing groups of student activists, stimulated by troublemakers from outside the universities, keen to make use of militant protest for their own ends. With the assistance of legislation, the university authorities succeeded in restoring order in their own affairs. The vigour of the peace movement subsided, with the war in Vietnam. Those elements in Japanese society which were subversive largely for the sake of subversion, apart from the hardest revolutionaries of the Japan Red Army, who mostly went abroad to work with terrorists elsewhere, turned their attention to opposing the construction of Tokyo's new airport at Narita. A good deal of damage had been done already to the reputation of Sato's government, which was in no condition to survive the 'Nixon shocks'.

Despite all these difficulties, the LDP had not done badly in the general elections held during Sato's premiership, in 1967 and 1969. Their previous gradual loss of seats in the lower House continued, but at a slow pace, leaving them still dominant. The JSP also continued its decline, but at a faster pace, losing a few seats to the DSP, but suffering even more seriously from the entry into the competition of the Komeito (the Clean Government Party), which was the political arm of the Nichiren Shoshu Buddhist sect, Soka Gakkai (the Value-adding Society). The Komeito, appealing primarily to that sector of the urban population which had derived the least benefit from the country's economic advance, won no fewer than 47 seats at its second appearance in the lists. It was a reminder, at a time when most people's incomes were rising steadily, and when this was naturally widely attributed to the skill of the governing party, that some had been left behind in the economic advance; perhaps even an intimation of deeper discontents.

The government did its best to prolong the sense of well-being which had been so marked in 1964. The Osaka Expo of 1970 gave a boost to the country's international image. In the next year, the Showa Emperor made the first imperial state visits to foreign countries. It was said that he looked forward to the visit to London, where he had last been fifty years before.

There was no future for Sato's government after the summer of 1971, though it was the next summer before Sato resigned. He favoured Fukuda Takeo, who was at the Foreign Ministry after a spell as Finance Minister, as his successor, but the outcome of a bitter contest, in which Ohira Masayoshi and Miki Takeo also stood in the first ballot, was that Tanaka Kakuei defeated Fukuda in the run-off, with consequences which are still apparent. It was a victory for money.

8

New Agenda: Domestic, Regional and Global, 1972–90

The full significance of Tanaka's influence on the conduct of domestic politics, primarily but not exclusively felt within the LDP, became apparent only gradually. The first exciting development in his premiership was the establishment of diplomatic relations with the People's Republic of China, accomplished as the result of Tanaka's visit to Peking in September 1972. For more than twenty years, the most important bilateral relationship in East Asia had been sustained by non-governmental ties; again the twenty years before that had been wasted in bitterness and war. The possibility of Sino-Japanese reconciliation, even of co-operation, could now be explored. Japan's strong links with, and increasing investments in Taiwan, and the Western orientation of Japan's policies, remained as limiting considerations for both parties. Despite the inherited burdens of mistrust and enmity, the resumption of official exchanges with China was accounted a triumph for Tanaka's government. This historic achievement could not, however, be exploited by them, since it was followed by an unsettled period in China, with the deaths of Chou and Mao, and the struggle of the party of economic reform against the Gang of Four.

It was Tanaka's idea, when he became Prime Minister, to consolidate his standing with the electorate, and at the same time to meet some of the American and European criticisms of the management of the Japanese economy, by shifting a substantial weight of the country's industrial effort into domestic development and reconstruction. A plan entitled *The Remodelling of the Japanese Archipelago*, devised by members of a think-tank recruited and directed by Tanaka, called for the establishment of new industrial centres, to be sited in the less highly developed provinces, away from the overcrowded and polluted Pacific coast of central Honshu; for the drastic improvement of the whole national infrastructure, including communications; and for environmental protection, modern sewerage and better amenities; in short, for the provision of a higher quality of life, for a society which could now afford it.

The publication and promotion of this plan had the effect of raising land prices in provincial areas expected to benefit from its implementation, and, although some dispersal of industrial activity was eventually achieved, with improvements in road and rail networks, it thus contributed to the onset of a severe bout of inflation. The main cause of this, however, was the first oil shock, of 1973.

The oil shock unsettled the Japanese economy, for a time severely. The steep rise in costs of energy, coupled with the threat of shortages of fuel, caused acute unease throughout Japanese industry. Stringent measures to conserve energy, and determined efforts to diversify sources of supply, were pursued by both government and industry. Equally firm steps were taken to bring domestic inflation under control. Economic policy was supported by a brisk campaign of public information, to the general effect that the era of almost automatic rises in prosperity must be regarded as having come to an end. Wage demands were moderated accordingly, and considerable reductions in biannual bonuses were widely accepted. For two years, Japan's balance of trade went heavily into deficit. After the export successes of the 1960s, and the dismantling of a range of import controls in the early 1970s, drastic adjustments were required in order to set new standards in industrial productivity, to accelerate technological innovation, and to intensify export marketing worldwide. By the autumn of 1975 recovery seemed to be assured, even if it was still slow.

Although Tanaka's government survived its onset, the oil shock frustrated the plan for the remodelling of the Japanese archipelago. (It amounted to a setback also for the more modest programme set out separately in successive comprehensive national development plans, of which the fourth, produced only in 1987, seemed to resume close to the point at which Tanaka had found himself obliged to shelve his project.) Tanaka was unable to survive the so-called Lockheed scandal, which arose out of allegations of the misappropriation of substantial funds connected with the purchase of aircraft, and which, combined with rumours of other suspicious dealings in Tanaka's circle, forced him to resign before the end of 1974. Owing to his continuing control of funds essential to the functioning of the largest faction in the LDP, Tanaka was nevertheless able to control most appointments to leading positions within the party as a whole long after his departure from office and his subsequent indictment by the public prosecutor.

The need for political reform, long advocated but never well defined, now became more insistent. Tanaka himself had been to some extent aware of this need: he was responsible for the second, failed, post-war conservative proposal for the adoption of a single-member constituency system, for elections to the House of Representatives. The overwhelming preoccupation with fund-raising, which came to afflict each lower House Diet member, with few exceptions, arose in part from his having to compete with other candidates from his own party in soliciting approval and votes within his own constituency. He had to spend not only much time in doing so, but also, more pertinently, all such funds as he and his supporters could raise, locally and in the capital; and still he depended crucially, in many if not most cases, on the sums which his, or her, faction might be able and willing to provide. Tanaka had built up a factional treasury of unparalleled wealth and scope.

The public, and many politicians, wanted release from excessive dependence on the financial resources of the factions within the LDP, because the system was so easily abused by the unscrupulous. The circumstances of Tanaka's resignation as Prime Minister gave rise to a demand for change to which LDP leaders responsible both for the system and for the selection of his successor felt obliged to pay attention. Miki Takeo was nominated by the party elders, and elected president by LDP Diet members, partly because he was reported to enjoy a public reputation not only for personal integrity but also as a serious proponent of reform.

There were various theories, and various possible components, of political reform, which now became and remained a central subject of national debate. To start with, it was a matter of long-standing concern to all political parties that the electorates in most rural constituencies, from which the LDP traditionally derived its most reliable source of strength, tended to have become much smaller in numbers than those in the most heavily populated urban constituencies. An attempt had been made in 1964 to adjust this anomaly. In 1975 there was a second reapportionment to correct discrepancies in the 'value' of votes, as between certain electoral districts. The demand continued, however, for further adjustments to constituency boundaries, or alternatively to the numbers of candidates to be returned from the more lightly populated districts. Finally, in 1985, the Supreme Court was to rule that the gap in the values of votes in the general elections of December 1983 had amounted to a breach of the Constitution. In 1975 Miki did his best to avoid this outcome, and was temporarily successful. He also secured revision of the Political Funds Control Law, but this revision did not solve the problem of excessive campaign spending. Miki then alienated important sectors of his own potential supporters by an unsuccessful attempt to strengthen the Anti-Monopoly Law. His desire to purge the party of any elements found to be tainted by suspicion of corruption attracted further criticism; and he resigned in December 1976.

Fukuda Takeo, having been nominated to succeed Miki, designated by the LDP's Diet membership, was duly adopted as president at the party convention; and having thus become Prime Minister, himself drew attention to the method of selecting their leader, as an aspect of political reform which the LDP might re-examine with possible advantage both to the transparency and fairness of the system and to their public image. The idea was to give ordinary, paid-up members of the party throughout the country the chance to participate in a preliminary process of selection. Fukuda presumably also hoped this would reduce the power of factional treasuries. Ironically, and although his premiership had enjoyed some success, including notably the achievement of a Treaty of Peace and Friendship with the People's Republic of China, the experimental introduction of the new procedure for the selection of the party president led to the withdrawal of Fukuda's candidature for a second term of office, in 1978, after his defeat by Ohira Masayoshi in the wider preliminary ballot. The general impression was that the experiment had merely led to the wider adoption of the capital's style of 'money politics'. The resources of the Tanaka faction were reported to have been deployed in support of Ohira.

As Prime Minister, Ohira, who also worked hard at consolidating Japan's international standing, especially in Asia and the Pacific, turned his attention, in domestic affairs, to the need for fiscal reform. His proposals for a consumption tax, though sound in terms of economic policy, were highly unpopular, and he was blamed within the party for the LDP's sixth consecutive failure to reverse the decline in the number of lower House seats they had held in general elections. In 1979 their share of total votes cast, though it recovered slightly, was no more than 45 per cent; and for the first time they held fewer than half of the seats in the lower House. This made it much more difficult to control work in the committees, and generally to manage the business of the House. The position could be retrieved to some extent by enlisting the support of some Independents. The handful of members who had defected to form the New Liberal Club, precisely because they deplored the style of 'money politics' adopted in the LDP, might also be relied upon to keep the opposition at bay. Nevertheless, the situation had deteriorated badly. Ohira was obliged to accept a further contest for the leadership, after the general elections of 1979, in which he again defeated Fukuda. Disunity within the party brought about the loss of a vote of confidence, in which disloyalty to Ohira's government was apparent within both the Miki and the Fukuda factions, and thus a further general election, in the following summer of 1980.

Ohira's untimely death during this election campaign inspired a rally by the LDP's supporters throughout the country, and the party won 284 seats in the lower House. As an apparently safe choice, Suzuki Zenko, who had inherited the leadership of Ohira's faction, was selected as president by the elders of the party, and approved as Prime Minister also by the Diet members, with no wider consultation. Suzuki's intention was to concentrate on the rehabilitation of the public finances. He, with Watanabe Michio as Finance Minister, first froze then cut government spending, in successive budgets, in the attempt to reduce and eventually to eliminate dependence on deficit-financing bonds. As part of the same strategy, he appointed Doko Toshio, former chairman both of Toshiba and of the Keidanren, as head of an advisory council on administrative reform. In his handling of foreign affairs, however, Suzuki made mistakes. He allowed a provocative reference, in the communiqué following a visit to Washington, to 'the Japan–US Alliance'; and there was also some fumbling over the difficult question of nuclear weapons in United States warships calling at ports in Japan. Criticism of Suzuki within the LDP was exacerbated by his appointment as Secretary-General of the party of one of the closest political associates of Tanaka Kakuei. But the resignation of Suzuki before his two-year term as president had expired was unexpected. In elections held among the party membership throughout the country, Nakasone Yasuhiro emerged as leader. He enjoyed the support of the Tanaka faction. Indeed, when he became Prime Minister, his administration was at first known as the Tanakasone government.

Nakasone's character and style enabled him to demonstrate that willingness to accept the responsibilities of leadership could secure freedom of action for the Prime Minister, even if he was denied control over funds on which his party must ultimately depend. But this independence of action would be linked very closely to the success of his policies. Nakasone's use of advisory bodies of distinguished membership to assist in the shaping and execution of administrative and educational reforms, and his energetic and constructive performance on the international stage, were among those factors which won for him an exceptional two and a half terms of office as president of the party. But the need for political reform reasserted itself. Nakasone's successor, Takeshita Noboru, who had taken over the Tanaka faction, and with it at least a dominant position in control of the party's finances, was forced out of office as the result of the Recruit scandal, named after a company whose founder had tried to buy influence, the repercussions of which threatened to be more damaging to the LDP even than the circumstances of Tanaka's downfall.

The party's difficulties seemed all the greater by contrast with the electoral triumph achieved under Nakasone's leadership in 1986, when they won 300 seats in the lower House, compared with 250 in 1983; and 72 in the House of Councillors. After the series of further scandals which followed, and because of the persistent unpopularity of measures of tax reform which Takeshita had forced through the Diet, the party for the first time lost its overall majority in the House of Councillors in the elections of 1989, and were seen to be in danger of suffering further losses in the summer of 1992. After the general elections of February 1990, the LDP were left with 286 seats in the lower House. This was still a strong position, but Miyazawa

Kiichi, as Prime Minister, remained insistent, in the spring of 1992, that the party must initiate measures of political reform.

The problems associated with 'money politics' affected some of the opposition parties, as well as the LDP, and the opposition also found difficulty in adjusting to changes in the international situation, with their obvious implications of ideology and principle. The JSP, although it was able, after a long decline, to recover some ground in the general elections of 1990, still won fewer seats then than it had held thirty years earlier. This was partly on account of the development of the Democratic Socialist Party, and latterly of the activity of the political wing of the new union federation, Rengo, which signified a great reduction in the direct support of organized labour for the JSP; and partly also because of the emergence from the late 1960s of the Komeito. This party, despite its strong initial appeal to those who felt themselves to have been left behind in the advance to prosperity, held no more than 46 seats in the elections of 1990, which was well below its best performance. The policies of Komeito's leaders were formulated in such general terms that they were able, at various times, to explore the possibilities of collaboration both with the JCP and with elements of the LDP; as well as with the centre-left parties, occupying the intervening political territory, with which Komeito came to discuss electoral tactics on a fairly regular basis.

Despite the potential strength of the opposition, if united, the multi-member constituency had the effect of keeping it divided in most electoral contests. That, and the renewed success of the Japanese economy after recovery from the oil shock of 1973, together with further achievements in foreign policy, meant that the LDP, for all its own factional divisions and in spite of the increasingly damaging scandals, was never very seriously challenged in the 1980s. Among the successful departures in foreign policy, the new relationship with China, inaugurated by Tanaka, was slow to develop, largely, as noted above, on account of the divisions which emerged within the Chinese leadership.

It was not until early 1978, therefore, that the Long Term Trade Agreement (LTTA) was concluded, providing for a detailed schedule of greatly enlarged purchases over eight years, Japan undertaking to supply plant, machinery and technology, on terms of deferred payment, and to buy Chinese coal and crude oil. On the Japanese side, this was largely the achievement of Inayama Yoshihiro, Vice-President of the Keidanren and president of Nippon Steel. The negotiations were conducted still without official participation, but the preamble to the agreement made clear that both parties to them had enjoyed governmental support.

This agreement was followed, later in the same year, by the Treaty of Peace and Friendship, signed by Sonoda Sunao, then Foreign Minister in the cabinet of Fukuda Takeo, and Huang Hua. In the preparatory negotiations there was difficulty over the insistence of the Chinese on an anti-hegemony clause, aimed unmistakably at the Soviet Union. To offset this, and to avoid prejudice to their prospects of improving relations with Moscow, the Japanese required the inclusion of a statement that the treaty would not influence the position of either signatory *vis-à-vis* any third power. The incident exemplified the suspicion and watchfulness which underlay renewed Sino-Japanese exchanges, notwithstanding the extraordinary scope for development which this renewal seemed to offer.

In commercial and financial relations, as it turned out, there were continual ups and downs. As early as February 1979, within a few months of the conclusion of the Long Term Trade Agreement, China found it necessary to cancel various developing projects, and to suspend very substantial orders for plant and equipment from Japan. This serious setback was followed by the gradual assertion of authority in Peking by the proponents of economic reform, and by the ascendancy of Deng Xiaoping. More immediately, however, uncertainty over the contracts for participation in major projects such as the Baoshan steel complex, which had originally enjoyed high priority in China's Ten-Year Development Plan, but which was first suspended, then partially revived, caused disappointment and dismay in Japanese industrial circles. The Chinese decision to seek loans from governments as well as from private sources, and to accept aid, served to put the relationship back on to a positive course. Many difficulties remained, notably over the transfer of technology, terms for the operation of joint ventures, energy supply, and access to markets; but Japanese trading companies, manufacturers and banks put great effort into the patient cultivation of what must, in their belief, prove to be fertile land for the development of business. Prime ministers who most strongly supported this effort included Ohira Masayoshi in 1979, and Nakasone Yasuhiro, who made available to China a second tranche of government loans in 1984.

By that time China had become Japan's second largest trading partner, but was running a large deficit in their bilateral exchanges. The Chinese government proceeded to restrict imports, and in 1986 the yuan was allowed to drop sharply in value against the yen. The drop in world prices for crude oil exacerbated Peking's problems. The Chinese had by then succeeded in supplying no more than about 5 per cent, in value, of Japan's imports. Much might depend on the future scale and quality of China's oil production. The discovery of rich new deposits could transform the prospects. But although trade had not developed as fast as was forecast in the Long Term Trade Agreement, and supplies of crude oil from Bohai and elsewhere in China and offshore had not reached the predicted levels, partly because of rising demand within China, Japan nevertheless accounted for 20 per cent of China's total foreign trade in the late 1980s, and Japanese banks had greatly increased their activities in support of manufacturing and trading companies established throughout China. Improvement in the terms available to would-be investors was among the principal objectives of Japanese corporations in their approach to the markets of China, and an agreement for the protection of investments was concluded, after prolonged negotiations, in 1988. The suppression of the demonstrations in Tienanmen Square in the following year led to a temporary decline in business exchanges, but the resumption of a policy of economic modernization by the Chinese government seemed unlikely to be long delayed. Japanese business interests expected patience and perseverance to be rewarded, in China as elsewhere. The extent of their investments in Hong Kong underlined these expectations. The high priority given to China in the Japanese government's aid policy was sustained. By the mid-1980s Japan was providing over half the total, in value, of all development loans made to China.

In Japan's bilateral political relationship with China there were similarly recurrent difficulties, in addition to the legacy of the long war, the continuing issue of Taiwan, and the overshadowing reality of opposing strategic alignments. These lesser difficulties included disputes over the coverage of the recent past, and of responsibility for causing suffering in war, as presented in Japanese history textbooks for schools; official Japanese government attendance at the Yasukuni Shrine, in commemoration of Japanese casualties in war; the treatment of 'war orphans', people originally abandoned in China when the Japanese forces withdrew in 1945; and title to the territory of the Senkaku Islands. Successive Japanese governments took action to contain these and other such disputes, which were never pressed beyond a certain point by Peking.

The influence of many of the larger international problems affecting Sino-Japanese relations became steadily less inhibiting after Washington's recognition of the Chinese government in Peking. With the ending of the Vietnam War, the decline in the international appeal of communism, the consequent loss of impetus in the Non-Aligned Movement, and the eventual disintegration of Soviet power, it became easier to identify national interests. It was evident that interests common to Japan and China should include the attainment of stability in the Korean peninsula. China's development of commercial exchanges with the Republic of Korea, and Japan's cautious support for the cause of reunification of North Korea with the Republic suggested that the strategies of Tokyo and Peking, if not explicitly co-ordinated, were recognized in both capitals as being compatible, even mutually supportive. Some continuing competition for influence in South-East Asia, and perhaps also in South Asia, need not inhibit the development of co-operation in North-East Asia, where stability in the territory of the former Soviet Union might become an even greater preoccupation than that of the Korean peninsula. The co-ordination of international efforts to assist

181

in developing the natural resources of the Russian Far East might offer a wider challenge, but it was one to which both Japan and China would surely aspire to respond.

During the tentative East–West détente in the 1960s, when there had been discussion of the Soviet Union's willingness to draw upon Japanese technology and American capital in order to develop the Tyumen oilfields, the prospect had seemed something of a threat to China. By the early 1990s, China's active partnership in any such project, together with that of Japan, the latter this time perhaps as the source of funding as well as of technical expertise, was predicted. The idea of co-operation rather than rivalry with China in North-East Asia was no doubt attractive to planners in Tokyo. A solution to the problem of the northern territories, however, presumably remained a precondition of serious Japanese commitment to any new scheme for the exploitation of Russia's natural resources.

In the interval between the first, illusory détente and the breakdown of Soviet power, against the lowering background of confrontation between the then superpowers, the prospects for Japan's participation in the programme of modernization to which China's leaders were becoming gradually more wholeheartedly committed were seldom loudly proclaimed. There had been many disappointments on the way. The resignation of Hu Yaobang in 1987 was a new setback, since he was accused of favouring 'over-friendly' relations with Japan. The expulsion from China of a Kyodo News Agency reporter made matters worse. Even after the collapse of Soviet power had opened up the international setting, the repercussions of the Chinese government's repression of dissent inhibited frank assessments of economic opportunities. Nevertheless, some major projects prospered. The persistent endeavours of Japanese corporations began to show returns. The Chinese market had been crucially important to the Japanese iron and steel industry when demand elsewhere for its products turned down sharply, in the early 1980s. The growth of student exchanges, of mutual language study and of tourism were evidence that the idea of a new era in Sino-Japanese relations was not illusory. By the mid-1980s Japanese tourists were going to China in their tens of thousands every year, and the subsequent setback was not prolonged. Moreover, the first-class seats on several flights a day between airports in Japan and China showed high occupancy ratios: such travellers had business in view.

Ideological, subversive and surrogate military methods, together with the threat of direct intervention, having failed, China had been unable to compete with Japan's great post-war effort to promote and participate in the economic advance of leading countries of South-East Asia. This effort, which had begun with a frugal approach to the necessary business of reparations, did not itself go smoothly at first. It was known that Japan had remained unpopular in much of South-East Asia since the end of the Second

World War, but the hostile demonstrations which met Prime Minister Tanaka in Indonesia and Thailand, during his tour of the region in 1974, caused considerable shock in Tokyo. The Japanese government reacted by increasing the availability of credit and stepping up its programme of grant aid for countries in South-East Asia; and by exhorting Japanese industrial groups to take full account of the interests of countries which were hosts to their investments in the extraction of raw materials, in manufacturing and in the development of communications and infrastructure. An attempt was made, on Prime Minister Fukuda's instructions, to lay down principles which should guide Japanese corporations in their activities in other Asian countries.

When the programme of reparations came to an end, in 1975, the scale of Japan's aid was expanded. As much as 60 per cent of Japan's total aid budget was disbursed in the region, and it was still so when Japan became the largest donor of aid throughout the world, towards the end of the 1980s. Japan provided more than half of all aid made available to Thailand, the Philippines and Malaysia, and a substantial proportion of Indonesia's allocation. The first oil crisis, of 1973, was immediately seen in Tokyo greatly to have increased the importance to Japan of sources of energy in the countries of East Asia, in which Japanese industry consequently accelerated and enlarged its investments. These investments were heaviest at first in what became known as the newly industrialized economies of the Republic of Korea, Taiwan, Hong Kong and Singapore; but they were later more evenly spread throughout the region. In the 1970s and 1980s Japan's bilateral trade both with the newly industrialized economies and with all Singapore's partner countries in ASEAN grew very rapidly. The composition and scale of these countries' exports to the United States also owed much to Japanese investment.

Successive Japanese governments were consistently supportive of the unity of ASEAN, and aware that any premature move to revise the Peace Constitution would be liable to excite suspicion and resentment in South-East Asia. Though generally sympathetic also with ASEAN's approach to the problems of Indo-China, they felt able to afford a more forthcoming attitude towards the economic requirements and aspirations of Vietnam. In so doing, they took a genuinely independent view, the political value of which might or might not be recognized by the international community at a later stage.

From the time of the first oil shock, Japan's imports from the oil-producing countries of the Middle East, like the trade with the newly industrialized countries of East Asia, assumed increasing importance, both statistically and politically. Political adjustment caused additional difficulties to relations with Washington. Direct investment in the Middle East proved undependable. A very large project to build an oil refinery at Bandar

Shahpur, in particular, incurred losses so devastating, after the outbreak of the Iran–Iraq War, that even Mitsui had to seek assistance in order to recover from them.

Nevertheless, there was a strong growth, from the latter 1970s, in Japan's exports overall. This was achieved despite the sharp decline in shipbuilding which, because of the oil shock, came so soon after Japan's assumption of world leadership in this sector. The agreement, reached within OECD, that shipbuilding capacity should be reduced by 35 per cent, was a serious blow to Japan's heavy industries. Great efforts were made to avoid the necessity of large-scale redundancies in companies which had offered lifetime employment. Diversification, primarily into land construction equipment, was managed in such a way as to absorb most of the labour in the shipyards. Rising demand from China was instrumental in the recovery of the iron and steel industry.

Japanese exports of manufactured goods were now causing increased dissatisfaction in North America and Western Europe, both because of the imbalances which resulted from their expansion and because of their impact on domestic industries in the receiving countries. The British motor-cycle industry had been an early casualty: it had looked in vain for protection to successive governments devoted to the principles of free trade, and had never seriously considered collaboration with any of the mutually competitive, leading Japanese makers. Motor manufacturers in all the other economies of the free world were progressively more seriously alarmed by the intensity of the competition from Japanese industry. Even before the oil shock, Japan had become the world's second largest manufacturer of motor vehicles. After the oil shock, Japanese cars gained added advantages, especially in North America, from their comparatively economical performance. Something of a resort to managed trade seemed inescapable. Already, in the 1960s, the Japanese textile industry had entered into a voluntary restraint agreement, to cover exports to the United States. In the mid-1970s Japanese car manufacturers began to make deliberately limiting annual forecasts of the combined market share they expected to achieve in Britain, after discussions with the Society of Motor Manufacturers and Traders, which spoke for the British industry. The Ministry of International Trade and Industry in Tokyo was the discreet referee, its whistle hardly heard outside the domestic stadium, where the competitive struggle was unremitting. Among and between the electronics industries of the leading industrialized countries, the general trend of development was similar.

It was in electronics that technological competition was most intense, primarily between Japan and the United States. Leadership in the production of semiconductors passed for a time to Japan, but remained in contention. Europe was equally deeply concerned, both in considerations governing the transfer of technology and in those determining the rules of fair trade. By the mid-1980s Japanese industry was beginning to invest heavily in the construction of manufacturing facilities both in Europe and in the United States. Japanese investment in the United States did not greatly reduce bilateral friction, because the Japanese surplus on visible trade reached levels which caused constant criticism both in American industrial circles and in Congress. Chronic United States budgetary deficits made matters worse, despite massive Japanese purchasing of US Treasury bonds. Japanese acquisitions of real estate and of industrial and intellectual property in the United States led to expressions of resentment and hostility towards Japan. Fortunately for Japan, the principal strain in the Uruguay round of the GATT negotiations lay between Europe and the United States, though any solution of the obstinate problems of trade in agricultural products seemed certain to involve renewed demands at least for the 'tariffication' of rice imports into Japan.

Inevitably, expressions of hostility were reciprocated. But there were also conciliatory voices to be heard on both sides of the Pacific, especially in official quarters. There was widespread recognition that the economies of Japan and the United States were deeply interdependent, and that their common interests, though reduced in urgency by the break-up of the Soviet Union, remained so extensive as to render a high degree of mutual co-operation in international affairs indispensable to both.

Throughout the 1970s and the 1980s, Japan's Western orientation in the struggle with Soviet power long having been assured in political terms, by far the country's most important bilateral relationship, that with the United States, was primarily dependent upon an intricate equation of strategic and economic factors. Ever since the earliest days of the cold war, and especially since the Korean War, there had always been a strong body of opinion in influential circles in Washington that Japan must be brought to contribute more, and more directly, to Western defence. Ever since the end of Hatoyama's premiership, however, the leaders of the ruling party in Japan had accepted that revision of Article 9 of the Constitution must await an evolution in public opinion, uncertain in its timing, not sure even to come about. They had, accordingly, determined to avoid inciting the lively popular reaction which they judged that any rapid expansion of the self-defence forces would incur, and, in line with this approach, it was decided in 1976 that the defence budget should not exceed 1 per cent of GNP. The significance of this informal decision, taken by the leaders of the Liberal Democratic Party in the interests of harmony within the Diet and of preserving public confidence in their policies, was, however, diminished by the sustained rate of growth of Japan's GNP, which was such as to permit the trebling of defence spending over the next ten years without its exceeding this limit. The first oil shock of 1973, though its principal consequences were of course economic, also stimulated continued examination of defence policy, and of the nature of interdependence.

In 1980 a study group set up by Prime Minister Ohira evolved the concept of 'Comprehensive National Security'. The idea was to work with like-minded countries to create a stable international peace. The 'low posture' was no longer an adequate description of Japan's position: as Foreign Minister, Sonoda Sunao disowned the phrase as being unworthy of a country which had a major role to play on the world's stage. In 1979 the Japanese government had denounced the Soviet invasion of Afghanistan in unusually forthright terms. Substance was given to the idea of comprehensive national security by stepping up economic assistance to strategically key countries, including Pakistan and Turkey. Later, Nakasone, as Prime Minister, was at pains to convince the Japanese people that greater expenditure on defence would be appropriate. But, although the conventional ceiling of 1 per cent of GNP may have been exceeded in the late 1980s, it was only by a very narrow margin.

The Japanese government, however, publicly undertook, in 1982, to assume responsibility for defence of the sea lanes out to 1,000 nautical miles from Japan's coastline, and, though the emphasis was placed on the lines of supply from the south, it was clear that this undertaking also involved a commitment to deny entry into the Pacific by Soviet naval vessels based on Siberian ports, if the necessity arose. Because of the threat posed to the whole region by Soviet power, the Chinese government, in turn, came to accept the scale of Japan's military capability as appropriate to the requirements of self-defence, and even agreed to hold occasional exchanges of view with Japanese officers and senior officials from the Defence Agency in Tokyo. After much discussion, the Japanese government subsequently found it possible to participate in the work envisaged in President Reagan's Strategic Defense Initiative. There were difficulties over the transfer of technology, and over projects for the collaborative development of military aircraft. However, by the time that the Soviet threat was dispersed, the Japanese self-defence forces were well equipped. In manpower, they were roughly equal to the strength of the British armed services.

The debate about Japan's military capability did not end with the ending of the struggle between the West and the Soviet bloc. The question whether approval should be given by the Diet for the employment of Japanese forces overseas, under the auspices of the United Nations, remained open after the Gulf War of 1991. Japanese minesweepers had by then taken part in operations sanctioned by the Security Council, and medical personnel had been made available. No consensus was reached at that stage among the political parties to cover future contingencies, despite the efforts of Prime Minister Kaifu. The larger step, of an amendment to Article 9 of the

Constitution, was not formally proposed, and there was no evidence that the Japanese people were ready for it. Meanwhile the dramatic reduction in East–West tension did not serve greatly to reduce the persistent friction between Washington and Tokyo.

In Tokyo, some held the view that difficulties with the United States could be contained more easily, and the growth of Japanese power and influence be more readily assimilated, in the context of an Asian-Pacific community of nations. This would embrace not only the members of ASEAN and the other newly industrialized countries of Asia, and those less advanced in economic development which needed shelter from outside threats, but also Australia, New Zealand and Canada, whose markets, or supplies of raw materials and food products, were so important to Tokyo and Washington alike, and whose contribution to the pursuit of common interests would be so valuable both in political and in strategic terms. The membership of countries of South America bordering the Pacific would be appropriate. Perhaps the Chinese themselves could be persuaded to participate. During Ohira's premiership these ideas were given some prominence in statements of Japanese policy. There was some response. It proved difficult to embody the concept of an Asian-Pacific community in specific proposals, but useful progress was made in the Pacific Economic Cooperation Conference (PECC), a consultative body with academic and commercial as well as official representatives, founded jointly in 1980 by Ohira and the then Australian Prime Minister, Malcolm Fraser. China and Taiwan became full members of this organization, whose essentially unofficial character enhanced its usefulness.

In addition to its constructive role in the PECC, Japan played a full part in the work of ECAFE. It usually provided the leading official in the Asian Development Bank, and also aspired to speak for the non-communist countries of East Asia at the economic summits.

At these meetings, of the seven leading economic powers, Japan's bilateral relations with the United States could be seen in the global context. From their beginning, in 1975, these economic summits served to moderate the tone of debate about issues of economic management, and to promote a limited trilateral consensus on policy. In 1984 the Japanese government supported the United States in pressing for a new round of negotiations on the liberalization of trade, in the GATT, at a time when the Europeans would have preferred to defer action. The following year, after discussions at the Economic Summit, the Group of Five reached the Plaza Agreement, which led to a dramatic strengthening of the yen against the dollar in the interest of reducing the imbalance of trade between Japan and the United States. The imbalance, and the United States' deficit, persisted, but the effect of this agreement, coupled with measures taken by the Japanese government to implement the recommendations of a committee set up by Prime Minister Nakasone under the chairmanship of Maekawa Haruo, a former governor of the Bank of Japan, to study the requirements of a more open domestic market, was greatly to increase the proportion of manufactured goods in Japan's imports; and thus to accelerate changes to the earlier post-war pattern of the country's foreign trade, which the oil shock of 1973 had first stimulated.

These changes came to have a considerable effect on Japan's relations with the countries of Western Europe. Despite the constant demand for Japanese consumer goods to supply the markets of Europe, and admiration for the famous economic miracle which had brought about the recovery of the Federal Republic of Germany, there was some scepticism in Japan in the mid-1970s as to Western Europe's prospects of resuming a vigorous growth in overall industrial activity, its capacity for innovation in manufacturing, its competence in production engineering, its management techniques, and its work ethic. The Japanese government, however, remained fully aware of the importance of Europe's contribution at that time to the strength of NATO, and thus to the deterrence of a more aggressive Soviet policy in Asia.

Both government and industry in Japan also recognized that the European Community, though it seemed a long time coming and was difficult both to assess and to understand, could transform the global balance of economic power. To the authorities in Tokyo, diligent as they were, it was by no means clear whether the Secretary-General of the Commission in Brussels was a rather grand civil servant or a reincarnation of Napoleon, in a business suit. But Japanese industrialists recognized that, if they did not establish manufacturing facilities in the territories of member countries of the EC, their products might be in danger of exclusion from the European single market, due to come into being in 1992.

After an uncertain start, and some setbacks, including the cancellation of a planned investment by a leading Japanese electronics company following hostile demonstrations in the north of England, the welcome subsequently given to Japanese investment in Britain, from the early years of Mrs Thatcher's premiership, led to its rapid growth, ultimately throughout the EC. Britain was host to about half Japan's total manufacturing investment in Europe in the period leading up to the completion of the single European market. Despite the greatly improved atmosphere, there was still pressure in Europe to contain further Japanese advances into European markets, and new arrangements were negotiated to manage and limit imports of motor vehicles from Japan, on a European basis, far into the 1990s.

By the early 1990s, moreover, the income deriving from Japanese overseas investments was itself reaching levels which, on a global scale, would soon constitute a further set of disturbing imbalances. The wider opening of Japanese securities and insurance markets was required, in order to create the 'level playing field' demanded by Japan's international partners. Rheto-

188

ric often failed, however, to respect the distinction between mathematical equality, or quantitative balance, on the one hand, and equality of opportunity, in equally open markets, on the other. This failure caused less misunderstanding in relations between Japan and the EC than it did between Japan and the United States. Nevertheless, Japan's relationship with the USA remained far deeper and thicker than relations with most European countries, or with the EC as a whole. With the Commission, of course, discussions concentrated on trade policy. On a visit to Brussels as Prime Minister of Japan, in 1978, Fukuda Takeo was reported to have said, 'Europe has not quite treated us as a true friend or a real partner, but rather as something alien to them [*sic*].' This was an early view, only slowly and partially superseded. Meetings with a troika of European Foreign Ministers for wide-ranging reviews of international affairs, at a time when individual member governments of the EC pursued distinctive foreign policies on issues of particular importance to them, were at first uninspiring and largely unproductive. Bilateral meetings with the representatives of European nations with which Japan had historic ties and with which there were shared constitutional and cultural interests remained generally more rewarding.

European countries, individually or collectively, sometimes provided useful cover when Japanese interests seemed to require a certain distancing from United States policy, as in respect of the Middle East, and especially after the first oil shock. Japan's attitude towards the Soviet Union was, by contrast, generally more rigid than that commonly adopted in Western Europe. The constant application of Soviet pressure over fisheries was partly responsible for this, and in the background the long heritage of mutual suspicion and latent hostility. Above all, it was the Japanese government's consistent position on the issue of the northern territories which governed the relationship. Of the islands in dispute, the Habomais and Shikotan were geographically very close to Hokkaido, of which they are clearly geographical or geological appendages, while Kunashiri and Etorofu equally evidently have the character of southern Kuriles. The strategic significance of the channels between particular islands and island groups was greatly diminished by the dissolution of Soviet power. Successive Japanese governments were uncompromising in their claim to the restitution of full sovereignty over all the northern territories. Nevertheless, the desirability of averting the complete collapse of economic and hence of social order in the territories of the former Soviet Union seemed likely to require a concerted effort by the international community, to the success of which the participation of Japan would be indispensable.

By the late 1980s the Japanese government was no longer constrained in approaching such questions by considerations involving the harmony of domestic society. The extreme, violently revolutionary elements on the left, which had caused so much trouble in the 1960s, had mostly abandoned hope of attaining their objectives, or of gaining international support, years before the end of the Soviet regime. Some groups retained affiliations with communist or Trotskyite doctrine, but their only practical co-operation with foreign movements was abroad, usually in the Middle East. The Japanese Red Army arranged for some cadres to be trained with other terrorist organizations in that region, and carried out various operations from bases there, including hijackings of aircraft, attacks on diplomatic premises, and the Lod Airport massacre. In Japan itself, apart from a few attacks aimed at prestigious targets, from fairly primitive rocket launchers or mortars, and occasional, more sinister exercises designed to disrupt communications, the extreme left confined its activity for most of the 1970s and 1980s to the siege of Narita Airport, and continued opposition to its extension. This was the only cause espoused by the extreme left which was found capable of drawing support, or even much interest, from the public; and attempted subversion at Narita was contained by the authorities without great difficulty, though at considerable expense. In the 1980s, extremists of the right were more often in evidence in Tokyo, where their paramilitary groups drove trucks and vans with loudspeakers round the Imperial Palace moat, or demonstrated in the neighbourhood of the Yasukuni Shrine.

Largely disregarding its own unreconstructed fringes, Japanese society as a whole continued along the path of evolutionary prosperity. The public awareness and enjoyment of steadily rising standards of living was maintained, interrupted only for eighteen months or so, after the first oil shock. In the 1980s, opinion polls revealed that about 90 per cent of the Japanese people looked upon themselves as members of the middle class. There was some disquiet about the educational system. Its control became increasingly centralized, though privately owned institutions proliferated. Competition at school and especially for places at the leading universities was intense; and, although the general level of performance was maintained satisfactorily, and the proportion of students going on to higher education was exceptionally high by world standards, the strains imposed were such as to give rise to much complaint about the 'examination hell' (*shiken jigoku*). The Japan Teachers' Union, although concentrating after the 1960s on economic rather than political objectives, remained the most militant union in its methods, and in its hostility towards the ruling Liberal Democratic Party, which was reciprocated.

The wider labour movement went through a period of shifting national and international affiliations, dominated for a decade from the mid-1960s by the alliances of Domei with the right wing of the JSP and with the Democratic Socialist Party; and of Sohyo with the left wing of the JSP. The influence of the JCP throughout the labour movement declined, and with it the strength of the smaller, communist-oriented union organization. There was a lessening of militancy generally, though the annual spring offensive

(*Shunto*) remained a central determinant of the rate at which wages rose on the national scale. Meanwhile, in the centre, a moderate group developed, concentrating at first on conciliation within the wider movement. By the late 1980s this organization, Rengo, looked capable of providing a new and responsible political focus for the whole labour movement. In early 1992, a candidate of its political affiliate, standing at a by-election for a seat in the House of Councillors, caused a modest sensation by defeating the LDP's candidate, at a time, admittedly, when there was a widespread desire, born of public distaste for the continuing succession of scandals, to see the LDP at least symbolically humbled.

Industrial relations came to be affected by fears of the process of 'hollowing out', which was believed to pose a threat of unemployment to the labour force in Japan allegedly as a result of excessive overseas investments. By the early 1990s, however, there was a shortage of labour in Japan, despite the availability of a substantial body of immigrant workers, many of whom were not officially entitled to seek employment but were permitted to stay in the country because of their usefulness. The greatest threat to continued prosperity was then thought to stem from the ageing of the Japanese population itself, which was forecast to begin to exert a downward influence on living standards from soon after the turn of the century.

Some qualified observers took the view that such forecasts, based on the simple extrapolation of existing trends, failed to take account of the likelihood that technological developments would counteract the effects of demographic change. The capacity of advances in automation and information technology, combined with those in medical science and biology, to transform Japanese society and to affect living conditions more widely, was not doubted by those familiar with the work of leading research establishments in Japan. The decision of Prime Minister Nakasone to sponsor an international seminar on the life sciences, as a special contribution to follow up the discussions at the Economic Summit during Japan's chairmanship, gave an indication of some likely priorities for the future.

During Nakasone's successive terms as president of the LDP and Prime Minister, and not least because of his style of leadership, Japan may be said to have secured full international acknowledgement of the attainment of the country's post-war goal of equality with the most influential and powerful Western nations. This acknowledgement was accorded on account of Japan's economic performance. There were some indications in the early 1990s that this performance might have reached its peak. Nothing in the history of the past century, however, has suggested that the capacity of Japanese society to adjust to changing circumstances will be easily exhausted. Nor were strictures passed on the younger generation, 'the new humankind' or *shinjinrui*, widely believed to foreshadow a steep decline in morale, ambition, capability or diligence.

191

The slogan popularized by Nakasone's government was the one word: internationalization. It came to be interpreted in various ways. For some, it suggested that Japanese methods and standards might come to be applied worldwide, and even, for a few, that Japan's national interests could confidently be regarded as paramount. For others, it signified the need for give and take, and served precisely as a reminder that international trade and politics were not zero-sum games in which a single winner could aspire to sweep the pool. Those who were chiefly responsible for Japan's industrial and financial successes, who led the corporations and organizations which would determine the lines of much future strategy, together with the senior officials in government departments, whose advice they valued (but whose guidance they no longer felt obliged invariably to follow), were generally aware that the international trading system had to be constituted fairly, and its rules and conventions operated considerately, if the achievements of their own generation were to be fully realized. They knew, for example, that the principles of reciprocity and equal opportunity must be applied internationally to the regulation of financial services as well as to that of trade.

Matters of such far-reaching importance were not always, at first, argued and decided on merit, in Japan any more than elsewhere. The power of the single-issue lobby to delay even moves arguably imperative in the national interest was a familar characteristic of the age. In Japan, the agricultural co-operative movement was, not surprisingly, strongly protectionist in its outlook. The power of the Nokyo, the organization which represented the movement, was substantial. The JSP, seizing an opportunity to supplant the LDP in its former rural strongholds, adopted a protectionist approach to trade in agricultural products. There were obvious environmental and conservationist considerations to be taken into account, as well as the economic consequences for rural communities of a more open market, where prices for rice had been supported artifically for longer than anyone could remember, and imports virtually excluded for decades. Could the Japanese rice-farmer hold a sufficient place in an open market, on the basis of quality and consumers' preference? If not, how could a satisfactory alternative livelihood be assured for him in the country, and how should the future development of Japanese agriculture as a whole be planned and managed? These questions were not unlike those facing farmers, and farming itself, in many other countries. They deserved to be treated with the greatest care, especially in the context of the Uruguay round of GATT negotiations. They were suitable subjects neither for megaphone diplomacy nor for treatment by power-broking lobbies; nor could they be tackled exclusively at the national level. Interdependence was inescapable, as members of the Diet representing rural constituencies inevitably came in the end to acknowledge, if only grudgingly in some cases, or indirectly.

'Money politics' tended to flood into such areas of controversy, like water through the ingenious irrigation systems of the traditional Japanese rice-farmer. This was why political reform came so high on the agenda, both for conscientious politicians and for the electorate in Japan. There was a desire to ensure that neither favourable treatment, nor inactivity, nor silence could be bought, and that political parties should be judged on the merits of the general policies they advocated and implemented. This desire applied above all in industry, where one of the main strengths of the Japanese corporations was considered to lie in their skill at keeping their employees informed of the larger aims and objectives of the board of directors. Improper distortions would be liable to early detection, in this industrial culture, with potentially widespread and disastrous results, as demonstrated in the scandals which actually came to light. The chairman of the Keidanren, Hiraiwa Gaishi, was accordingly prominent among those calling for political reform in the spring of 1992.

There were of course other areas, in addition to education, agriculture and the environment, trade and financial regulation, in which reforms were demanded, if less urgently. It was alleged that 'money politics' was linked with the underworld of crime and protection rackets. The authorities showed a gradually firmer readiness to contemplate extended, systematic action against the hitherto half-tolerated gangsters and mobsters, the *yakuza* and the *sokaiya*, the former involved in all manner of crime, the latter specializing in the 'protection' of corporate directors from potentially troublesome 'shareholders' at annual general meetings. There was a similarly gradual improvement in the handling of social problems such as those of the formerly outcaste *burakumin* or *eta*, of the Korean minorities, and of immigrant labour. Thanks partly to the example set by foreign firms in their employment, more and more Japanese women were pursuing independent careers. The majority of the electorate, conscious of the continuing improvement in their own living conditions and standards, saw no likelihood of obtaining better economic management through any of the other parties; nevertheless, there was a public sense that the LDP ought to be constrained to demonstrate in action the sincerity of the party's long-professed belief in political reform, and that such action should go beyond the reapportionment of seats among multi-member constituencies.

The responses of successive Japanese governments to persistent pressure for change, whether in compliance or in resistance, and whether the pressure came from foreign or from domestic sources, tended to be cautious and slow. The impression that they moved only when forced to do so was in part the result of the importance they attached to the careful preparation of public opinion. The concept of consensus was applied not only to their supporters. It was considered bad form to force measures through the Diet when the intensity of opposition exceeded a certain level, regardless of the size of the majority in favour of the proposals in question. It was sometimes done, but seldom without leaving a feeling of failure and distaste among all concerned. There had been violent storms in the Diet in the early post-war decades, but LDP leaders after Kishi were especially careful not to parade or flaunt their majorities.

The reasons for this were complex. They included a prudent regard for the unity of the LDP itself. The danger that complete factions, undervalued or inadequately rewarded by the leadership, might make common cause with one or more of the opposition parties was always present, in the background. Besides, the sovereignty of the people was not merely a polite constitutional fiction. The political strategists in the ruling party knew better than to forget that the LDP was accountable to the people. They recognized that a thoroughly shameful or inept performance could forfeit the confidence of the electorate beyond possibility of recovery. Were this to happen, the intimate understandings built up over decades with both the bureaucracy and the industrial organizations would not save them. If they were to suffer an electoral defeat sufficiently severe as to deprive their united forces of control over proceedings in the Diet, the coalition of factions of which the LDP was composed might finally fall apart.

If they faced the future with confidence, however, it was because they felt they had earned a substantial share of the credit for Japan's firm establishment as a leading economic and industrial power, in a world in which economic strength was, for the time being at least, more often decisively influential than military strength. Even at the highest level of strategic negotiation, too, the Japanese government had after all succeeded in influencing the provisions of the Intermediate Nuclear Forces Treaty concluded between the United States and the Soviet Union in 1987. Japan's expenditure on conventional forces, moreover, was expressed in one of the world's three largest national defence budgets. Prime Minister Kaifu had been unable to muster sufficient support for the United Nations Peace Cooperation Bill in 1991, but it was significant that the debate had been conducted in a reasonable spirit, such as might easily permit of its resumption. Uncertainty in the sensitive area of defence and security was more than compensated for by Japan's status in economic affairs as, for example, in the recognition that Japan carried approximately equal weight in the GATT negotiations with Western Europe and North America.

Such large comparisons were regarded with some apprehension by those in Japan who remained conscious also of the country's weaknesses. Some fear of continuing or even of sharpening differences with other nascent regional blocs was balanced by consideration of the strength of Japan's position in the Asia-Pacific region. The absence in East Asia of a North–South problem of hopelessly unbalanced development was in part a tribute to Japan's commercial and industrial enterprise. The emergence of Asian-

Pacific Economic Co-operation (APEC), following a proposal by the then Australian Prime Minister, Robert Hawke, in a speech in Seoul in early 1989, gave promise of a formal structure founded on the consultative work of the PECC. On a visit to Bangkok in 1991, Miyazawa Kiichi was reported to have said, 'The Asian economic zone will outdo the North American economic zone and European economic zone at the beginning of the 21st century, and assume a very crucial role in the world.' If developments in the region were to reduce Japan's dependence on oil from the Middle East, the stability and security of the country's economy and industry could be strongly reinforced. Meanwhile, even the disintegration of Soviet power had not greatly reduced the importance of Japan's bilateral relations with the United States, to both parties.

It seemed, in the spring of 1992, that the great unexplored territory of a China more firmly bent upon economic reform might once again seem to offer an open door; but not this time one which any foreign powers were likely to aspire to keep open by their own efforts. Developments in China would also have far-reaching effects externally, going far beyond Hong Kong and Taiwan, and touching Japan's interests everywhere. The stability of the Korean peninsula was, as ever, a key concern for Japan, especially following reports of Pyongyang's capability in the production of nuclear weapons. Russia's weakness required the attention of Western Europe, as well as of the United States and Japan; but it was to the latter that discontent in Siberia brought the closest new preoccupation. This heavy and extensive agenda of unfinished business in North-East Asia, though of great consequence for the world at large, was most intimately related to the security and prosperity of Japan. The greater Japan's global influence became, the more pressing this unfinished business must grow. There were times when the outlook for Tokyo in the 1990s would recall the circumstances of a century before; but the viewpoint of the Japanese people, their attitudes towards and knowledge of the outside world, and the technology and resources available to them had all been transformed in the interval. Internationalization meant, above all, that there were limits to what any country could set out to do on its own.

Author's Note

The author has many acknowledgements to make, and will fail to do justice to his creditors, in the following note. It needs to be prefaced by a reminder that any opinions given in the book are his own, and should, above all, not be taken as expressions of official British government policy.

Sir George Sansom's first and greatest book, *Japan, A Short Cultural History*, has retained the absorbing interest and authority which it held, for this reader, on the slow voyage from Southampton to Kobe, more than forty years ago. *The Western World and Japan*, and Sansom's last major study, *A History of Japan to 1867*, in three volumes, also command wholehearted admiration. The lectures which Sansom gave in Tokyo in December 1950, and which were published originally by the International Secretariat of the Institute of Pacific Relations, New York, under the auspices of the Japan Institute of Pacific Relations, and the title *Japan in World History*, go far beyond his own introductory reference to 'a modest contribution to the work of Japanese scholars'. Tuttle did a service in reprinting and republishing these lectures, in Tokyo, in 1977. They are the more remarkable when considered in the context of the Occupation and the work of the Far East Commission. The background to Sansom's work as a whole is depicted in Katharine Sansom's *Sir George Sansom and Japan: A Memoir*. Some of his official economic reports, often composed jointly with colleagues, were published by HMSO for the Board of Trade and the Foreign Office, and show a keen and realistic appreciation of the strength of Japanese industry in the 1920s and 1930s. Many others, not intended for publication, are available in the F.O. Series in the Public Records Office: they go back, for example, to notes on the role of State Shinto towards the end of the Meiji period.

Sansom also completed and saw to the publication of Sir Charles Eliot's book on *Japanese Buddhism*, another work which has retained its importance, as part of the general background to Japanese studies as well as for the specialist. In his address at the Annual Ceremony of the School of Oriental and African Studies in 1956 (of which Professor Hagihara Nobutoshi kindly gave the present writer a copy) Sansom explained why great works of scholarship, such as those to which he had paid tribute earlier in his address, might no longer be expected from active servants of the British Crown and government. He spoke of a time when 'young secretaries were encouraged to interest themselves in the life of the people among whom they lived', and when 'it was even thought rather priggish to attend the Chancery in the afternoon'. He would be relieved to know that Sir Hugh Cortazzi, who was often constrained to attend the Chancery far into the night, had nevertheless produced, in *The Japanese Achievement*, an introductory, chronological guide to the development of Japanese civilization, in all its human aspects, which is unlikely to be superseded in our time. *The Cambridge Encyclopedia of Japan* now gives a comprehensive thematic survey by a group of distinguished scholars.

It is customary, and indeed natural, to regard 1868 as the starting point of modern Japanese history. Professor W. G. Beasley's *The Meiji Restoration* is indispensable to the foreign student for an understanding of this historical phenomenon, both as event and as process: it can be combined with the same author's skilled presentation of *Select Documents on Japanese Foreign Policy 1853–1868*, for insight into the perception within Japan of the international context. This is a good way of approaching the official papers published, for example, by the Foreign Ministry in Tokyo in the series of volumes of Japanese diplomatic documents, *Nihon Gaiko Bunsho*. It may be appropriate to note here that the experience of the present writer testifies to the courtesy and helpfulness with which visitors are received by the directors and staff of both the National Diet Library and the Diplomatic Record Office, where the Japanese Foreign Ministry (Gaimusho) archives are made available for study in Tokyo.

Another work of distinction, analysing the Meiji settlement, is E. H. Norman's study, *Japan's Emergence as a Modern State*, originally published for the Institute of Pacific Relations and subsequently also made available, in New York, with a selection of his other writings, edited by John W. Dower, in *Origins of the Modern Japanese State*. As a first-hand account in English of the events and movements surrounding the Meiji Restoration, as fresh and exciting as if written yesterday, that given in Sir Ernest Satow's *A Diplomat in Japan* remains invaluable.

Among works on the intellectual life of the Meiji period, Carmen Blacker's study of the writings of Fukuzawa Yukichi, *The Japanese Enlightenment*, is outstandingly helpful and perceptive. Instructive biographies of great figures emerging in the Meiji period include Roger F. Hackett on *Yamagata Aritomo*, C. E. Cody on *Itagaki Taisuke*, Hamada on *Prince Ito*, and Iddittie on *Okuma Shigenobu*. For studying the nature of the work of the military leaders of the period, J. N. Westwood's *Illustrated History of the Russo-Japanese War* is still a reliable guide. Later biographical studies which are especially illuminating are Lesley Connor's *The Emperor's Adviser*, on Saionji Kinmochi, and J. W. Dower's *Empire and Aftermath: Yoshida Shigeru and the Japanese Experience, 1878–1954*; the latter most conveniently consulted together with his son, Yoshida Kenichi's translation of *The Yoshida Memoirs*.

Great debts are owed to the authors of general histories of the whole modern period, most notably to the late Professor Richard Storry, for *A History of Modern Japan*, to Professer Beasley for *The Modern History of Japan*, and to Professor Reischauer for *Japan*. Each of these established authorities has extended these debts; Reischauer with *The Japanese*; Beasley with *Japanese Imperialism 1894–1945*, and *The Rise of Modern Japan*; and Storry with *Japan and the Decline of the West in Asia*, *The Double Patriots*, on Japanese nationalism, *The Case of Richard Sorge*, in collaboration with F. W. Deakin, and *The Way of the Samurai*.

The present writer has drawn especial benefit also from the work of Professor Ian Nish, including his book on *Japanese Foreign Policy 1869–1942*, as well as *The Anglo-Japanese Alliance* and the *Alliance in Decline*, his study of Anglo-Japanese relations, 1908–1923, and *The Origins of the Russo-Japanese War*. His article in the *China Quarterly* (1990), 'An Overview of Relations between China and Japan, 1895–1945', is a key contribution to a subject of outstanding interest and importance. His latest book on the Manchurian crisis, *Japan's Struggle with Internationalism*, was awaited with great expectations, now amply satisfied. There is also much to be learned from Ogata Sadako's *Defiance in Manchuria: The Making of Japanese Foreign Policy 1931–32*.

It seems likely that Mrs Ogata's impression of the Showa Emperor's attitude towards what might be called the insubordinate tendency will stand. We have, too, an article by Ian Nish on 'The Showa Emperor and the End of the Manchurian Crisis', in *Japan Forum* (October 1989). The same number of that useful periodical carried a note by Stephen Large on 'Imperial Princes and Court Politics in Early Showa Japan', which was later followed by his *Emperor Hirohito and Showa Japan*. There is no lack of books touching on the Showa Emperor's role, but not all exhibit an equally scholarly approach. Large's work and Professor Takeda Kiyoko's book on *The Dual-Image of the Japanese Emperor*, with its Foreword by Ian Nish, and her paper on 'The Emperor System in Modern Japan', given as the third Richard Storry Memorial Lecture in 1989 and published by St Antony's College, Oxford, set a standard here.

To return to the general history of the period, we now have Volumes 5 and 6 of the *Cambridge History of Japan*, in which internationally recognized experts range over the nineteenth and twentieth centuries, providing chapters of separately distilled wisdom rather than a continuous narrative. The consistently high quality of the contributions is reminiscent of those volumes of thematic studies from universities in the United States, for which students of Japan have so long has cause to be grateful. Among those most often consulted by the present writer were *Changing Japanese Attitudes toward Modernization*, edited by M. B. Jansen, *Political Development in Modern Japan*, edited by R. E. Ward, *Dilemmas of Growth in Prewar Japan*, edited by J. W. Morley, and *Japan in Crisis*, edited by B. Silberman and H. D. Harootunian. Two extremely stimulating volumes published within the last decade are *The Japanese Colonial Empire, 1895–1945*, edited by Ramon H. Myers and Mark R. Peattie, and *The Japanese Informal Empire in China, 1895–1937*, edited by Peter Duus, R. H. Myers and M. R. Peattie. Among collected papers of distinction published in Britain, mention should be made of *Modern Japan, Aspects of History, Literature and Society*, edited by Beasley, the outcome of a conference held in Oxford and London in 1973.

Rewarding works on political thought in Japan include the essays of Maruyama Masao, a collection of which was published in English as *Thought and Behaviour in Modern Japanese Politics*, and Najita Tetsuo's *Japan: The Intellectual Foundations of Modern Japanese Politics*. Papers edited by Nish following the Anglo-Japanese Conference on the History of the Second World War, and published under the title *Anglo-Japanese Alienation 1919–1952*, included notable contributions by a galaxy of Japanese historians, Professors Hosoya Chihiro, Hagihara Nobutoshi, Usui Katsumi, Ikeda Kiyoshi, Nomura Minoru, Watanabe Akio and Iriye Akira, as well as by Nish himself, Peter Lowe, Gordon Daniels, Donald Cameron Watt, Christopher Thorne and Air Commodore Henry Probert.

The late Professor Christopher Thorne's books, especially *The Limits of Foreign Policy* and *The Issue of War*, clearly display the international scenery for the whole period of and between the two world wars, and contain much wise comment and judgement. *The Origins of the Second World War in Asia and the Pacific* is a brilliant study by Iriye Akira, who deepens his treatment in *Power and Culture: The Japanese-American War 1941–45*. On the period leading up to the war, the reflections of the United States and British ambassadors in Tokyo are available in Joseph Grew's *Ten Years in Japan* and Sir Robert Craigie's *Behind the Japanese Mask*. The latter's final report, together with a memorandum by the Far Eastern Department of the Foreign Office in London on developments from mid-1940 to the outbreak of war, and comments by both Churchill and Eden, are to be found in the Public Record Office at Kew, under the reference Premier 3/158/4. Together with the records of official views on the pros and

199

cons of allowing the Anglo-Japanese Alliance to lapse, as set out in the course of preparation for the Washington Conference of 1921 (surely a model debate of its kind, in depth and even in muted passion) these papers are among the greatest treasures available to the student of these events.

Official histories of the Second World War itself were consulted, together with numerous memoirs, including some of those which emerged in the proceedings of the International Military Tribunal for the Far East. In Japan, memoirs of the 1930s and 1940s are still coming to light, for example in the concluding issue of *Bungei Shunju* for 1990, and the first issue for 1991; and in the *Yomiuri*'s monthly magazine for August 1991. Among officially sponsored studies of the war, that by Bateson, from an Australian point of view, gives a particularly vivid account of campaigns in mountainous jungle territory, such as was encountered on all the fronts of the war in Asia. The volumes of the British official history, together with the memoirs of leading commanders, including Field Marshal Viscount Slim, give a full account of the later campaigns in Burma, while Major-General Lunt's *Retreat from Burma* is a first-hand record of the opening scene in that theatre of operations, following the fall of Singapore. A masterly survey of the decisive struggle in the Pacific is given in *The Two-Ocean War* by Admiral Samuel Eliot Morison, whose ability to combine detailed description with clarity of general exposition can have been matched very rarely. F. C. Jones on *Japan's New Order in Asia, 1937–45*, was an early post-war study of the external objectives of Japanese policy in wartime. The domestic situation in Japan is observed perceptively in Professor Ben-Ami Shillony's *Politics and Culture in Wartime Japan*.

Though Ivan Morris's *The Nobility of Failure* deals with the theme of tragic heroism in the history of Japan as a whole, and has only one chapter on the kamikaze fighters of our period, it must be mentioned here. Morris's best known work was on the Heian court, but he also wrote *Nationalism and the Right Wing in Japan: A Study of Post-war Trends*. This was for the Royal Institute of International Affairs (RIIA), which also, with the Institute of Pacific Relations, commissioned *New Paths for Japan*, by Harold Wakefield.

There is naturally an extensive literature by writers in the United States about this early post-war phase, of which we may take Professor Michael Schaller's *The American Occupation of Japan* as a good representative, with its short, explosive Appendix about General MacArthur's relations with President Roosevelt and other 'liberals' in Washington. Richard B. Finn's *Winners in Peace: MacArthur, Yoshida and Postwar Japan* is a new account based on first-hand experience. An exceptionally well educated view of basic factors in the early post-war period is given in Sir Esler Dening's *Japan. The Occupation of Japan 1945–52* is the subject of papers by Professors Iokibe Makoto and Amakawa Akira in a collection edited by

Nish for the Suntory-Toyota International Centre at the London School of Economics. Roger Buckley has written perceptively on *Occupation Diplomacy: Britain, the United States and Japan, 1945–52*. Professor Ronald Dore's *Land Reform in Japan* is an authoritative study of one of the most important aspects of this phase.

Post-war history as a whole is, of course, not yet ripe for definitive treatment. There is a great deal of published material in the United States, much of it in leading periodicals such as *Foreign Affairs* and the *Journal of Japanese Studies* (Seattle). In *An Empire in Eclipse, Japan in the Postwar American Alliance System*, John Welfield has covered a lot of ground, in considerable detail. There is a useful collection of papers on *Europe and Japan, Changing Relationships since 1945*, edited by Gordon Daniels and Reinhard Drifte; and Professor Drifte has also published a study of *Japan's Foreign Policy* for the RIIA (Chatham House Papers). Laura Newby has written on *Sino-Japanese Relations, China's Perspective*, also for Chatham House. Sir Hugh Cortazzi has contributed a paper on *British Influence in Japan Since the End of the Occupation (1952–1984)* in the Nissan Occasional Paper Series, for the Nissan Institute of Japanese Studies in Oxford.

Beasley's *The Rise of Modern Japan*, already mentioned, gives a general account right up to the death of the Showa Emperor. *The Emergence of Modern Japan: an Introductory History since 1853,* by Janet Hunter, also reaches the present Heisei period. The same author's *Concise Dictionary of Modern Japanese History* gives the full composition of Japanese cabinets up to 1980, and records a wealth of information in convenient form for reference.

But, though it may be too early for extended and definitive historical assessments of the post-war period, there is already a mass of material on particular developments and aspects of contemporary Japan, much of it of the highest quality. On government and politics, a selection must include Professor Hans Baerwald's *Japan's Parliament: An Introduction*, Professor Arthur Stockwin's *Japan: Divided Politics in a Growth Economy*, Professor Gerald L. Curtis's *The Japanese Way of Politics*, and *Politics in Modern Japan* by Kishimoto Koichi, senior specialist in the National Diet Library in Tokyo.

On the Japanese economy, there is also much distinguished work available to supplement the sound foundation established in G. C. Allen's *A Short Economic History of Modern Japan*, and *The Japanese Economy*. Allen's other books include his enjoyable memoir, *Appointment in Japan*. W. J. Macpherson's *The Economic Development of Japan c.1868–1941* is impressively condensed. As to how the Japanese do it, there is Chalmers Johnson's famous book, *MITI and the Japanese Miracle*. Ronald Dore's analyses are of the greatest value, for example, *Flexible Rigidities: Industrial Policy and Structural Adjustment in the Japanese Economy, 1970–80*; and

Taking Japan Seriously: A Confucian Perspective on Leading Economic Issues. James Abegglen has written books and articles closely based on practical experience, including, in collaboration with George Stalk, *Kaisha: The Japanese Corporation.* Trade imbalances are the subject of continuing discussion on all sides, some of it in need of a greater clarity of analysis such as is given, in a closely related field, in Sir Fred Warner's recent study of *Anglo-Japanese Financial Relations.*

A glance through the notes above is enough to remind the writer of unacknowledged debts, for example to scholars such as Scalapino, Bisson, Borton, Farley, Lockwood, Emmerson, Yanaga; the names would come pouring out. There is scholarship and there is sensation, sometimes both: Morris, Gibney, Kahn, van Wolferen, and so many vivid accounts by creative and conscientious journalists. With Emmott in particular, on the economy and finance; Tasker; and Horsley with Buckley, contemporary commentary merges with scholarship. Among interpreters, in the larger sense, we should do well to remember Vere Redman; as well as Dick Storry; and it is instructive to contemplate the distance between, say, Basil Hall Chamberlain and Professor Brian Moeran. In his talks for the tenth Ishizaka Memorial Lectures, Ronald Dore took up the question *Will the 21st Century Be the Age of Individualism?* (Remembering Ishizaka Taizo, we may also ask, Was not the twentieth?)

Whole areas of reading about religion, education, the arts, Nihonjinron, literature and life itself in Japan are surrendered here, in the interests of brevity. To say nothing of China, Korea, Asia and the Pacific. It may be worth drawing attention to the Anti-Bibliographic Note with which John King Fairbank concludes his splendid book *The Great Chinese Revolution 1800–1985;* also to the impetus given to work on Asia and the Pacific by the addition of the *Pacific Review* to the company of distinguished journals essential to students of contemporary developments, especially; and to the work of its editor, Dr Gerald Segal. Much is being achieved, too, in Australia, New Zealand and Canada, far-off countries about which we used to know more. Perhaps it is worth recording that his reading list for the present writer's first voyage to Japan in 1951, besides Sansom, included K. M. Panikker's *Asia and Western Dominance*, and Guy Wint's *The British in Asia.*

Personal debts to friends and colleagues in Japan and Britain and more widely can never be settled, but they are not forgotten. It would be right to mention here the kindness and hospitality of Professor Arthur Stockwin and his colleagues at St Antony's College, Oxford, and in the Nissan Institute of Japanese Studies. Much generous encouragement was also given to this endeavour by Michael Hurst of St John's College, Oxford, who knows more about the footnotes of history than most of us about its main text.

Finally, the present writer is conscious of owing something altogether indispensable, including enjoyment, to the work of Tanizaki Junichiro, of Kawabata Yasunari, of Yoshida Kenichi, of Donald Keene and of Edward Seidensticker, to end with a few more names of the very highest distinction.

Berwick St John   S.G.
Wiltshire
1993

Glossary of Selected Japanese Terms

bakufu

Government based on the military (literally, tented) headquarters of the Shogun; especially the system of administration established by the Tokugawa Shogunate, *c.* 1600–1867.

burakumin

'Hamlet people' (also *eta* or *hinin*) long since formally emancipated, but still suffering discrimination; originally, communities with no caste or status, on account of their occupations as, for example, butchers or tanners.

Daimyo

Grand baronial vassals of the Shogun, and holders of fiefs; in some cases, hereditary rulers of extensive domains and leaders of powerful clans, before the Restoration of 1868.

dokudan senko

Doctrine of supreme command; justification of authority claimed for commanders of fleets and armies, up to the Second World War.

Domei

The All-Japan General Federation of Labour, formed in the mid-1960s, in a merger of anti-communist trade unions, supporting the right wing of the JSP, and the DSP.

Edo

Now Tokyo. See Tokugawa, and Bakufu.

fukoku kyohei

A rich country and a strong army.

Gaiko Chosakai

Advisory Council on Foreign Relations, established in 1917, but lapsed in the 1920s.

Gaimusho

Ministry of Foreign Affairs, Tokyo.

gekokujo	Domination of seniors by their juniors.
Genro	Elder statesmen, a group constituted informally, but which was influential, at times dominant, in political affairs from the 1890s for nearly half a century.
Gensuikyo	Movement for the abolition of atomic and nuclear weapons, often connected with the wider ideological aims of the peace movement.
habatsu	Factionalism. (cf. Hanbatsu)
Hakko Ichiu	All directions (regions of the world) under one roof.
Hanbatsu	Clan-faction; used to donote the concentration of political power in the hands of men from Satsuma (the domain of the Shimazu family, centred on Kagoshima in Southern Kyushu) and Choshu (modern Yamaguchi Prefecture), in the west of Honshu, with Hagi as its capital.
Heisei	The era name for the reign of the present Emperor Akihito, from his accession in 1989, following Showa, Taisho, Meiji.
Jiyuto	Liberal Party, with a conservative connotation, often used to denote the Liberal Democratic Party.
Jushin	Former prime ministers; mostly used to refer to them collectively as constituting an advisory council.
Kansai	The region west of the barrier at Hakone set up by the Shogunate to control movement, e.g. of arms and women, into and out of Edo (Tokyo); commonly used to denote the area of Osaka, Kobe and Kyoto.
Kanto	The region east of the barrier (see above) at Hakone, especially the plain north of Tokyo Bay.
Keidanren	The Federation of Economic Organizations, the body which represents the business world of private enterprise in Japan.
keiretsu	Group of industrial enterprises.
kiheitai	Auxiliary militia formed shortly before the Meiji Restoration to strengthen regular Choshu troops.
Kodoha	Party of the Imperial Way, the army faction led by Generals Araki and Mazaki, in the 1930s.

Glossary of Selected Japanese Terms

kokutai	Concepts of an essential national polity.
Komeito	Clean Government Party, the political wing of the Soka Gakkai, q.v.
ManKan kokan	Thesis that control over Manchuria could be traded with Russia for the dominant position in Korea.
narikin	Nouveau riche, often, after the First World War, also profiteer.
Nokyo	The agricultural co-operative organization.
Rengo	The Japanese Trade Union Confederation, also in action as a political party.
samurai	The military (officer) class of society under the Shogunate, ranking above the farmers, the artisans and the merchants.
Satcho	The Satsuma and Choshu interests; see Hanbatsu.
seikanron	The argument for the invasion of Korea, as debated among the leaders of Meiji Japan.
Shakaito	The Japan Socialist Party (JSP).
Sodomei	Federation of Labour, politically moderate.
sogo shosha	The leading trading companies.
Sohyo	Labour Unions General Council; supported the left wing of the JSP in post-war Japan.
Soka Gakkai	Value-Adding Study Society, a lay organization sponsored by the Nichiren Shoshu sect of Buddhism; see also Komeito.
sokaiya	Crooks specializing in the 'protection' of boards of companies at annual or periodical general meetings. See Yakuza.
tei shisei	Low posture, used to characterize Japanese foreign policy in the decades following the Second World War.
Tokugawa	Family whose Shogunal administration at Edo, or Yedo (Tokyo) was the *de facto* government of Japan throughout the period to which their name is given; see Bakufu.
tonarigumi	Neighbourhood associations, established in wartime.

Toseiha	Control Party, the army faction dominant after the 26 February Incident of 1936; opposed to the Kodoha, q.v.
yakuza	Gangsters, usually referring to large criminal organizations.
Yuaikai	Friendly Society, an early welfare and embryonic labour organization.
zaibatsu	Big business (literally, financial clique), used in particular of the largest and most influential industrial concerns of the inter-war years, especially Mitsubishi, Mitsui, Sumitomo and Yasuda.
zaikai	Financial circles, the City.
Zengakuren	All-Japan Federation of Student Self-Government Associations; militant, influenced for a time by the Japan Communist Party.

Index

Index

210

Index

Index

Index